# Metaphysics

**Also available from Continuum:**

*Critical Thinking*, Robert Arp and Jamie Carlin Watson
*Phenomenology*, Michael Lewis and Tanja Staehler
*Philosophical Logic*, George Englebretsen and Charles Sayward
*The Philosophy of the Social Sciences*, Robert C. Bishop
*The Philosophy of History*, Mark Day
*The Philosophy of Mind*, Dale Jacquette

**Forthcoming:**

*Classical Chinese Philosophy*, Im Manyul
*Ethics*, Robin Attfield
*Introduction to Indian Philosophy*, Christopher Bartley
*Pragmatism*, John Capps
*Philosophy of Language*, Chris Daly
*Philosophy of Law*, Jeffrey Brand-Ballard
*Philosophy of Science*, Emma Tobin

# Metaphysics
## An Introduction

Jonathan Tallant

continuum

**Continuum International Publishing Group**

The Tower Building      80 Maiden Lane, Suite 704
11 York Road           New York
London SE1 7NX      NY 10038

www.continuumbooks.com
Online resources for this book are available at http://philosophy.
tallant.continuumbooks.com

**British Library Cataloguing-in-Publication Data**
A catalogue record for this book is available from the British Library.

ISBN: HB: 978-1-4411-6239-7
       PB: 978-1-4411-0454-0


**Library of Congress Cataloguing-in-Publication Data**
A catalogue record for this book is available from the Library of
Congress.

Typeset by Newgen Imaging Systems Pvt Ltd, Chennai, India
Printed and bound in India

# Contents

# 1

# An Introduction to Truth-making

Let's begin by considering a seemingly straightforward question: if the sentence 'my cat is on the mat', is true, how does it get to be true? The most obvious answer to the question would seem to be that the sentence is true because my cat exists, the mat exists and the cat *is* on the mat. The world includes my cat being on the mat. Likewise, that 'a tomato is red' is true, is due to there *existing* a red tomato. As I write, the claim that 'Barack Obama is president of the United States' is true, because Barack Obama exists, the United States exists and Barack Obama *is* the president of the United States. Thus, we might think, some existing thing or things makes the sentence 'Barack Obama is the president of the United States' true.

The very natural thought, seemingly underpinning these explanations, is that sentences are true because of what exists. So, when we say that ' "the tomato is red" is true', we say this because there *exists* a red tomato. In anticipation of some terms that we will deploy later on, we may say that it looks like these sentences are *made true* by what exists. Perhaps you think that's a trivial result; *of course* our claims are true *only* if they are made true by what exists in the world. It's obvious from consideration of the forgoing and many other sentences like them that the world makes true what it is that we say. What could be more obvious?

Let's pause, just a moment, to state that intuition in a semi formal fashion. To begin with we will follow convention and allow that when we wish to indicate that something is a proposition we will deploy triangular brackets around it, such that <p> states *the proposition that p*. Roughly speaking, a proposition is taken to be that which is expressed by a particular sentence and sentences in different languages can be used to express the same proposition. Thus, 'it is raining' and 'il pleut' both express the same proposition.

Using this notation, we can then say that the proposition that p – which we write as <p> – is true if, and only if, something (that exists) *makes* it true. Call this the 'truth-maker' thesis.

> TM: <p> is true if and only if p makes it true.

Now although it might seem as if TM is a natural and intuitive principle, one that should be adopted without a second thought, a moment's consideration of TM reveals that it will have surprising and far-reaching implications for a variety of different sorts of discourse. Consider, for instance, the proposition that <it's possible that I not write this book>. At least intuitively the proposition seems true (and for the time being let's assumes that it is). So let's ask the obvious question: we've accepted TM, so what makes it true that <it is possible that I not write this book>? According to the very plausible principle TM *existing thing must* make it true: but what?

What are our options? Perhaps, we might think, it's *my actions* that make it true that <it is possible that I not write this book>. But at least upon first inspection that doesn't look right. After all, I am writing the book! So the actions that I in fact perform don't seem to tell me anything about what I could, but do not in fact, do. It's unclear how my actions can then also make it true that <it's possible for me to not write this book>. By way of refinement we might then say that I make it true by having particular abilities: since I might have chosen to exercise those abilities in a different way (perhaps by writing research papers instead), so it is the case that *I* make it true that it is possible that I not write this book.

Although this looks more promising as an account of what makes it true that <it's possible that I not write this book>, problems arise. For instance, we said that it was my having particular abilities that made it true that <it's possible that I not write this book>. But what sort of abilities? Presumably, what we mean to say is that I *could* have behaved in a way that I did not, and that I *could* have behaved in that particular way (lying on the sofa, rather than writing a book) makes it true that <it's possible that I not write this book>. But what we might find potentially troublesome about such thoughts is that we're now saying that what makes it true that <it's possible that I not write this book> is simply that *I could have behaved in a way that I did not*. That, in turn, looks to say nothing more than it's possible for me to behave in a way that I did not! It seems, therefore, that we're still lacking an account of what it is that makes it true that <it's possible that I not write this book>. What is it, then, that exists and makes true our talk about what is *possible*?

Clearly, the forgoing is far from exhaustive and appears a little in the abstract at this stage. We'll return to a discussion of what makes true claims about what's possible (and necessary – the so-called *modal* truths) in Chapter 4. For the time being, though, my intention is simply to point out that endorsing TM leads us to search for truth-makers for *all* truths. That is, every single true claim that we make is such that some existing portion of reality *makes* it true. This is, indeed, the attitude taken by a number of contemporary metaphysicians. For our purposes, then, we are going to treat metaphysics as a quest for truth-makers.

That is going to lead us to make some surprising claims. Just to whet the appetite a little, consider the following putative truths.

> 2+2=4 – what makes that true? Are there really such things as numbers? (Chapter 3)
>
> There were dinosaurs – what makes that true? Does the past really exist? (Chapter 7)
>
> The collapse in the sub-prime mortgage market caused the recent financial crisis – what makes that true? What *is* it for one thing to cause another? (Chapter 9)

Questions like these have excised philosophers for years and in this book we'll be considering these questions and others like them. Of course, there are other questions that have vexed philosophers, too. Questions such as 'is killing wrong?' and 'is the Mona Lisa beautiful?' all fall within the purview of philosophy, and, if one thought that the answer to these questions is 'yes', then it may well be appropriate for us to seek out truth-makers for these claims. However, considering the nature of truth-makers required within these domains would take us away from what may be considered to be mainstream metaphysics into the domains of (meta)ethics and aesthetics. Our focus here is narrower and concerns debates that are, as a matter of historical fact, more often treated as core subjects in metaphysics.

It's perhaps appropriate here for me to alert the reader to an issue that they ought to be aware of. Many of the debates that we look at during the course of the book were not, at least when originally considered, presented in terms of either seeking or providing truth-makers for true propositions. Indeed, the endorsement of TM as a philosophical theory is both recent (only really being brought to light in Mulligan, Simons and Smith (1984)) and contentious (as we shall see in Chapter 10).

I have deliberately chosen to present the issues that we will cover in this book as ones dependent upon the idea of truth-making for two principle reasons: first, treating TM as a means by which to present the various different areas allows a particularly clean presentation of the issues and provides the reader with a constant theme that runs through the book; second, it's at least plausible that something very much like TM has underpinned much metaphysical thinking, both in the last hundred years or so and much earlier.[1] So, although it is a little inappropriate to present all of metaphysics as in the thrall of truth-making, presenting these issues in the way that I do is not without some justification. Nonetheless, the reader should keep in mind that there is more to metaphysics than the quest for truth-makers. Some of the dialectically significant features of the debates will be discussed in a moment.

# §1.1 Truth-making: Maximalism and necessitarianism

In the last section we noted that TM is pretty plausible, but you might then have been somewhat taken aback at the suggestion that propositions like <2+2=4> need truth-makers. Surely, we might think, although true propositions about things like cats, mats, tables and chairs need to be made true by what exists, it's altogether more radical and less intuitive to think that true mathematical propositions require some existing thing to make them true.

Although such sentiment is understandable it seems to sit uneasily with TM. It seems that if we're going to think that some truths have truth-makers, then we should think that they all do. And since we do think that some propositions require truth-makers, so we should think that all truths require truth-makers. As Cameron (2008a: 107) puts it, with something of a flourish: '[w]hat possible reason could one have for thinking of some propositions that they need to be grounded in what there is that doesn't apply to all propositions?'

Let's flesh out this thought a little. Suppose we think that propositions such as <my cat is on the mat> need truth-makers in order to be true. Presumably, the intuition that is in part motivating this thought is that what is true depends upon what exists. Certainly, one finds that idea ably expressed in the literature on truth-making:

> My hope is that philosophers of realist inclinations will be immediately attracted to the idea that a truth, any truth, should depend for its truth on something 'out-side' it, in virtue of which it is true. (Armstrong (2004: 7))
>
> [T]he root of the idea of truthmakers is the very plausible and compelling idea that the truth of a proposition is a function of, or is determined by, reality. (Rodriguez-Pereyra (2005: 20))
>
> we are looking for reasons from the side of the world as to why a certain proposition is true. (Simons 2005: 254)
>
> Truth must, one expects, depend in some way on reality. (Mumford (2005: 263))

To borrow the language from the last of these quotations and relate this back to number talk: if we think that <2+2=4> is true, then, presumably, we are looking for some portion of reality upon which the truth of <2+2=4> can depend; some existent that is responsible for the truth of the proposition. *That* is a request for a truth-maker.

In any case, if we think that propositions about cats and mats need to be made true by existing objects, then we'll need some pretty good reasons to think that true talk about numbers *doesn't* need to be made true in exactly the same way. If we only endorse TM with regards to some truths, and not others, then it looks as if we will be charged with an unprincipled application of TM to some domains and not others: this looks decidedly *ad hoc*. It looks very much as if by endorsing TM we just are endorsing the thought that what's true depends on what exists. So, let us proceed on the basis that *all* truths need truth-makers.

We have found that a natural extension of TM is that for *every* truth, some *thing* or *things* makes that proposition true. This view is described, in the literature, as Truth-maker Maximalism.[2] Thus:

> TM-Max: *For all* <p>, <p> is true if and only if *p* makes it true.

# §1.2 The nature of the relation

Suppose we grant TM-Max. It still seems as if we have an important question to answer: what is it for the world to *make true* a particular proposition? More precisely, what *is* the truth-making relation? It would be good if we could say something informative about this relation, if only to get clear on the details of the view.

Typically, the relation is thought to be something like necessitation. That is, whenever something exists, it necessitates certain truths about it. To see why, let us return our attention to my cat, sat on the mat. The thought of the truth-maker theorist is that the cat sitting on the mat necessitates the truth of the proposition <the cat is on the mat>. It is impossible for the proposition to be false if the cat is sat on the mat. That sounds plausible. Likewise, the existence of the cat, the mat and the cat's being on the mat, will necessitate the truth of <there is a cat> and <there is a mat>.³ It is impossible for there to be a cat and the proposition <there is a cat> not be true and it is impossible for there to be a mat and the proposition <there is a mat> turn out false. We can give countless other examples. The existence of the red rose necessitates the truth of the proposition <the rose is red>. The existence of an electron necessitates the truth of the proposition <there is an electron>.

Another concept worth making plain at this stage is that of a minimal truth-maker, although I think that really in spelling this out we are doing nothing more than making something explicit that was present in TM all along. The rough idea underpinning this concept is that a minimal truth-maker is the 'smallest' portion of reality required to make a given proposition true. To illustrate: we might reasonably say that the minimal truth-maker for <a cat is on the mat> is the state of affairs of a cat sitting upon the mat. By way of contrast, the minimal truth-maker for <there is a cat> will presumably be only a cat. However, we could of course offer up a different truth-maker for <there is a cat>. We could cite as a truth-maker for this proposition the existence of a cat, my house, Mars and a corkscrew. This truth-maker is not *minimal* and I hope that it is intuitively obvious why we are interested in minimal (as opposed to non-minimal) truth-makers. There is something very strange about thinking that the reason the proposition <there is a cat> is true is that there exists a cat *and* a house *and* Mars *and* a corkscrew. In contrast, it looks perfectly obvious that the reason <there is a cat> is true is simply that there exists a cat.

When metaphysicians attempt to locate the parts of the world that make true our claims, they typically seek the minimal truth-makers for their claims.

So let us recap what has been said so far. In order for a proposition, <p> to be true, something exists that makes it true. Specifically, we are looking for the *smallest* portion of reality whose existence necessitates the truth of <p>. The truth of <p> is necessitated by what exists.

# §1.3 Metaphysics and physics

We're now in a position to begin to assess how we might do metaphysics. Consider any proposition that we think of as true; we must identify some existing feature of the world that makes that proposition true – some feature of the world that necessitates the truth of the proposition. Working out what it is that make these claims true will then be the job of the metaphysician.

Of course, it's tempting to think that the project of working out what exists is really the job of the scientist. After all, we're asking questions about what exists (what the truth-makers are for our true propositions) and uncovering what exists is *clearly* the job of the scientists. Why, then, ought we to engage in metaphysics?

To defend metaphysics properly is a substantial project in itself, so let me simply make a few remarks that will (hopefully) be enough to persuade the reader that the metaphysician is engaged in a viable project.

Consider the humble tomato. It is red. That's a true claim that we could make about it. So, what makes it true that <the tomato is red>? A natural temptation would be to say that what makes the proposition about the colour of the tomato *true*, has *something* to do with the microphysical structure of the tomato and that clearly specifying the precise detail of that structure is the job of the physicist. Partly, that's true. But now consider a second tomato, under the same conditions, that appears to be precisely the same colour as the first tomato. Presumably we want to say that the proposition <the two tomatoes are the same colour> is true. What makes it true? Here, again, we might simply say that it's the microphysical structure of the two tomatoes that is responsible and that, once again, specifying the nature of this is the job of the physicist.

This example then permits us to get to the heart of a distinctively metaphysical question. What does it mean to say that the two tomatoes have 'the same microphysical structure'? More specifically, what makes it true that <the two tomatoes have the same microphysical structure>? Is the truth-maker for this proposition some property that both tomatoes share, or is it merely the case that the two tomatoes resemble one another, but are not *literally* the same colour? Further, if this is a case of mere resemblance, in what does resemblance consist? Is resemblance a relation? If resemblance is a relation, it certainly doesn't look like the sort of relation that the physicist studies. We certainly won't find in any physics text-book an account of the physical properties of the 'resemblance' relation.[4] Uncovering the nature of that relation might then be a job for the metaphysician.

Of course, we could say that two objects resemble one another iff they have the same arrangements of sub-atomic particles. But then we merely ask a variation on our first distinctively metaphysical question: what makes it true that two arrangements of particles are *the same*? Once more, these questions concerning sameness and resemblance simply seem not to be questions with which scientists engage. These tentative steps are, I think, enough to point to the fact that there is *some* scope for doing metaphysics even in the presence of a complete physics.

But, at the same time, good metaphysics ought to be carried out in the light of our best physics. To see why, consider the following thoughts in the analysis of causation. We might (*very* crudely) be tempted to think that causation has something to do with the way in which objects crash into one another. Perhaps this is why when we see one snooker ball strike another, and the latter move off, we think that the first ball causes the second to move. But these tentative thoughts about causation may be meaningless at a micro level, the level of reality at which we find quarks, electrons and the like, if the fundamental constituents of reality are not, in fact, snooker-ball-like particles crashing into one another, but fields. Fields surely do not 'crash into one another'.[5]

Clearly, then, although metaphysics and physics are independent – in that there are questions that metaphysicians try to answer that the physicist does not explicitly consider, and vice versa – they are also related. Whatever our best metaphysics says ought to be compatible with our best physics. If physics tells us that the micro-physical level is constructed out of fields, then assuming that we think that causation occurs at the micro level, our theory of causation had better not require that causation only occurs where objects 'crash into' one another.

But now suppose that we have a philosophical theory that tells us that a proposition <p> is true and a scientific theory that tells us that <p> is false. Should we then believe that <p> is true or false? I think that the intuitive answer is that we ought to believe that <p> is false, and that we ought to follow the science where science and philosophy clash. But we must then offer some argument. If we simply say that we ought to believe in our best science because *it's intuitive to do so*, then the metaphysician will likely ask us to defend the claim that our intuitions are of any particular weight. Moreover, scientific theory and intuition come into conflict on a semi-regular basis. For instance, intuition tells us that, for any two events, there is a fact of the matter as to whether or not they occur simultaneously with one another; as we shall see (Chapter 7) science plausibly requires us to deny this. It is also extremely unintuitive to think that there are entities that have the properties of both waves and particles; but this is precisely how electrons are described. Surely, if science requires us to deny our intuitions in many cases already, then the scientist ought to give up intuition as a motivating force for thinking that science is prior to metaphysics.

Perhaps, if we wish to try and deny that there is any role for metaphysics, we will instead claim that science has made clear progress; philosophy has not. Perhaps this fact can then be used to launch an attack on metaphysics. But then yet more argument is needed. In particular, we need answers to at least some of the following questions: what is progress in science and what is progress in philosophy? Why think that progress in science is evidence of truth? Absent answers to these questions, it's hard to see how to prosecute the case against metaphysics. It may be, for instance, that progress in philosophy and science appear very different and, thus, that it is no blemish upon the record of philosophy that it does not make the same sorts of progress that science does.

There are attempts to provide answers both by those who see metaphysics as prior to physics and those who see things the other way around. My intention here is not to adjudicate upon these matters. For the purposes of our inquiry here we will leave it an open question as to which discipline (if either) is prior, and proceed on the assumption that physics and metaphysics will both play an important part in our attempt to uncover the nature of reality.

# §1.4 Metaphysical desiderata and tools

What we also need to have in hand, before proceeding to try and engage with some metaphysical issues directly, is some sensitivity to the kinds of dialectical issues that concern metaphysicians. To begin with we should consider plausibly the most famous of these: Ockham's razor:

OR: Do not multiply entities beyond necessity.

Perhaps more revealingly we might say that our best metaphysical theories ought to do as much explanatory work as possible with as few entities as possible. Let me give a slightly glib example. Suppose we have a theory of the world that posits two sorts of objects – call them Fandangos and Bandangos (their natures need not concern us here) – and a competing theory that posits only Fandangos. Setting aside for a moment what, precisely, might be meant by the terms involved, it seems that the natural position for us to adopt is that there are only Fandangos. If we can make do with *only Fandangos*, then a theory that posited both Fandangos and Bandangos is multiplying entities beyond necessity, and so is falling foul of OR. Think about a real life example. Suppose that you are the unfortunate victim of burglary. You come downstairs one morning to find the back door ajar, and many electrical items missing from your home. Specifically, you have lost your DVD player and 20 DVDs. You might then formulate the hypothesis that a burglar broke in and stole these from you. In this instance, you posit a single burglar. Now, of course, what you *could* do is posit two burglars. We could imagine that the first burglar broke in to your home and stole the DVD player and that a second burglar then came along, spotted the open door and came in and stole your DVDs. So we could suppose that there exist two burglars and two distinct acts of burglary; we could suppose that there exists only a single burglar and only a single act of burglary. Indeed, we *could* argue that each individual DVD was stolen by a different burglar and that there were in fact 21 burglars! In this case it is clear, I think, that we naturally think the case of the single burglar and single act of burglary the most natural and reasonable explanation. This is another instance of OR at work. What underpins OR is the presumption that theories positing fewer entities (or kinds of entities) are preferable to those that posit more. We call this a preference for ontological parsimony. It is this preference for parsimony that we can think of as driving and motivating OR.

However, ontological parsimony needn't be the only virtue of a good philosophical theory. Thinking again about the possibility of invoking the existence of abstract objects, such as numbers, suppose that we find ourselves in a situation where there is some phenomena in need of explanation, and that the phenomena *is* explained by the invocation of abstract objects, though not explained if we deny that there exist any abstract objects. In that case, where we have an explanatory burden in place, we might reasonably suppose that the theory that supposes the existence of abstract objects is preferable to the theory that does not.

What is becoming clear is that theories can have a number of distinct virtues. A theory may be virtuous because it gives us all of the truth-makers we require, but it may be troublesome because it posits a lot of ontology and so not be very parsimonious. How we weigh these matters is complicated and there are no hard and fast rules. We must proceed with caution.

A further tool that the philosopher has available to them is that of reduction and/or elimination. Although both contentious notions in themselves, having a loose grasp of them here will help us in our later discussions. Let's begin with reduction and consider a case from the philosophy of mind.

It's a seemingly obvious truth that people have minds; it is not so obvious as to what that mind is supposed to be. There are those prepared to endorse the mind as an entity or substance that is distinct from the body, or any aspect thereof. For such 'dualist' philosophers, there is both mind and brain and they are genuinely distinct.

Drawing on what we learned above, it is I think easy to see how the dialectic might progress from here. The natural first thought is that the truth-maker for talk about a 'mind' will be the mind itself – this non-physical substance alluded to a moment ago. However, pressure from Ockham's razor can then be brought to bear: we don't want to posit a mind *over and above* the brain, unless we have to. Recall, we are not to multiply entities beyond necessity. Thus the temptation is to try and get rid of the mind altogether. We could then eliminate commitment to a mind and be eliminativists about the mental. In following this line of thought, we might say that there are no truth-makers for claims like <I have a mind> and, since the proposition lacks a truth-maker, it is false.[6]

But now we have to think about matters: is there anything that might be explained by the positing of a mind, that isn't explained if we do not posit a mind? One thing that might leave us tempted to answer in the affirmative is that we seem to think and on the reasonable assumption that a thing may only think if it has a mind, so we find ourselves needing an explanation of how it is we can think, that is best provided by the postulation of some mind.

What we need is a mid-point between the eliminativist's denial of the existence of a mind, and the dualistic claim that there is a mind *as distinct from* a body. The way that people have proceeded, traditionally, is some form of reductionism: that is, there is a mind, there is a brain, and the mind can (in some way) be reduced to, or identified with, the brain. Notice, this is not the same as eliminativism (which claims that there is no mind); reductionism claims that there is some part of the world that deserves to be called a 'mind', but then goes on to say that this mind is to be understood as reducible to something purely physical.

Undeniably, these are complicated notions and philosophical disagreement over what they accomplish and are to be understood is rife, but another example may help to illustrate further. Think about an Orchestra: would you say that it exists? That is, do you think <there exists an Orchestra> is a true proposition? If you do, then presumably you think it requires a truth-maker. So, you will think that there are such things as Orchestras in the world. But given Ockhamistic reasoning, the natural thought would be that if we can withhold from including Orchestras in our ontology, we ought to do so. In other words, where possible, we should probably want to be eliminativists about Orchestras. Of course, in that case <there exists an Orchestra> lacks a truth-maker. If we thought that this was an indefensible view, then we might just be prepared to say that the eliminativist about Orchestras is obviously wrong. But, if we wanted to be a little less flat-footed, then we might want to find some explanatory purpose to which we might put Orchestras. So, perhaps we don't think that many people simply playing music at the same time is sufficient to explain how it is that all players play the same piece of music at the same time, same tempo, following similar alterations in tempo and dynamics. What is needed to explain these goings on is the existence of Orchestras. To that end we might propose that Orchestras *do* exist, but reductively analyse them as being 'collections of instrumentalists coming together and playing a particular piece of music'. Thus, Orchestras do exist, it's just that we can reductively analyse what it is to be such a thing.

This pattern of reasoning is one that we will see many times in the discussions that follow. It's important to keep in mind that although many of the arguments that we'll be exposed to are complex, a good many of them end up with us deliberating upon whether or not some feature that seems to be in need of explanation can be explained; and, if it can, whether or not the explanation is worth the cost to our ontology. Are we prepared to posit the existence of a new entity given our preference for ontological parsimony?

In summary, then, we have various weights and measures to keep an eye on. We want to try and keep our theory as parsimonious as we can, but we also want to make sure that our theory explains what it sets out to.

Another concern, or dialectical tool, which we need to keep in mind concerns our knowledge of what we posit. Suppose, for instance, that we end up arguing that there are objects (numbers, perhaps) with which we have no causal contact. Since we have no causal contact with said objects, it becomes an immediate concern as to how it is we could ever know that such objects exist. Although there are a variety of responses to such objections (as we shall see later on) what is essential to our metaphysics is that we must be able to come to know about the entities that we posit in our ontology. Indeed, metaphysicians typically argue that the posits of our best theory ought to be no more epistemically problematic than those entities that we posit in our best science. If, for instance, it's acceptable for the physicist to endorse the existence of unobservables via some particular line of reasoning, then employing that line of reasoning to also posit unobservables in metaphysics ought to be acceptable, too.[7] Thus, we may hope, metaphysics ends up on an epistemic par with science, and since science is taken to be an inquiry that is successful, vibrant and useful, so metaphysics too is in a solid position to inquire into the nature of the world and what exists within it.

# §1.5 Intuitions

The final theoretical virtue that I'm going to mention before moving on to case studies is that of how intuitive a particular view is. This might strike you as a little odd. Why do we think that it matters that a particular view is intuitive? Why should we think that our intuitions are any guide to truth, at all?

I'll mention one reason, here. Without our intuitions, inquiry (of any form, at all) may well not be possible. In defence of the role of intuition, we might (borrowing from Zimmerman (2008: 222) record the following). We have learned, from the history of epistemology, that *certainty* about the world is an unattainable goal. We cannot rule out the *possibility* that we are being deceived by a Cartesian Demon (an evil demon, intent upon systematically deceiving us). The best we can do in response to the (epistemological) sceptic (maybe) is to say that it *seems intuitive* to think that we have knowledge of the world.

So why think that we ought not to be (epistemological) sceptics? Simply because it is intuitive for us to not be so: that is, it's just commonsense to believe that we know about the world; it's *intuitive* to think that we do. In order to get inquiry off the ground, we must give at least some positive weighting to our intuitions, else we remain snared in scepticism. Thus, in order to engage in *any* inquiry about the world, we need to believe the hypothesis that there *is no Cartesian Demon*, where the only substantive *reason* for that claim is that it seems like a commonsense result.

We might then be tempted to claim that intuition can tell us about epistemology, but not about metaphysics. This would still threaten the reasonableness of deploying intuitions in metaphysical inquiry. The trouble with such a line of argument is that by making the claim that *we are not deceived* by something akin to a Cartesian Demon, we *are* making a metaphysical claim; to wit, 'it's not the case that there exists a Cartesian Demon who deceives us'; or, 'it is the case that the world exists in such a fashion as to give rise to the experiences we have in roughly the way that we think that it does'. Further, we are not systematically deceived by an evil demon – we really do perceive objects in the world and our perceptions afford us a reliable guide to the nature of those objects we perceive. In that case, not only do we deny the existence of such a demon but we also make more positive claims. For instance, we each assent to the truth of the proposition <*I* exist>. These are metaphysical claims (existence claims) if ever there were any.

It's hard to see how any theorizing can proceed without permitting intuition or commonsense *some* role. Absent a non-ad-hoc demarcation criterion for when intuition can, and cannot, be applied, it seems that we must think that our intuitions play some role in proper inquiry. Of course, if our intuitions *cannot* play any role, then rational inquiry *of any sort* into the nature of the world must fail; but I think we can be more optimistic than that. It certainly seems to us as if inquiry is possible and successful – just look at the great strides made in the sciences! It seems that it may be legitimate to deploy our intuitions to at least some extent in what follows.

# §1.6 Summing up and using this book

There are certainly many other issues that we could explore in an introduction to the methodology that will underpin the remainder of the book. But some of these are best introduced with explicit discussion of cases and examples from the literature. To that end, I'll close our discussion of the methodology here. One potentially useful way to proceed is for us to keep in mind the theoretical virtues of a good theory that have been discussed here.

- How ontologically parsimonious is the theory?
- How much explanatory power does the theory have?
- How do we come to know about the posits of the theory?
- How intuitive is the theory?

We seem to need truth-makers in order to preserve the truth of our discourse; we also need to explain various phenomena. In order to satisfy both of these requirements, it seems that we will be required to posit existing entities. These existing entities will necessitate the truth of propositions. When positing such truth-makers we ought to be concerned to posit only *minimal* truth-makers; the smallest portions of reality that will suffice for the truth of the proposition in question. Every such true proposition has a truth-maker (maximalism). However, pressure from Ockham's razor and the possibility of reduction will seemingly militate against the positing of existents (parsimony is a virtue). When faced with pressures from both directions it is incumbent upon us to carefully weigh-up the competing claims made by either side before using the evidence to generate a cautious conclusion.

To be clear, this book is intended only as an introduction to topics and it is not intended to go any further than *mere introduction*. So, if you're looking for high-level analysis of the cardinality argument against genuine modal realism, then you'd be better served looking elsewhere. Given the voluminous literature in metaphysics I have, of necessity, had to cherry pick particular topics. For the most part, I have focused upon views and objections that I *enjoy* teaching and thinking about. As pedagogical virtues go, I think that teaching topics that are enjoyable and interesting, is important. It may well be the case that, for instance, in discussion of Lewis' theory of possible worlds the cardinality problem is more powerful than the island universe objection; but the island universe objection seems more readily tractable; seems more intuitive (to me) and is a much more engaging problem to present.

The reason that I enjoy the material presented here is that I think it clever, insightful and interesting. Thus, I hope that the critical reader will spare me the barbs of criticism for not focusing upon what they think is the most pressing topic. Since I find myself presented with too much to hope to cover, I hope the reader will indulge me in my preferences.

At the end of each chapter the reader will also find three further resources. The first of these is a list of recommended reading by topic. In these lists I've tried to pick out reading that will help the reader to develop their understanding of the topics and arguments covered in the chapter. This is not intended to be exhaustive; rather, I recommend texts that I think make clear and develop the key themes of the chapter. There is also a list of 4–5 study questions. These are the kinds of question that could, I think, reasonably be used as the starting point for a tutorial discussion, or simply to prompt the reader to think about the material that has been covered. Finally, at the end of each chapter I have included a 'mind-map'. These are intended to be pictorial representations of the subject matter discussed.

# Recommended introductory reading

Armstrong, D. 2004. *Truth and Truth-makers*. Cambridge: CUP, chapter 1.

Cameron, R. 2008a. 'Truthmakers, Realism and Ontology', in *Being: Contemporary Developments in Metaphysics*, LePoidevin, R. ed. Cambridge: CUP, 107–28.

Cameron, R. forthcoming, a. 'Truthmakers', in Glanzberg, M. ed. *The Oxford Handbook of Truth.* Oxford: Oxford University Press.

Rodriguez-Pereyra, G. 2006. 'Truthmakers', *Philosophy Compass*, 1/2, 186–200.

## Study questions

1) List all of the theoretical virtues of a metaphysical theory that have been described in this chapter. Are there any other potential features of a theory that you think would make it a good theory?

2) The methodology described in this chapter sees us positing truth-makers for all truths. Do you think that this is the right way to proceed? If not, how would you proceed instead?

3) In this chapter I suggested that we often find ourselves weighing and balancing competing theoretical virtues. Of the virtues you listed in response to question 1, which do you think most important and which least important? Why did you opt for that ranking?

4) Describe what you think the minimal truth-makers are for the following propositions, be as precise as you can be:
   a) <the cup of tea is hot>
   b) <there are three people between me and the door>
   c) <the window is rattling>
   d) <the desk is in my office>

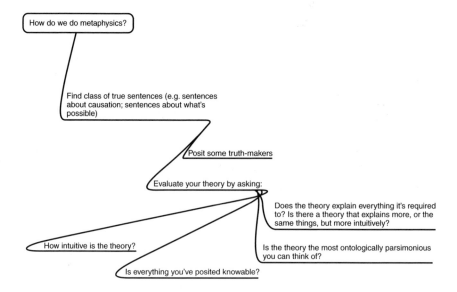

How do we do metaphysics?

Find class of true sentences (e.g. sentences about causation; sentences about what's possible)

Posit some truth-makers

Evaluate your theory by asking:

Does the theory explain everything it's required to? Is there a theory that explains more, or the same things, but more intuitively?

How intuitive is the theory?

Is the theory the most ontologically parsimonious you can think of?

Is everything you've posited knowable?

# 2

# The Special Composition Question: 'Physical' Objects

Let us begin this section with the special composition question[1]:

> SCQ: what necessary and jointly sufficient conditions must any xs satisfy in order for it to be the case that there is an *object* composed of those xs?

To get a sense of what is being asked, let us think about an example. In my office I have a chair. It is composed out of many different parts. There are chair-legs, the back of the chair (which includes some cushioning) and the seat of the chair (which also includes some cushioning). These different parts (the chair-leg, the chair back and the chair seat) are composing a chair. Contrast this arrangement of objects with another. I have a desk in my office. On top of my desk are a coffee-cup, a computer and a printer. These distinct objects (the desk, the coffee-cup, the computer and the printer) do not compose an object. So, what are the legs, back and seat doing that the cup, desk, computer and printer, are not? It seems to us as if the legs, seat and back, come together to form a unified whole – a composite object that we call a chair – whereas the cup, desk, printer and computer remain a plurality and do not compose. So, when does unity arise from plurality?

Consider another example. My house is made from bricks. It certainly appears, then, that the bricks compose my house. The plurality of bricks somehow has a unity and composes something new – my house. In contrast, imagine a pile of bricks strung out across a building site. This plurality of bricks does not compose an object. In what does the difference between these disparate collections of bricks consist? In virtue of what does one collection compose and the other not? In language with which we are now familiar: why is it that one plurality of bricks makes it true that <this is a composite object>, but the other plurality does not?

# §2.1 Basic options: Contact and fastening

To sensitize ourselves to some of the dialectical issues at hand, let's consider two answers to the question as to when unity arises from plurality. The first answer is called 'Contact':

> Contact: To get the *xs* to compose something, one need only bring them into contact; if the *xs* are in contact, they compose something; and if they are not in contact, they do not compose anything. (Van Inwagen (1990: 33))

Why might we be tempted by *Contact*? Consider the following: suppose you wake up on Christmas morning to find that someone has given you a Lego model as a present. At the point you receive the gift it is boxed up and the pieces are contained in small see-through plastic bags. The pieces are to be built into a toy castle. But, at the point when the pieces are spread out in the bag, they do not yet compose a toy castle. Indeed, part of the fun of receiving the gift is putting together the pieces in such a way as to get them to compose a castle. Our natural thought, then, might be that once we bring the pieces into contact with one another (hopefully in the way described by the instructions!) the pieces *compose* an object – a castle. We build a toy castle from the pieces and we achieve this by bringing the pieces into contact. Thus, where we bring entities into contact, they compose, but not otherwise. If Contact were correct, we'd have an answer to the SCQ.

But Contact, at least as it is stated above, fails. Think carefully about the Lego bricks: do we really want to say that we get them to compose some further object, *simply* by bringing them into contact with one another? Upon further reflection, don't we really think that, in order to make the bricks into a castle, we'd have to fasten the bricks together? Think about another example: when we put a pen on a desk we don't think that, just by bringing the two objects (the pen and the desk) into contact, we do enough to generate a composite object – call it 'pen-table'.

Indeed, think back to the second case cited in §2 – that of a house being composed of bricks and a pile of bricks lying on a building site. Suppose that we arranged the building-site-bricks such that they were laid out next to one another (touching), running end-to-end across the building site. These bricks are in contact with one another, but it would seem very strange to think of them as composing an object.

So, to coin some terminology, (due to Markosian, 2008) *Contact* looks too *liberal*: if we endorsed *Contact* it would force us to admit into our ontology objects that we don't think exist, such as pen-tables. Any view that forces us to introduce too many objects into our ontology, we'll call *too liberal*. And it seems to matter if a view is too liberal. What we are trying to do, in answering the SCQ, is specify when composition occurs. If an answer to this question is too liberal, then it would appear that there will be situations in which the proposition <there is a composite object> is true, but where we do not, think such a proposition should be true.

It also looks like *Contact* faces a different sort of problem. Think, for a moment, about a hydrogen atom. A hydrogen atom consists of one proton and one electron. It is a thing; plausibly, a composite object. However, according to *Contact* hydrogen atoms fail to be composite objects. Why? Because the proton and electron are not in contact with one another. To give a sense of this: were a proton scaled up to the size of the sun, then a similarly scaled-up orbiting electron would be orbiting at a distance much greater than that which the earth orbits the sun. That leaves a lot of space between electron and proton!

So, not only is *Contact* too *liberal*, it's also too *conservative*. That is, *Contact* would have us say that a hydrogen atom is not, contra what is seemingly our best physics, a composite object. Any view that permits too few objects into our ontology, we'll call *too conservative*. Once more, this is important. We are trying to specify when composition occurs. It seems that if a view is too conservative then it is failing to do justice to our sense of when this is. If our account is too *conservative*, then there will be situations in which we think that a collection of objects *ought* to make it true that <there is a composite object> – such as the case of the atom, just discussed – but in which it turns out that the proposition is not true.

The second answer that we will consider is fastening, or fastenation.

> Fastenation: To get the xs to compose something, one need only cause them to be fastened to one another. (c.f. Van Inwagen (1990: 56))

To see the intuitive pull of *fastenation*, let's return to the Lego-brick case. Our concern when we considered *Contact* was that we don't get the Lego bricks to compose a castle simply by placing them next to one another. What we needed in order for composition to have occurred was for the bricks to be disposed to stay together in some way. That being the case, *fastenation* has appeal; in order to get the Lego-bricks to compose a castle, we'll have to not only bring them together, but cause them to be *fastened* together.

Now, does that deal with the two further problem cases that we raised for contact, above? It looks like it might. When we simply place the pen onto the table, we don't fasten the pen and table together. Thus, we don't generate a new composite object: there is no 'pen-table'. That's the result we wanted. Also, we *might* be tempted to say that although not in contact, there is some force of attraction that holds the electron and proton together, such that they compose a hydrogen atom. Of course, this would require us to say that a force is a fastening, but perhaps we can say that. *Fastenation* thus looks like it has quite a bit to recommend it.

But despite that intuitive lure, there are problems. Consider the pair of cases that we just looked at, but in more detail. In the case of the 'pen-table' we said that there's nothing fastening the pen and the table together. Is that right? Is there *nothing* binding them together? Plausibly, there is something. Gravity. Gravity is a force and so in precisely the same way that the force holding the electron and proton together suffices for them to be fastened to one another, so the force of gravity suffices for the pen and table to be fastened together. Since gravity is a force that holds the pen and table together, so there is some form of fastening between the table and the pen.[2]

The natural response to this is to say that the force of gravity (at least in this case) isn't strong enough to generate a new composite object. So, even if we allow that a force can act in such a way as to fasten two objects together, what is crucial is that we get *enough* of a force between them. If this was right then we would have to argue that the force between the electron and proton is enough to fasten them together (and, thus, lead to their composing a hydrogen atom) whereas the gravitational force between the pen and the table is not enough to count as a fastening (and so not enough for composition to occur).

Suppose that's right. It raises an obvious question: how strongly fastened would two objects have to be in order to compose a new object? If gravity is not enough, but the clicking together of Lego bricks *is*, then we look to need some definite account of quite where this line is to be drawn.

We face a rock and a hard place, here. The rock: if we specify too weak a force requirement for two objects to count as fastened, then the 'pen-table' gets to count as an object, which runs counter to our desire to avoid being too liberal. The hard place: if we specify too strong a force for fastening to occur, then we'll lose certain objects from our ontology that we might well want to keep. That seems problematic as it would be too conservative. What would be needed if we were to preserve fastenation is some way of specifying the force requirement for fastening in a way that satisfies both our liberal and conservative intuitions *and* that isn't ad hoc. Such a constraint looks very difficult to find. For any strength of force that we posit, it would look most reasonable to ask why we have fixed on *that* strength of force and not something just a *little* weaker or stronger.

That is not, of course, to say that such a thing is impossible. But, absent some way of specifying a non-ad-hoc answer to the question of how securely fastened two objects must be in order to compose, I shall move on.

# §2.2 A very liberal reply

As indicated, we are at the moment stuck between having too conservative a criteria for when composition occurs (such that we admit too few objects into our ontology) and having too liberal a criteria for when composition occurs (such that we admit too many objects into our ontology). Although this seems like a problem to be overcome, some philosophers have denied that this is so. Indeed, some have chosen to become what we might call *maximally liberal* and endorse a view called *Universalism*, such that:

> Universalism: for any non-overlapping xs, there is a y such that y is composed of the xs.[3]

The consequence of this? Quite simply, that whenever we have two distinct things, they compose a further object. The pen-table exists! But that's not the least of it: there also exist Eiffel-tower-dolphins, cat-cheeses and tonsil-cups! Indeed, if God and the Devil both exist, then so does a 'God-Devil'.

Let's begin our consideration of Universalism by setting to one side the intuitive reaction that Universalism is *obviously* false (though we'll return to this later). Why might one be tempted to think Universalism is true? First, *Universalism* doesn't suffer from any problems of conservativeness: that is, it doesn't rule out the existence of any of the objects we wanted in our ontology. Given that we raised this as a problem for both *Contact* and *Fastenation*, this is surely a virtue of Universalism.

Second, Universalism permits us to provide definite answers to other difficult questions. In particular, Universalism helps us with the issue of vagueness. Consider the example of the chair with which we began this chapter. It seems quite plausible that there will be a particle that exists *right* at the boundary of the chair. Is the particle a part of the chair? If that particle is *right* at the very edge of the chair – right at the boundary between the chair and its surroundings – then it might seem as if there really is no answer to this question. It is, to use some philosophical parlance, we may say genuinely vague as to whether or not the particle is a part of the chair.

But vagueness in the world is, to many metaphysicians, not acceptable. There is always a fact of the matter. Either the particle is a part of the chair, or it is not. It cannot be a vague matter as to whether or not the particle is a part of the chair. It will not do to say that it is *genuinely* vague as to whether or not the particle is a part of a composite object. Thus, Lewis (1986a: 212)

> The only intelligible account of vagueness locates it in our thought and language. The reason it's vague where the outback begins is not that there's this thing, the outback, with imprecise borders; rather there are many things, with different borders, and nobody has been fool enough to try to enforce a choice of one of them as the official referent of the word 'outback'.

It had better not turn out, then, that there is genuine vagueness in the world.

Happily, given Universalism, there is no vagueness in the world; there is not a chair that has 'imprecise borders'. Rather, there are many different composite objects in the vicinity, with many different parts. Some of those composite objects have the particle that we described as 'at the boundary' as a part; others do not. But the crucial point is that there is no imprecision in the borders in any of the objects that exist. Vagueness only appears, here, because we have not decided which of these composite objects is the right one to be picked out by the term 'chair'. So, if it is more plausible to think that vagueness is in our language or in our epistemology, rather than *in the world* and (many metaphysicians claim that it is), then Universalism seems motivated.

Third, it's worth pointing out that *Universalism* isn't a purely *ad hoc.* answer to the SCQ. Whatever else we might say about *Universalism*, it's not *ad hoc.* We have a clear set of criteria as to when objects compose some further thing: always. Contrast this with 'fastening'. We saw that if we are to consider fastening a viable solution, then we must specify some particular strength of force as sufficient for fastening (and thus sufficient for composition). The trouble was that any strength of force that we specify looks arbitrary; we have no obvious reason to think that one particular strength of force is sufficient for composition, rather than another. Universalism simply faces no analogous problems.

## §2.2.1 Problems

Let's now consider a problem that a proponent of Universalism might face – that *Universalism* is just *obviously* false. After all, any criteria for object-hood that would include pen-tables, tonsil-cups and Eiffel-tower-dolphins is not a criteria that succeeds in capturing what we intuitively think of as objects, at all. None of the three aforementioned putative objects would be ones that *I* would naturally think of as actually being objects. Let us call these strange objects 'gruesome' objects (following the convention in the literature).

But, although it might be right that these objects are deeply counterintuitive, it's worth taking a moment to consider one way in which proponents of Universalism have attempted to explain away the fact that the result is so counterintuitive. Let us begin by noting that all agree with the Universalist *inasmuch as* all of the objects that we intuitively believe to exist, are counted as existing composite objects by *Universalism*. Where we disagree is in the further objects that Universalism claims exist. Thus, what we require is an explanation of why we think that there are no gruesome objects.

What has happened here, says the Universalist, is that our language suffers from certain anthropocentric tendencies, such that our tendency to not think of there being such things as pen-tables is merely a matter of our ignoring them – plausibly due to their not being that interesting to us. Given the sort of creatures we are, and the particular needs and plans and projects we have, we recognize pens and tables as objects, but do not recognize pen-tables (and the like) as objects. After all, how regularly would we need to invoke something as abstruse as a pen-table in an explanation? How frequently would we feel the need to talk about such a thing in such a way that we couldn't simply talk about there being both a pen and a table? Not very often at all. And so it is that we have come to believe that there are no such things.

In slightly more formal terms the idea is fleshed out by the claim that, in natural languages like English, we implicitly 'restrict our quantifiers'. Thus, the claim is that when we talk to one another using English, outside the philosophy class, we have already tacitly agreed to certain standards of use, such that the term 'exists' applies to tables, chairs and so on, but not to pen-tables, or other similarly gruesome objects.

There's a temptation to think such moves as underhand and a bit sneaky, but clearly English conversation does function in this way to at least some degree. We have conventions in place to ignore objects when we're assessing the truth of particular propositions. Consider, for instance, someone who says that 'it's raining'. Clearly, that person doesn't mean that every inch of the earth's surface is being rained upon; rather, they mean that some particular location is being rained upon. Likewise, if a cinema go-er remarks that 'everyone was eating popcorn' we would typically suppose that the context of the utterance in some way contributes to the truth-conditions of the utterance, such that for us to regard the claim to be true we would require nothing more than that everyone in the *cinema* was eating popcorn. In both the case of the rain and the popcorn what we have is an instance of context contributing to the truth-conditions of the sentence; context contributes to whether or not the sentence is true.

What the *Universalist* is drawing upon is precisely the same phenomena. They are claiming that our use of 'object' or 'exist' is restricted by the fact that when most of us use such language we are specifically ignoring all of these strange objects, such as pen-tables. But, once we remove these restrictions, the claim that 'there are no pen-tables' turns out to be false (in the same way that if we removed the implicit restriction to talking about only people in the cinema, the claim 'everyone was eating popcorn' would turn out to be false). We might then add to this the further claim that since we so rarely move beyond the context in which we agree that there are no such things as pen-tables (indeed, the only context in which we might be tempted to do such a thing is the context in which we engage in metaphysical theorizing), we've become *very* used to thinking that pen-tables are not objects. So used to it, in fact, that it's become a habit. And habits can be hard to kick. All of this being the case, we have a perfectly reasonable explanation as to why we might be tempted to think that Universalism is *obviously* false, even if it's not.

The shape of the dialectic here bears some thinking about. We began this chapter with the assumption that there were many different sorts of answer one could give to the SCQ; we've considered *Universalism* and although the theory seems motivated by sensible considerations and can deal with at least our intuitive worries about it, there remains the impression that *Universalism* is an extreme answer to the SCQ. If nothing else, Universalism posits *so many* different objects that it must do at least some violence to Ockham's razor, even if the objects posited are all of a kind with one another.

Perhaps what we should agree upon, then, is that Universalism seems internally coherent, and although it has some motivation, we might do well to see if other theories can generate better answers to the SCQ since *Universalism* seems like an extreme metaphysical position. It requires us to posit a very large number of objects – objects that we do not, at least intuitively, believe in.

# §2.3 Restricted theories of composition

If we're to avoid the rock of excessive conservatism and the hard place of excessive liberalism, we need a middle ground. We need to find an answer to the SCQ that includes objects such as tables, chairs and cups; but not pentables, Eiffel-tower dolphins and their gruesome fellows. One attempted answer to the question is due to Ned Markosian. His 'Brutal' view of composition is just this:

> *Brutal Composition*: There is no true, non-trivial, and finitely long answer to the SCQ. (Markosian (2008: 352))

Here is Markosian's explanation of the view:

> Suppose that there is no rhyme or reason as to when composition occurs and when it doesn't, as the view in question suggests. There could still be a truth of the form 'Necessarily, for any xs, there is an object composed of the xs iff –.' It would just have to be an infinitely long list of every possible situation involving some xs that compose a further object. (*op cit*)

Why believe that composition is Brutal? First, it's worth noting that the view accords with our intuitions (or, at least, it's plausible to think that it does). In any situation where we *think* that composition occurs, the most likely explanation of this – according to the proponent of BC – is that composition in fact occurs. *Why* is there composition in those cases? There *is* no reason; it's just a brute fact that there's composition in these cases.

Second, the proponent of BC might think that they can solve particular historical problems that have been raised. For instance, suppose that we have a cat called Tibbles, and that we identify some part of Tibbles as Tib: let's say that Tib consists in Tibbles, minus her tail. Thus, at some time t, Tibbles and Tib are distinct. However, suppose that at some later time, t*, Tibbles loses her tail, such that Tibbles and Tib become identical. If that turned out to be the case then, since identity is transitive, Tibbles and Tib ought to be the same thing as each other today – which is clearly an absurd result.

(A little more slowly: Tibbles at t is identical with Tibbles at t*; Tibbles at t* is identical with Tib at t*. But if Tibbles at t is identical with Tibbles at t* then Tibbles at t is also identical with Tib at t*. And since Tib at t* is identical with Tib at t, so Tibbles at t is identical with Tib at t. But that's wrong. Tibbles at t has a tail and Tib at t does not.)

Although there are many different solutions to this problem, it seems clear that BC offers us a straightforward time of it. I take it that, prior to my stipulation to the contrary, there was no temptation to think of Tib as a thing at all. In other words, Tib was not, according to our intuitions, an object. That being the case, there was no *thing* Tib, prior to t*, since there was no such thing that was composed out of the various parts of Tibbles, prior to the removal of Tibbles' tail. Since Tib didn't exist prior to t*, so there existed no such thing, Tib, with which Tibbles might be identical at t.

Third, it's also worth noting that BC is consistent with there not being vague objects in the world. We saw above that this was an advantage of *Universalism*: so, too, it must then be an advantage of BC. Is the particle at the end of your nose a part of you? If we thought BC correct, then we would surely concede that we do not know whether or not such a particle is a part of you. But, if BC is true, our *knowledge* of whether or not the particle is a part of you does not matter. The infinitely long list stipulated by BC will specify that the particle is a part of you, or it is not. It is not, therefore, a genuinely vague matter as to whether or not the particle is a part of you. This is the result that we were looking for.

## §2.3.1 Brutal problems

But BC suffers from problems too. To begin, let's look at an objection raised by Ted Sider. Consider, first, a case in which my body exists – C1. Now consider another case, C2, which consists of my post-cremation body's ashes scattered to the wind. Clearly, in C1, we want to say that my body is composed; equally clearly, in C2, we want to say that my body is not composed. Sider's thought, then, is that we can construct a sequence of cases connecting C1 to C2, within which each case is extremely similar to each case either side of it. Since we *do* have composition in C1, but not in C2, there must be some point in the series from C1 to C2 at which composition ceases to occur. The worry, then, is that the sequence of cases from C1 to C2 can be expanded so that the cases resemble one another *so* precisely at any particular point that it will appear arbitrary as to where we should say that composition is no more. As Sider has it:

> Why is the cut-off here, rather than there? Granted, everyone must admit *some* metaphysically 'brute' facts, and it is a hard question why one brute fact seems more or less plausible than another. Nevertheless, *this* brute fact seems particularly hard to stomach. (Sider 2001: 124)

Our concern then will be this. At some point in the continuum of cases between C1 and C2 we must specify that composition occurs in one case, but does not occur in the next. But given how closely these cases will resemble one another, it is 'hard to stomach' the idea that one of these states counts as composition, but the next one does not.

What to say in reply? Markosian puts the plausibility of this argument (what he calls the 'continuum' argument) down to the assumption that the qualitative resemblance between the various cases has, or ought to have, some impact on whether or not objects compose. So, the thought might be, because the various instances of C will differ only *slightly* with respect to some condition such as contact, so to suppose that one of these cases is sufficient for there to be composition, but not another, *would* be arbitrary.

Markosian aims to show that Sider's reasoning is faulty. To illustrate, he considers the following type of case that is not quite the same but reveals to us the way in which Sider's reasoning has gone astray. Suppose we construct a series of cases that resemble one another *almost* precisely at each point in the sequence, but such that there is a good variation in the series – perhaps a series of people who differ only minutely with respect to their height. To add colour to the case, suppose that there are, in fact, 1,000 people in this series. With this series in mind, suppose we were then presented with someone who was concerned with the thought that height dictated handedness, such that short people are left-handed and tall people are right-handed. In order to prove their thesis to us they ask us to conceive of a sequence much like the one described, where the first hundred or so people *are left*-handed and the last hundred or so are right-handed. They then argue that *at some point* there will have to be a sharp cut-off between those people who are right-handed and those that are left-handed. But, they say, this is clearly implausible since the people will resemble one another so closely: the cut-off will simply be arbitrary. Clearly, this is a bad argument: in part, it's a bad argument because it treats height as a determining factor in handedness, and then tries to show that once we've endorsed that assumption, there's no way to generate a distinction as to where in the scale right-handedness kicks in: that is, there's no *obvious* reason to think that any particular height generates right-handed people. But, of course, the argument is bad precisely *because* there is no connection between height and handedness. Thus, although any cut-off would be arbitrary, that fact is in and of itself uninteresting. What we must now do is tie this in to the case of composition.

Markosian's thought is that the case of height and handedness is just the same as the case of composition. The continuum argument seems appealing because we're *tempted* to think that composition has something to do with how closely the cases resemble one another with respect to some quality or other (perhaps contact, or fastenation). But once we recognize that there is no such connection (between e.g. contact or fastenation and composition), we ought to recognize that there's *no* problem in drawing a sharp cut-off in the sequence. There just is no connection between the facts of composition and the facts of contact or fastening, any more than there is a connection between height and handedness.

Another objection that we might put to the proponent of BC is that positing Brute metaphysics is to do *bad* metaphysics. We are, after all, at least to some extent in the business of explaining the world; positing primitives does nothing to explain anything.

But if we're going to push that line, then we need to be careful. As indicated in the passage from Sider, quoted above, *all* theories will need *some* metaphysical primitives. And, if all positions need some primitives, then it hardly seems fair to Markosian to object that his theory posits some primitives.

Perhaps the most obvious way to argue against Markosian is to look at the wider shape of the arguments that we have been considering. We allowed, above, that it was a virtue of Markosian's view that it helped us to preserve our intuitions about when composition occurs and when it does not. We said, in the introduction, that intuition preservation is a theoretical virtue. But the critic of BC might reasonably respond that this isn't the *only* intuition in the neighbourhood that might be worth considering. When we asked the SCQ we had the intuition that it could be answered. The SCQ *sounds*, intuitively, like the sort of question to which there ought to be informative answer that can be written down. Since Markosian is denying that there *is* an answer of this sort, so Markosian's view *in fact* fails to preserve some of our intuitions.

Of course, there is scope for a reply here: perhaps Markosian can say that he isn't interested in intuition preservation *in general*, only in particular cases. Although such a reply might work, we might then need to be told why to hold this form of particularism about intuitions. It's not entirely clear how we would provide such an explanation.

Markosian might, instead, say that intuition preservation *in general* is good, but since our inability to answer the SCQ points to the fact that the SCQ *can't* be answered, so BC is the best way to preserve at least *some* of our intuitions. This latter approach will depend upon whether or not other solutions turn out to be viable. One might be sceptical, though, since we've already seen that *Universalism* looks at least coherent. In any case, it will pay dividends to turn, once more, to another competing answer to the SCQ.

# §2.4 Nihilism

In the same way that *Universalism* might be seen to be the liberal extreme, endorsing the existence of a plethora of hitherto unconceived of objects, *Nihilism* represents the conservative extreme:

> *Nihilism*: Necessarily, for any non-overlapping *xs* there is an object composed of the *xs*, iff there is only one of the *xs*.

In less precise, though more colourful, language, the only objects that exist are mereological simples – those objects that lack parts. It is not clear what these will be, but perhaps we can simply describe them as the most fundamental particles. Our current best candidates may be quarks.

Granting the (seemingly) plausible assumption that tables, people, atoms and the like would have parts if they existed, so tables, people, atoms and the like do not exist. Indeed, it seems as if the *Nihilist*'s view of reality will be such that there exist some fundamental particles that have no parts, but nothing else.

Clearly, *Nihilism* is counterintuitive. Intuitively true propositions like <there is a table> turn out, on this view, to be false. So, like the proponent of *Universalism*, the Nihilist must take some steps to explain away the counterintuitiveness of their position. In fact, things are perhaps worse for the Nihilist than they are for the Universalist. Whereas the Universalist had to explain the truth of propositions that we typically don't think about (e.g. <this is a pen-table>), the Nihilist has to explain to us why the propositions about which we seem *most certain* (such as <this is a table>) are, in fact, false.

But other challenges abound, too. Nihilism might, at first blush, seem to be at odds with our best physics. For example, physicists study the earth; they study atoms. Both the earth and atoms look to be composite objects and so if Nihilism denies that there are composite objects, then parts of physics dealing with these topics will be mere elaborate fiction. That would be a highly controversial result.

The Nihilist thinks that they have a response to both points. To begin with, although they think that propositions like <this is a table> are false, the Nihilist doesn't deny that sentences such as 'this is a table' are warranted, even though they expresses a false proposition. According to the Nihilist, the world is arranged in a particular sort of way, and it is due to that arrangement of the world that it is *appropriate* for us to say 'there is a table', even if it is strictly speaking false. Thus, although our talk about tables and other composite objects lacks truth-makers and so is false, the intuitive pull of our talk is explained by the fact that some very similar proposition *is* true.

Here is the Nihilist's explanation in more detail. There are no composite objects, but there are mereological simples (objects with no parts) arranged in particular ways. In the case of the table we might say that although <there is a table> lacks a truth-maker, the very similar proposition <there is a collection of simples arranged table-wise> has a truth-maker: namely, a particular arrangement of simples arranged table-wise. Because we don't *typically* think of there as being a distinction between the two propositions (<there is a table>, <there is a collection of simples arranged table-wise>) so we think of the first being true, where, in fact, only the second proposition is true.

The Nihilist thinks that they can use this pattern of explanation to make sense of the putative objection from science, too. Nothing in our best science, they will contend, requires that here be any such *thing* as a 'composite object'; instead, our best physics can be understood as compatible with the view that there are no composite objects, there are merely simples arranged object-wise.

Thus the Nihilist is even able to offer us the following canonical re-interpretation of our physical theories:

(i) replacing every occurrence of 'there is something which' with 'there are some things which'
(ii) replacing every occurrence of 'for every thing' with 'whenever there are some things'
(iii) replacing every occurrence of 'is part of' with 'are among' (the xs are among the ys iff whenever something is one of the xs, it is one of the ys)
(iv) replacing every occurrence of 'is identical to' with 'are the same things as' (the xs are the same things as the ys iff for any thing, it is one of the xs iff it is one of the ys)
(v) replacing every singular predicate in the theory with a new plural predicate. Thus, 'is a molecule' is replaced by 'are arranged molecule-wise', 'has mass M' is replaced by 'have mass M'. (Rosen and Dorr (2002: 163))

All of which is well and good, but the Nihilist then owes us at least two further arguments. First, although they might have told us how our everyday talk about composite objects comes to be thought of as true, even if it is not, and they may have circumvented the arguments from physics, they haven't yet spoken directly to the concern that their theory is deeply unintuitive. Second, given that the view seems so counterintuitive, without some strong motivation to believe it we might well think that we ought to not endorse Nihilism. Motivation thus becomes a pressing issue.

Let's begin with considerations of motivation. Why might we be tempted by Nihilism? Three reasons are prominent, here. First, there is no vagueness in Nihilistic worlds because there are no composite objects about which it might then be a vague matter as to whether or not some x is a part of that object. Second, the theory is extremely elegant; not only that, but it also scores highly when we think about ontological parsimony. It's hard to conceive of a simpler theory than one that posits nothing other than mereological simples. Third, we might reasonably argue that, in the face of none of the other answers to the SCQ looking that appealing, Nihilism begins to seem a reasonable option.

One further argument can be brought forward in favour of Nihilism – though it is certainly controversial. Consider a cricket ball: if that entity exists, then it is composed of a collection of particles. Now suppose that, as seems probable, the physical explanation of the flight and behaviour of the ball can be explained completely by explaining and describing the behaviour of the sub-atomic particles that compose the ball. Add to our case a window. Similarly, the window is composed of a collection of sub-atomic particles and a description and explanation of the behaviour of the window requires *nothing* other than a complete description and explanation of the behaviour of the sub-atomic particles that compose the window.

With the context described, now consider how we should think about what happens when the ball strikes the window. A natural thought is that the ball causes the window to break. However, if there is nothing to describing and explaining the behaviour of both ball and window over and above a description of what happens at the micro level, then it looks as if all of the causal work that will be done at the micro level in our scenario. That is, the sub-atomic particles that compose the ball behave in a particular way; the sub-atomic particles that compose the window behave in a particular way *and that's it*. There is nothing more to be said. If we also thought that the ball and the window were genuinely involved in the case then, as well as the sub-atomic particles causing other sub-atomic particles to behave in a given way, we'd *also* have the ball causing the window to break. This would leave us with the ball causing the window to break *and* one set of sub-atomic particles causing another set of sub-atomic particles to behaving in a particular way. Now that seems odd.

In fact, it seems more than odd. It seems that the ball and window would, if they existed, 'overdetermine' the outcome: the behaviour of both the particles and the ball and window seem to account for the outcome. Now, if the particles are doing all of the work, then it seems that the ball and window have no real part to play in the scenario. And if that turned out to be true, if we had no role for window and ball to play, and so no reason, presumably, to think that they exist, then it would look to be a violation of OR for us to posit the ball and window in addition to the sub-atomic particles. We might then argue that this favours Nihilism. According to Nihilism, there is nothing other than the mereological simples. There is no ball; there is no window. All that we have are the elementary particles that lack parts.

This will be where Nihilism can make gains. Since Nihilism posits no composite objects, so Nihilism will never entail that there is over-determination and, if that is the case, then Nihilism is *obviously* preferable to other theories of composition.[4]

This leads us on to the other question: how do we deal with the charge that the view proposed is deeply counterintuitive and defies common sense? To an extent, this is a charge that must be met head-on. The view just *is* counterintuitive. However, the charge can be mitigated. Metaphysicians are typically prepared to allow that, all things being equal, it is preferable for our best theory to be one that is intuitive. But, even then, we do not want to cling dogmatically to our intuitions. After all intuitions are often fickle things affected by the media, gender, race and so on. There is more to metaphysics than simply asserting your preferred view and declaring it to be intuitive.

With that in mind, consider two sentences.

(a) There is a table in my office.

(b) There are simples arranged table-wise in my office.

The point we must then concede is that although unreflective commonsense favours (a), it is equally clear that (b) has never occurred to us (outside our theorizing at any rate). We surely cannot rule out (b) on the grounds that it's counterintuitive if we've never given it a moment's thought before. Clearly, what is needed is time and space for reflection. Nihilists will then claim that, once we have given this some deeper thought, it is far from clear that (a) is obviously true and (b) obviously false. Our intuitions, once better informed, will not tell between the two – or so claims the Nihilist (cf. Rosen and Dorr (2002: 158).

# §2.5 Organicism

Van Inwagen claims that we do have reason to think that there are composite objects. Thinking cannot occur without composition. Van Inwagen's claim is that there must be at least some composite objects because a mere collection of objects can never think. That is, a collection of simples arranged person-wise is not a collection that is capable of thinking. This, Van Inwagen thinks, motivates a move to Organicism.

Organicism: necessarily, for any *xs*, the *xs* compose, iff their activity constitutes a life.[5]

Two points are worth making, however. First, Van Inwagen's argument against the Nihilist looks like it fails; second, it's opaque as to what Van Inwagen's view really entails.

Van Inwagen's argument against the Nihilist proceeds via an examination of Searle's Chinese Room thought experiment. Suppose that an English monoglot is placed in a sealed room with a collection of Chinese ciphers and a manual: the manual tells our English monoglot which ciphers to respond with when given Chinese ciphers. Our native English speaker then has various Chinese ciphers fed into the room and then, as per the instructions, proceeds to feed various Chinese ciphers out of the room. The (not uncontroversial) Searlian conclusion is that this system of inputs and outputs fails to display what we would think of as understanding, and so no model of mind that treats thinking as mere 'inputs and outputs' can be correct. There must be more to thought than these mere inputs and outputs.

Van Inwagen claims, though, that we can put this case to other work. Since what we have in the Chinese Room case is clearly a case of co-operative activity, but not also an instance of thought, so we can conclude that *mere* co-operative activity is insufficient for thought. The Nihilist only has mereological simples in their ontology, and would be forced to describe thought as a mere co-operative activity of many distinct simples. Thus, Nihilism is false and there are composite objects – thinking objects.

But, at least as far as it goes, the argument fails since it looks to draw a general conclusion from a specific instance. That is, Van Inwagen infers that *no* instance of co-operative behaviour is sufficient for thought simply because *an* instance of co-operative behaviour is insufficient for thought. Since generalizations from singular instances aren't valid, so Van Inwagen's argument has less force than it might initially appear.

But even if the argument did have some force, Van Inwagen's view is less clear than we might like. For instance, what, exactly, is it for the activity of some simples to constitute a life? How is it that simply by thinking occurring, composition occurs? On this last point, consider the following case, that seems highly counterintuitive. Suppose that Smith is in an extremely serious car accident and suffers severe neurological injuries, to the extent that in the operating room, Smith's neurological activity occasionally ceases, though is then restarted. In such a case, it looks very much as if the object we might refer to as Smith is going out of and coming back into existence. Not only that, but we go from there being a composite object one second, to it ceasing to exist, to it returning to existence, from one moment to the next. That appears strange. Somehow we are obliged to say that Smith is constantly drifting in and out of existence, despite the fact that to all intents and purposes it seems to us as if Smith is continuing to exist all along.

# §2.6 Monism

If we were tempted to believe in Nihilism, then there's plausibly another view that might be even more appealing: Monism. For the purposes of this chapter, at least, Monism is the view that there exists only *one* material object – the world.[6] (I should make clear, here, that when philosophers talk of 'the world' they typically mean something like 'this universe'.)

Why might we think that Monism is preferable to Nihilism? Two reasons appear salient. First, it looks to be an empirically open hypothesis that the world is such that there is infinite descent – that is, there is no lowest level. So, even the 'fundamental' particles that we fixed upon earlier are not simples. If that were to be the case, then the Nihilist is in trouble. How can there exist *only* simples if there is no 'bottom level' at which the simples might reside? If the picture just sketched is correct then Nihilism is false because there *is* no level at which the simples may reside. The Monist, in contrast, has no problem here. According to the Monist, it will *appear* to us that the world can be divided in such a way as to permit infinite descent: but that doesn't mean that the world has many *parts* (for if there *were* parts then these would be objects, and then more things than just the world would exist). But, the Monist thinks, merely that we can point to different areas of 'the World' does not show that these are *parts*. Indeed, since there is only one object, there *are* no parts. One way to try and conceptualize this is to think of a photograph. We can specify from the outset that this picture has no parts. However, it is nonetheless true that we can imagine keeping on zooming in on some particular area of the picture and finding more and more detail. Indeed, we could keep zooming in *forever* and still keep finding more detail.

Second, the Monist might claim that their view takes parsimony more seriously than does Nihilism. After all, the Nihilist posits a whole world of simples. By contrast, the Monist posits *only* a single concrete object – the world. Thus, Monism fairs better than Nihilism given considerations of parsimony.

Of course, Monism must deny, just as Nihilism did, that there are such things as people, chairs etc. So in precisely the same way that we saw that Nihilism does violence to our intuitions, so too does Monism. But that argument is only of tangential interest at this point in the dialectic. The claim made by the Monist is not that Monism is *right*, but that if you're persuaded by the virtues of Nihilism then you should be persuaded to take a further step and endorse Monism. Whether you then also think this only trivially interesting, perhaps because you *do* think that both Nihilism and Monism are ruled out by simple consideration of our intuitions, is something to be decided elsewhere.

# §2.7 Really a debate?

So how are we to decide what the best answer is to the SCQ? A number of considerations have already been raised: vagueness, intuitions as to how conservative or liberal our ontology ought to be, concerns over criteria being *ad hoc*, and we've also raised concerns as to whether or not consideration of the putative causal powers of objects has any role to play in determining which composite objects we ought to endorse.

But there might remain a suspicion that the various different positions that we've been surveying aren't, in fact, substantive metaphysical positions, and that the disagreement that seems to have been going on here is a disagreement about the way that we should use language, not a disagreement about the nature of the world. For example, compare the Nihilist and the Universalist positions. Both positions are compatible with the existence of simples (objects that themselves lack parts). Further, the proponent of Nihilism allows that there are collections of simples arranged (e.g.) table-wise. The difference between that view and the view that those simples compose a table *simply by existing* (Universalism) seems to be nothing more than a matter of what we *say* is required for composition. Universalism says that all that you need to do to be a part of something else is to exist; Nihilism, denies that this is sufficient for being a part. So, isn't this really a debate about the meanings of the word 'part' and 'exist'?

It's hard to see how to resolve this issue. What is certain, however, is that proponents of the views sincerely believe themselves to be having a substantive argument. The Nihilist and Universalist really do think that they are arguing about the existence of composite objects; they do not take themselves to be arguing merely about how we do and should use the words 'part' and 'exist'. If we are then sceptical about their debate and whether or not it is a debate that cuts to the heart of a metaphysical issue, then we must find a good argument that shows our opponent that they are *not* engaged in a substantive debate. Our doubts that the debate is genuine are not sufficient. If we are to convince our opponent that there is no genuine debate going on then we owe some argument.

# Recommended reading

### General

Van Inwagen, P. 1990. *Material Beings*. Cornell: Ithaca.

### Universalism

Lewis, D. 1986a. *On the Plurality of Worlds*. Oxford: Blackwell, 211–13.

Van Cleeve, J. 2008. 'The Moon and Sixpence: A Defence of Mereological Universalism', in Sider, T., Hawthorne, J. and Zimmerman, D. eds. *Contemporary Debates in Metaphysics*, 321–40.

Van Inwagen, P. 1990. *Material Beings*. Cornell: Ithaca, 74–80.

### Restricted theories of composition

Markosian, N. 1998. 'Brutal Composition', *Philosophical Studies*, 92, 211–49.

Markosian, N. 2008. 'Restricted Composition', in Sider, T., Hawthorne, J. and Zimmerman, D. eds. *Contemporary Debates in Metaphysics*, 341–63.

### Nihilism

Rosen, G. and Dorr, D. 2002. 'Composition as Fiction', in Gale, R. ed. *The Blackwell Guide to Metaphysics*. Oxford: Blackwell, 151–74.

Schaffer, J. 2007. 'From Nihilism to Monism', *Australasian Journal of Philosophy*, 85, 175–91.

Williams, R. 2006. 'Illusions of Gunk', *Philosophical Perspectives*, 20, 493–513.

### Organicism (and similar)

Merricks, T. 2003. *Objects and Persons*. Oxford: OUP.

Van Inwagen, P. 1990. *Material Beings*. Cornell: Ithaca, chapter 9 onwards.

### Really a debate?

Hirsch, E. 2002a. 'Against Revisionary Ontology', *Philosophical Topics*, 30, 103–27.

Hirsch, E. 2002b. 'Quantifer Variance and Realism', *Philosophical Issues*, 12, 51–73.

Sider, T. 2009b. 'Ontological Realism', in Chalmers, D., Manley, D. and Wasserman, R. eds. *Metametaphysics* Oxford: OUP, 384–423.

## Study questions

1) Write out each of the main theories of composition. Which theory do you think is best? What made you pick that theory?
2) Do you think it matters whether a view is too liberal/too conservative? Explain your answer.

3) Both Nihilism and Universalism look to explain away our intuitions about when composition occurs: how successful do you think these strategies are?
4) A number of competing methodological considerations were raised in this chapter. What were they? How important did you think them?
5) Do you think that there is any connection between thinking and composition?
6) Do you think that the debate between Nihilism and Universalism is *substantive*?

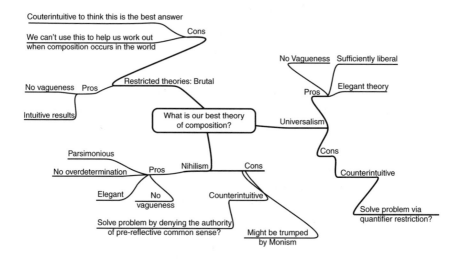

# Other Objects: 'Abstract' Objects

Our topic in this chapter is abstract objects; in particular, numbers. Are there such things as numbers? If so, what sorts of entity are they? In part, this chapter also serves to introduce a number of types of argument. These arguments will play a prominent role in the chapters that follow. Before we look to see quite what sorts of things numbers might be, let's first consider why we might be tempted to believe in the existence of such things.

## §3.1 As if by magic . . .

To begin with, consider the following sentences, paying particular attention to the underlined portions:

(1) <u>Jonathan</u> is hungry.
(2) <u>The cat</u> is sat on the mat.
(3) <u>The table</u> is square.

These sentences have a particular grammatical feature in common: they are subject predicate sentences. Crudely, these are sentences that name some object (the subject) and ascribe some property to it (the predicate). So, in (1) the subject of the sentence is 'Jonathan'; the predicate 'is hungry'.

Now, one thing that I take it we would agree upon as relatively uncontroversial is that in order for any of those sentences to express true propositions, the subject must exist. Thus (1) cannot be true unless Jonathan exists; (2) cannot be true absent a cat; (3) cannot be true unless there is a table. Granted, there may be further requirements in order for the sentences to express true propositions (the predicates may also have to accurately characterize the subjects, such that, for instance, Jonathan must *be hungry*), but it is at least a necessary condition that the described subjects exist if the sentences are to express true propositions.

That seems right. If we have a true subject–predicate sentence, we need the subject to exist. The moral of this tale, then, is that subject–predicate sentences are true only if the subject exists.

But now consider the following sentence:

(4) I have two cats.

This sentence is true: I do have two cats. But notice that (4) seems to entail (5):

(5) Two is the number of cats that I have.

To bring this out more clearly, consider (5) as a response to the question, 'what number of cats do you have?'.

A striking feature of (5), of course, is that it has 'Two' in the subject position; that is, a *number* appears in a true sentence as the subject of that sentence. We noted, just a moment ago, that where we have true subject–predicate sentences, the subject must exist, else the sentence cannot be true. Thus, 'Two' must exist in order for the sentence to be true. It seems that we can construct similar cases for all numbers. For example, 'there are nine planets' seems to entail that 'nine is the number of planets' which in turn entails that 'Nine' must exist; 'I have three pens' seems to entail that 'three is the number of pens that I have' which in turn entails that 'Three' must exist and so on. Unless we then want to deny that sentences like 'I have two cats' and 'there are nine planets' express true propositions, it would seem that we have little choice but to accept that numbers exist. Since sentences such as 'I have two cats' and 'there are nine planets' *clearly* do express true propositions, so we are obliged, or so it seems, to believe in the existence of numbers.

To be sure, the preceding argument seems suspicious. There is a definite sense that the existence of numbers has been generated almost out of nothing. After all, we began with a meagre claim about my cats and have now ended up believing in the existence of numbers. It rather seems as if we've inferred from the structure of our language to the nature of the world. Intuitively, that we can re-order a true sentence like (4) ought not to then require that we make substantial addition to our metaphysic. Because of that intuitive suspicion it's all too tempting to dismiss the thought that numbers exist out of hand. At least for the time being let's set that temptation to one side and consider the putative *natures* of numbers.

# §3.2 The nature of numbers

If there are numbers, how should we think of them? Typically, we are entreated to think of numbers as abstract objects; objects much like physical objects, but objects that (at least to a crude approximation) are 'outside space and time'. This loose notion needs to be tidied up.

A number of features seem to characterize abstract objects.

(i) Abstract objects, such as numbers, are *a causal* – that is, they do not causally interact with physical objects
(ii) Abstract objects, such as numbers, lack spatial or temporal location and extension
(iii) Abstract objects, such as numbers, are unchanging

Why might we be tempted to endorse that characterization as apt? Well, take for example the number 'two'. I've never seen the number 'two' cause anything: certainly, I've never seen it; I've never tripped over it; I've never smelt it. Granted, I may have seen instances of it if it exists (my two hands, two of my toes, my two cats), and I've seen an inscription of the token that we use to refer to the abstract object: that is, I've seen '2' written on a page. But I haven't seen 'two' itself. Neither am I aware of any causal role that the number two has played. For instance, I've never been aware of the number two breaking a window, mowing the lawn or throwing a stone. So all things considered, whatever else numbers do, they don't seem to cause anything to happen.

Further, to think that numbers have a spatial or temporal location would be odd. For instance, do we think that the number two is in my office, but not also in the south of France? Do we think that it resides in 2020, but not 2378? No, we do not. Indeed, to ask of numbers where or when they exist seems to mistake the very kind of entity that they are supposed to be – *abstract* objects. Because the very idea of numbers *being at* locations in space or time seems to make so little sense, it seems right to think that numbers lack spatial or temporal location. Of course, if they are not *in* time and space, then it's hard to see how numbers could have either temporal or spatial *extension*, either.

Finally, it's tempting to think of numbers as unchanging. In part, it's tempting to think of them as unchanging because it's hard to think of quite how numbers could change. It seems ridiculous, for instance, to suppose that where once 2+2=5, it is now the case that we have moved to a situation in which 2+2=4. Quite simply, the interrelations between numerical values have not and could not have changed. Thus we have support for the idea that numbers cannot change.

There remains the temptation to think that this is something of a thin characterization of abstract objects; just about everything that has been said has stipulated that abstract objects are *not* particular sorts of thing: they *do not* stand in causal relations to other objects; *do not* exist in space; *do not* exist in time; *do not* change. Is there a way in which we can offer a positive definition of what it is to be an abstract object?

One refinement suggested in the literature is due to Lowe and a brief diversion through Lowe's views gives us some space to consider some of the ways in which we might attempt to give a more positive characterization of abstract objects.

Lowe's (2002) suggestion is to start off with an initial claim about what it would be to be 'inside' and 'outside' time, and then use that distinction to characterize the further distinction between concrete and abstract objects. We begin with:

(6) To be in time is 'to be a possible subject of true tensed predications'.

Consider an example of an object that is obviously 'in time' – my cat Berkeley. Is Berkeley also the subject of true tensed predication? Yes. The sentence, 'Berkeley is scratching the sofa' has Berkeley as the subject of the sentence and includes tensed predication ('is scratching the sofa'). Likewise, the sentence 'Berkeley was ill, so we took him to the vet' has Berkeley as its subject, and includes tensed predication, 'was ill'.

However, numbers are not the possible subject of true tensed predications. Instead, they are only the possible subject of true tense*less* predications. The thought behind this is that although it makes good sense to say that '2+2 is 4', where we read the 'is' as tenselessly true – true at all times – it makes little sense to say '2+2 *was* 4'. One might, for instance, think that the latter incorrectly implies that although 2+2 *was* 4, it won't be in the future.

But, Lowe argues, (6) doesn't quite succeed. The number '12' appears as the subject in the following tensed predication, '12 used to be my favourite number'. Since this is a true tensed sentence that treats '12' as the subject, this is a direct counterexample to the proposal that we treat (6) as capturing what it is to be outside time – assuming we are to think of numbers as existing outside time.

One refinement, thinks Lowe, would be to suggest that all tensed discourse about number is purely *contingent* in character. That is, sentences such as '12 used to be my favourite number' could be true, but could also be false. We would then use this condition to augment (6). That deals with the putative counterexample since it's pretty clear that 12 might never have been my favourite number.

But, again, we can find counterexamples to even this augmented version of (6). For instance, 'either the number twelve is now being thought of by me or it is not the case that the number twelve is now being though about by me' (2002: 371). Since this expresses a logical truth (of the form P v ¬P; 'P or not P'), so it's necessarily true. This is an instance of a number being the subject of necessarily true tensed sentence and so is a counterexample to our augmented version of (6).

Lowe (2002: 371–2) finally settles upon:

> the sense in which such abstract objects as numbers do not exist 'in' time is that the only true tensed predications of which they can be the subjects *and which are not necessary truths quite independently of the fact that it is these objects that are their subjects* are contingent ones.

Since the last counterexample is necessarily true *only* in virtue of the fact that the truth is necessary independently of the fact that it's a tensed sentence (because it is a sentence of the form P v ¬P) so that *putative* counterexample no longer provides us with a problem or *genuine* counterexample.

But it seems that we can still ask *metaphysical* questions about what Lowe says. After all, to simply stipulate that numbers aren't the subject of one particular mode of predication, isn't to commit to a readily understandable notion of the nature of abstract objects. By way of analogy, suppose I were to tell you that to be 'possible' is to be the subject of modal predication (i.e. for x to be 'possible' is for x to be the subject of sentences that say that 'x is possible'). Plainly, that doesn't then tell us anything about the *nature* of modality. All that it tells us is that x is possible only if we can say that 'x is possible'. If that's right, then telling us that to be an abstract object is to be the subject of true tensed predication isn't to tell us anything at all.

In the end, our inability to say very much more than (i)–(iii) may present us with some difficulty. But let us allow that the proponent of abstract objects has said enough for us to be going on with. Abstract objects are exactly like concrete objects other than that abstract objects are *a causal*, are not located in time or space and are unchanging. We must now return to the issue of whether or not to believe in such entities.[1]

# §3.3 Why believe in AOs?

The argument I presented, above, was suspicious, because it seems as if we have begun with a true sentence about something mundane, and ended up with some extravagant ontology. What might we do?

One strategy we might adopt is to say that sentences like (4) do not entail sentences like (5). That;

(4) I have two cats.

does not entail,

(5) Two is the number of cats that I have.

But such moves look *prima facie* to be a dead-end. Witness:

(6) The table is brown.
(7) Brown is the colour of the table.

Just like (4) and (5), (6) appears to entail (7). That (6) entails (7) seems to be nothing more than a feature of the grammar of our language. It is a purely structural matter that (6) entails (7).

Now the relationship between (4) and (5) seems to be the same as the relationship between (6) and (7). The same change in structure seems to occur.

If that is right, then denying that (4) entails (5) seemingly requires us to give up on the claim that (6) entails (7). It is the structure of the sentences that preserves the entailment, so if we deny that (4) entails (5), then we must be denying that these kinds of structural changes are entailment preserving. Thus, we must deny that (6) entails (7).

But this looks a steep price to pay. It requires us to give up on our intuitive way of understanding entailments between sentences. It would require us to say, for instance, that it is possible that the table is brown, and that brown is not the colour of the table! Equally, we would have to give up on the claim that 'Barack Obama is the president of the United States' entails that 'The president of the United States is Barack Obama.' Surely that is a step too far. We ought not to give up on our language and logic so swiftly.

A slightly more drastic response might be to deny that sentences like (5) are true. We might concede that (5) is entailed by (4), but because we are reluctant to believe in the existence of abstract objects, argue that this shows that (4) must be false.

The thought, in rather more detail, might be this: we are all familiar with philosophy generating odd results. Philosophers have argued that time is unreal, that nothing ever changes, and that there are no tables. So, we might think, to give up on the truth of a few sentences about which, prior to this, we'd never given much consideration, is simply no great loss. And, in any case, simply that we've always *thought* that these sentences are true, is no sort of guide to their *actually being so*, is it? Doesn't this just appear to be an instance of our pre-theoretical beliefs being allowed to run riot, generating metaphysical commitments without proper consideration? We allowed in Chapter 1 that our intuitions are of some weight and so we should agree that denying the intuition that there are mathematical truths is a heavy theoretical cost, but perhaps given the ontological cost that we seem to be incurring in positing a whole new type of object, we should simply accept this theoretical cost. We might well think that even if we grant that the denial of these pre-theoretical intuitions *is* a cost, it is a better cost to bear than having to posit a whole different *type* of object. Ockham's razor might favour such an approach.

In response we might consider both the physical and mathematical sciences.

(8) 7 is greater than 5.
(9) There is a largest prime number.
(10) Force equals mass multiplied by acceleration.

Clearly, (8) is true – and is known to be by anyone with even the most elementary grasp of mathematics. Notice, also, that (8) is a subject–predicate sentence, and so given our earlier reasoning it can only be true if the subject of the sentence exists. Thus, numbers must exist else our elementary mathematics is false. Likewise, (9) is taken to be an open mathematical hypothesis: that is, it is held to be a claim that mathematicians might falsify or prove. But the proof lies, we think, solely within mathematics. It is not, or so we might think, within our purview as philosophers to deny that (9) is so.

What both of these sentences have in common, then, is that they are expressions of mathematical hypotheses. In particular (8) is a well-supported mathematical claim. If it is a well-supported mathematical claim then it would make sense to think that it is true. One might even go so far as to suggest that philosophy simply could not show the likes of (8) and (9) to be false. As Lewis puts it (Lewis (1991: 58–9)):

> Mathematics is an established, ongoing concern. Philosophy is as shaky as can be . . . I'm moved to laughter at the thought of how *presumptuous* it would be to reject mathematics for philosophical reasons.

Part of the thought behind this assertion runs as follows. Mathematics, historically, has done pretty well at tracking the truth. There aren't *many* mathematical claims that were once thought to be true that are now thought to be false. Philosophy, however, has done pretty badly. There are a number of philosophical claims that were once thought to be true that are now thought to be false. Once we take all of this into account, we might think it pretty obvious that we should not allow a philosophical overturning of mathematical truths. So these claims that are purely mathematical look to be ones that philosophers ought to take great care to avoid overturning.

Sentence (10) will take a little more unpacking: why think that a sentence that purports to be about force, mass and acceleration entails the existence of numbers? Well, we do not think that force, itself, is *equal* to mass multiplied by acceleration. After all, force is not mass and is not acceleration. It's hard to see how some physical force might be equal to two things that are so obviously not identical to it. Furthermore, multiplication is a mathematical operation. We cannot, then, literally multiply acceleration; properly speaking we can only multiply numbers. Hence, a more perspicuous reading of (10) might be:

(11) The number of units of force is equal to the number of units of mass multiplied by the number of units of acceleration.

Now although (11) makes no explicit appeal to the existence of specific numbers, and the existence of no particular number seems to be entailed by (11). But what is clear is that any particular application of the general scheme *will* end up so doing. For instance, consider the (admittedly rather wordy):

> (12) The force exerted by the hammer was equal to its mass of seven kilograms multiplied by its acceleration of 3ms$_{-2}$, which is to say that there was a force of 21 Newtons exerted by the hammer.

We could focus upon many different parts of (12), but simply consider the final clause: 'there was a force of 21 Newtons exerted by the hammer'. Using the strategy we outlined above, we can see that this entails;

> (13) 21 is the number of Newtons of force exerted by the hammer.

Once more it seems as if we have an argument for the existence of numbers. Notice, though, that this is not exactly the same as the purely mathematical sentences described by (8) and (9). The line of reasoning that we have just deployed has taken us through a way in which the *application* of mathematics is essential to science. Since ((13) (and (12), and many other sentences like them) must be true, as they express well-founded scientific claims, and since numbers appear to be an essential ingredient of our scientific theories, so numbers must exist.

# §3.4 Formalizing indispensability

This last kind of argument, that treats mathematical truths as indispensible to science, is known in the literature as the indispensability argument. It is, typically, taken to be the strongest argument that the Platonist has for the conclusion that there are numbers and may be regimented, thus:

> (14) We ought to have ontological commitment to all and only the entities that are indispensable to our best scientific theories.
> (15) Mathematical entities are indispensible to our best scientific theories.[2]
> (16) We ought to have ontological commitments to mathematical entities.

It seems a straightforward matter that (14) together with (15) entails (16); the argument appears valid. So we must now determine whether or not the argument is also sound; are (14) and (15) true? Our cursory examination in the preceding section may suggest so, but there are a number of ways in which we might respond.

One very appealing and natural way in which to object to the forgoing is to try to deny (15) by trying to deny that mathematical entities *are* indispensible to our best scientific theories – we still allow that mathematical claims are true, of course, but we deny that we need numbers as truth-makers for these propositions.

To see how this will work, let's consider a case.[3] Suppose that we have good evidence for the claim that:

(17) The average mother has 2.4 children.

No-one (who isn't a philosopher, at any rate) thinks that this entails the existence of 'the average mother'. Instead, we will explain the appearance of 'the average mother' in (17) by some other means. Consider, then, a sentence that is entailed by (17)

(18) 2.4 is the number of children that the average mother gives birth to.

(18) would *seem* to suggest, not only that there *really exists* the average mother, but that it *really* has 2.4 children. Presumably, this would involve chopping up the third child in a rather drastic fashion! But if we don't believe that such things as 'average mothers' exist, then what *do* we think is going on in cases like (17) and (18)?

# §3.5 Paraphrase

There is, on the surface of it, a very straightforward answer to that question. When we say that (17) is true what we commit to is nothing more than that, if we were to count up all of the mothers, and all of the children of those mothers and then divide the number of children by the number of mothers, the result would be 2.4. What we can do, then, is give a *paraphrase* of talk about 'average mothers', in terms of entities that are not remotely ontologically suspect: mothers.

The hope, then, is that we might be able to perform some similar task with number talk. That is, in the same way that we were able to preserve the truth of (17) but without committing to the existence of 'the average mother', perhaps we can preserve the truth of number talk, without committing to the existence of numbers. Instead, we can use a paraphrase that makes mention *only* of concrete objects. This is mathematical nominalism.

So how will the nominalist paraphrase work? Let's take a relatively straight-forward sentence, to begin. Suppose that we wish to make sense of sentences (4) and (5). Consider a slightly simplified version of (4):

(4)* There are two cats.

To paraphrase away any potential commitment to a 'number of cats', what we might then say is that (4)* expresses nothing more than the following claim, where 'C' stands for the predicate 'is a cat'. To make things slightly more perspicuous, I'll use first-order logic (plus the identity relation) in the paraphrase.

(4-para) $\exists x \exists y \, Cx \, \& \, Cy \, \& \, x{\neq}y \, \& \, \forall z \, Cz \rightarrow (z{=}x \lor z{=}y)$

In words: there exists an x and a y; x and y are cats and are not identical to one another, and anything that is a cat is identical to either x or y. The net result is that there are precisely two cats, despite the fact that *nowhere in (4-para) is there any mention of numbers*. (4-para) commits us to the existence of cats, but it does not obviously commit us to the existence of numbers.

It's relatively easy to see how we can expand this strategy. Whenever we're presented with a sentence that might *appear* to entail the existence of numbers, all that we have to do is paraphrase it using a quantified logic, plus identity. We call a theory that tries to preserve mathematical truths without positing numbers, and by explaining our number talk by recourse to particular entities (such as the cats in the above), 'nominalism'.

Before moving on to consider some of the serious problems that this view faces, it's worth considering an intuitive response that you might have. In the case of the sentence 'The average other has two children' we were happy enough with the paraphrase. We might even say that, once we thought about it, that the paraphrase captures what we really meant. That makes the paraphrase appropriate.

But the latest paraphrase has been offered using logic. Now although *we* can make sense of logic, there are plenty of people who can't – they haven't completed a course on logic. If these people haven't completed a course in logic, then how can they *really mean* (4-para) by 'there are two cats'? And, if people don't understand (4-para) then they can't mean to express it when they say 'there are two cats'.

What's important to keep in mind is what the paraphrase actually says, rather than the form in which it is presented. Think carefully about how you might explain the sentence 'there are two cats' to someone who didn't know what you meant by 'two', but who does know what a cat is. What would you say? I imagine that you would say that what we have is a cat, and another cat. Now, really that is all that the paraphrase says. It says that there exists a cat, x; there exists a cat, y, and that it is not the case that x and y are the same. The logical representation is simply a very precise way capturing that highly intuitive explanation of what is meant. This doesn't seem so extravagant.

But before we get too enthusiastic about this line of response, it's worth pointing out that there are at least three problems with this sort of manoeuvre. First, not all scientific theories will admit of ready paraphrase as is demonstrated by the following case borrowed from Melia (1995). Suppose that we had good evidence for the claim that 'every star is orbited by 2.4 planets'. However, suppose that, although we do have good evidence for this claim, it turns out the number of stars is uncountable. Simply, there are too many stars to be counted. If that were to be the case, then it would presumably also be impossible to construct the paraphrase, since any such paraphrase will require as many instances of the existential quantifier as there are stars. If the stars cannot be counted, then the paraphrase cannot be written and if we cannot write the paraphrase, then there *is* no paraphrase and the mathematical claim 'every star is orbited by 2.4 planets', is false. Consider, also, cases like $\pi$; how would we paraphrase uses of $\pi$ that appear in mathematical formulae?

Second, there might remain a worry that it's unclear as to what, precisely, this has achieved. Suppose we thought that (4-para) captured the meaning of (4)*; we might still think that (4)* entails (5)*:

(5)* Two is the number of cats.

If we think that (4)* entails (5)*, then it seems that ought to regard (4)* as having the following entailment, where 'N' stands for the predicate 'is the number of cats'.

(5*- para) $\exists x\ Nx$

That is, that there is some x such that x *is* the number of cats. If that's right, then even (4*-para) will entail the existence of numbers.

The whole of this worry concerns quite what paraphrase is and what it does. If the idea of paraphrase is to preserve the whole meaning of the original sentence, but the *original* sentence entails the existence of numbers, then paraphrase fails since we still have the original entailed commitment to the existence of numbers. If the idea of paraphrase *is not*, to preserve the meaning of the original sentence, then we have a problem because it was the truth of the original sentence (and scientific sentences like it) that we were so keen to preserve. If the nominalist is to take this line, then what they require is some account of the role of paraphrase that disposes off this dilemma.

The third problem is simply this: as yet it simply has not been shown that all scientific theories *can* be nominalistically paraphrased. Although, for instance, Field (1980) has been able to successfully paraphrase the theory of gravity, there are many other theorems (relativity, quantum mechanics and even some biological theories that we will come on to in a moment) that have not been successfully paraphrased. That being the case, the current nominalistic position is quite simply hopeful. At best it amounts to the claim that, since we've been able to paraphrase some scientific talk that appears to talk about numbers, we'll be able to paraphrase all of it.

It's hard, dialectically, to see quite why the Platonist ought to allow the nominalist that conclusion. Might they not suggest that we ought to wait and see whether or not that's true? There is, of course, more that can be said about the issue of paraphrase, but there is more to be said about the debate concerning numbers more generally, so we shall now move on.

# §3.6 Weaseling and the *new* Indispensability argument

Another way in which we might challenge the claim that mathematical entities are indispensible to our best science is due to Melia (2000). Melia (2000: 469) allows that scientists frequently do seem to use numbers in the way we have been describing, but denies that this ought to be thought ontologically interesting. In order to substantiate and illuminate this, Melia makes use of a particular semantic device.

On occasion, Melia thinks, we often talk in the following way: 'everyone F-ed, except Harry; he's the exception'. Less formally, we might say something like 'everyone was at the party, apart from Harry'. Clearly, there's nothing inconsistent about making such a claim. But if there's nothing inconsistent about making such a claim, then there ought not to be anything inconsistent about saying something, following on from (13), along the lines of,

> (19) 21 is the number of Newtons of force exerted by the hammer *but there are no numbers.*

The case Melia presents, in favour of moves like (19), is roughly this. Scientists frequently appear to talk about numbers in the way we've described, yet when pressed they also appear to deny the existence of Platonic entities, such as numbers. That presents us with a choice. We could think of scientists as hypocrites, constantly contradicting themselves. Alternatively, we might simply think that we've misrepresented what scientists were saying when they asserted sentences like (13): we *thought* they really meant something like (13), in fact they *really* mean something *weaselly* like (19).

Melia thinks, then, that we ought not to try and offer a paraphrase of the sentence as we were before. We simply ought to re-interpret scientists as meaning something like (19) when they utter sentences like (13). As Melia (2000: 469) puts it, '[i]t is surely more charitable to take scientists to be weasels rather than inconsistent hypocrites'.

According to Melia, the nominalist should say that the way our language has evolved is such that there is no way to give a complete description of reality, without using number talk, but that once we're done, we can then subtract away any commitment to numbers. Thus, the mathematical components of our theory do not *explain* anything; they simply serve as a descriptive device with which we can describe particular features of the world. Number talk is mere 'indexing':

> [A]lthough we may express the fact that a is 7/11 metres from b using a three place predicate relating a and b to the number 7/11, nobody thinks that this fact holds *in virtue of* some three place relation connecting a, b and the number 7/11. Rather, the various numbers are used merely to index different distance relations. (Melia 2000: 473)

So, granted, it may be the case that we cannot adequately describe the world without using number talk, and yes, that talk might *appear* to commit us to the existence of numbers, but look: no-one really thinks that the numbers *themselves* are really doing any explanatory work here. The numbers are certainly an essential part of the description, but not one that we have any reason to think exists outside of the story. That being the case, there's nothing at all wrong with retracting our number talk, once we've given a complete description of the world. To use a particularly evocative turn of phrase from Melia (2000: 469),

> [T]he mathematics is the necessary scaffolding upon which the bridge must be built. But once the bridge has been built, the scaffolding can be removed.

Thus we should be weasels.

Were we to reject this 'weaselly' line of argument, then what we would require is some reason to think that, contra Melia, mathematical entities are *required* in order for mathematical descriptions to be adequate. Ideally, we would be able to find some phenomenon that is explained by numbers themselves. At the moment we lack such a phenomenon.

Things, at this stage, do not look promising for the indispensability argument. They are about to get worse. Over the next three sections we'll look at reasons to think that *even if* Platonism is motivated by the arguments we've given, it's still far from clear that the view is one that we should endorse.

# §3.7 Epistemological concerns[4]

One very natural, though fairly poor, objection to the positing of mathematical objects is that we have no means of detecting them; that, because they are *a causal*, by definition, we cannot perceive them. If we cannot perceive something, then surely we can have no good reason to believe that it exists.

As I say, this argument is poor. Quarks are too small to be *seen directly*, yet we believe in them. Typically, of course, we believe in quarks because we believe that their existence plays some kind of explanatory role in our best theories. But, of course, that's precisely what we've just tried to demonstrate in the case of numbers: there are situations in which the existence of a number *would* play an explanatory role in our best theory. We have, admittedly, run into a situation where that claim now looks to be false – but in §3.9 we will return to the question and look at a case where numbers might be said to have an explanatory role. Certainly, we shall have to identify such a role if we are to believe that numbers exist and, thus, our epistemological argument should best assume that there *is* some such putative role for numbers to play.

It will not do, then, to deny that there are numbers simply because we cannot directly interact with them. If we were going to argue that there is some kind of epistemic concern, it looks like we're going to have to say that there's some general principle, such that, for all propositions, p, we cannot know p unless . . . and then both fill in the blank and explain why it is that no mathematical proposition can be known in that way.

Roughly, then, the structure of the epistemic argument against Platonism that we've just considered is:

(20) For all propositions, p, one cannot know p unless X.
(21) For no mathematical proposition is it the case that X.
(22) Therefore, one cannot know any mathematical propositions.

The trouble is that this argument is hard to make against the Platonist. What are we going to put in for X that doesn't beg the question against the Platonist? Whatever we give in lieu of X, it looks like the Platonist can just dig their heels in and object that any account of knowledge that rules against them is inappropriate as a means with which to approach this debate. After all, if the Platonist *does* think that we know mathematical propositions then it is unlikely that they will acquiesce and endorse a theory of knowledge that rules out our knowing mathematical propositions! Even more worrying is that contemporary epistemologists seem not to be able to agree on quite what X ought to be: if that's right then it will be difficult to force any particular theory of knowledge on the Platonist.

What we can do, though, is argue as follows. It seems that the Platonist is required by the lights of their own arguments to accept that the majority of mathematical beliefs that are had by mathematicians are true. We have allowed, after all, that mathematicians, and scientists, claims about numbers are to be regarded as true. Clearly, that means that our mathematical beliefs are highly reliable. It means that, for the most part:

(23) If most mathematicians accept 'p' as an axiom, then p.

What we *can* ask for, then, is an explanation of the *reliability* of these beliefs. As Field (1989: 232) has it:

> there is a big gap between the consistency of an axiomatic theory and its truth. In the case of physics we can presumably fill this gap at least in sketch: we can sketch the route whereby the assumed properties of, say, the electromagnetic field lead to various observable physical phenomena, and thereby affect our perceptual beliefs, and thereby affects our belief about the electromagnetic field. But nothing remotely analogous to this seems possible in the case of mathematics.

So the thought is this: grant the Platonist the assumption that most of their mathematical beliefs are true. What is then required from the Platonist is some account of *how* it is we track these *a causal* objects so reliably.

We need to be careful, here. There are two different things that we might be asking. One of them is important and useful; the other is not. First, we might be asking how our mathematical beliefs come to be justified. Absent an answer, we might then claim that because we can't specify, accurately, how our mathematical beliefs are justified, so we ought to claim that they're not justified. Thus, to flesh the case out with an example, we might *think* that 2+2=4, but, at least so we're supposing, since we have no justification for thinking that 2+2 is equal to 4, so we ought not to believe that 2+2=4. But that's a weak argument. The obvious parallel in the perceptual case seems utterly implausible. Suppose I can't tell you *how it is* that my perceptual beliefs are justified. Does that then mean that they *aren't* justified? No. We proceed all of the time on the assumption that beliefs formed on the basis of our perceptions *are* justified. The same point ought to apply to the mathematical case; simply that we cannot explain *how* the beliefs come to be justified does nothing to show that *they are not justified*.

The second, more subtle, line to take would be that the Platonist cannot give an explanation of *how* it is our beliefs come to be *reliable*. To illustrate, think about the perceptual case. When we think of how it is we perceive objects in the world, we give some complex story about how it is that the brain and eyes work such that we perceive objects. That story makes reference to regular sorts of behaviour: for instance, if a light beam strikes my eye, then, *most of the time* my brain will register this in a specific sort of way. Thus, in the perceptual case we can give *some explanation* of how it is our perceptual beliefs come to be reliable, by giving some explanation of how the physical mechanism involved in the perceiving generates that reliability.

But what sort of a story can we possibly give in the mathematical case? Can we say how it is that we, as physical beings, *reliably* come to true beliefs about abstract objects? It seems that we cannot! After all, we have no causal interaction with them – indeed, we have *no* interaction with abstract objects of any sort. The thought, then, may be that if we can give no account *at all* of how our mathematical beliefs are reliable, then, in the end, it is a complete mystery as to how it is our mathematicians are so often right about mathematical propositions. It would appear to be nothing more than an incredible coincidence. The best theory we can offer will *surely* not require that it be mysterious as to how we reliably tend towards truth in our mathematical reasoning.

The conclusion of such an argument is far-reaching. If there is no *possible* way to explain how it is that our mathematical beliefs reliably tend towards the truth, and it really is desirable that our best theory of mathematics not leave it mysterious how we come to know the content of mathematical propositions, then we really ought to deny mathematical Platonism as we have no explanation of how it can be that our belief-forming processes about mathematical propositions are reliable.[5]

# §3.8 Back to nominalism

Since it would appear that we face substantial epistemic concerns if we endorse Platonism, perhaps we should return our attention to nominalism. One problem we faced concerned the role played by paraphrase. It appeared that, if the paraphrase was to be considered adequate, it must wholly translate the original sentence, but by so doing, it would still entail the problematic sentence.

One way we might try to modify the paraphrase strategy is suggested by Hofweber (2007). He begins with consideration of some sentences (I've changed the numbering):

(24) Johan likes soccer.
(25) It is Johan who likes soccer.
(26) It is soccer that Johan likes. (p. 11)

Hofweber thinks that each of these sentences conveys the exact same information, but he thinks that they do so in different ways. The sentences each have a different focus. To illustrate this, consider the question: 'who is it that likes soccer?'. Though true, (26) seems inappropriate as a response to the question. The ordering of the words in the construction seems to stress 'soccer' as information to be conveyed (so is more appropriate as an answer to the question, 'what is it that Johan likes?').

Now why is this interesting? Sentences of a subject–predicate form are all *traditionally* taken to have the same structure of truth-conditions as one another. For any sentence, 'x is F', we commit to the existence of x and it's being F. Thus, 'the number of children is four' commits us to the existence of a number of children, and it being four.

But what Hofweber has done is point out that the syntactic form of a sentence can do more than merely generate truth-conditions: it can also stress particular items of information as salient. Compare the cases we looked at above, with a case that Hofweber (2007: 14) cites.

(27) What did you have for lunch?

Reply:

(28) The number of bagels I had is two.

That's odd, though not obviously false. Clearly, what should be said is:

(29) I had two bagels.

But, Hofweber thinks, there's no new information conveyed by (28), contrasted with (29). (29) is just a way of bringing out some particular feature of the sentence.

Here's Hofweber (2007: 24) in his own words:

> it [the term 'number'] is moved from its canonical syntactic position into an unusual position for the purpose of achieving structural focus. And this solves the puzzle. We don't get something from nothing. [the terms] have the same denotational terms. There is no new referring term . . .

So, if you were a nominalist about numbers, then you could say that there's no new information conveyed by *seemingly* ontologically committing sentences. They simply bring out the old, nominalist, information in a new way. We can put to one side the problems associated with paraphrase.

We then need to consider the overall shape of the dialectic. What's motivating the move to believe in abstract objects in the first place is that sentences that we use, that we take to be true, appear to entail (in conjunction with the claim that truths require truth-makers) that there are such things as numbers. If we can, instead, understand these modifications as merely providing a change of emphasis, rather than entailing that numbers exist, then we have provided a way to block that argument. Platonistic theories are far less parsimonious than their nominalistic counterparts. As we saw in the introduction, we value parsimony in a theory and so it would appear that we ought to prefer nominalistic theories – provided we have a way of blocking indispensability. Perhaps, then, we do not *need* paraphrase: rather, we can understand seemingly committing number talk as simply placing a different stress on particular items of information in given sentences.

# §3.9 Baker and the 'enhanced indispensability argument'

So what can the Platonist say? They will need another argument if they are to persuade us that numbers exist. One argument, that might well give us *some* reason to think that numbers exist, has been offered by Baker (2005, 2009). Thus,

(30) We ought rationally to believe in the existence of any entity that plays an indispensible explanatory role in our best scientific theories.
(31) Mathematical Objects play an indispensable role in science.
(32) Hence, we ought rationally to believe in the existence of mathematical objects [the numbering is mine].

The point to which we ought to pay particular attention is just how much stronger this argument is than the preceding indispensability argument discussed in §3.4. The previous argument tried to move from the *truth* of the mathematical component of scientific theories, to the existence of mathematical entities. As we saw, there is logical space for the nominalist to block this argument by arguing that mathematical propositions can be true without the need to posit mathematical entities. But, against this version of the argument, no such moves are available, for it is not merely the *truth* of mathematical claims that is at issue; rather, the claim is that mathematical entities play an explanatory role. Nor, importantly, can we take Melia's weasel route. If *mathematical entities* really are indispensible for scientific explanation, then we have a powerful argument for Platonism.

Baker thinks that there is at least one instance of a mathematical entity playing such an explanatory role. The case that Baker offers is that of the life cycle of the periodical cicada, 'an insect whose two North American subspecies spend 13 years and 17 years, respectively, underground in larval form before emerging briefly as adults' (Baker 2009: 614). There is, of course, a question in the offing: why are these life cycles prime? The answer to which is that prime cycles minimize overlap with other periodical organisms – specifically, predators and insects of similar sub-species. In the case study (Baker (2005: 229–30) Baker cites a paper by Goles, Schulz and Markus (2001) to demonstrate why prime life cycles may be preferable in relation to predators:

> a prey with a 12-year cycle will meet – every time it appears – properly synchro-
> nized predators appearing every 1, 2, 3, 4, 6 or 12 years, whereas a mutant with
> a 13 year period has the advantage of being subject to fewer predators. (Goles
> et al. 2001: 33)

Thus, Baker claims, at some point in their evolutionary history it would have been advantageous for cicada to develop prime life cycles.

Further, Baker also cites the works of Cox and Carlton (1988, 1998) and Yoshimura (1997), who offer a different explanation as to why prime life cycles may be advantageous.

> A crucial factor for periodical insects is to have sufficient mating opportunities
> during their brief adult stage. Almost as important, however, is to avoid mating
> with subspecies that have different cycle periods to their own. For example, if
> some of a (hypothetical) population of synchronized 10-year cicadas were to mate
> with some 15-year cicadas then their offspring would likely have a period of
> around 12 or 13 years. These hybrid offspring would emerge well after the next
> cycle of the 10-year cicadas and hence their mating opportunities would be
> severely curtailed. Yoshimura considers a putative stage in the evolutionary past
> where there were several subspecies of cicada with periods in the 14- to 18
> 18-year range. He shows how 17-year cicadas would intersect last often with
> cicadas of other periods in this range. Yoshimura explicitly connects these results
> to the fact that 17 is a prime number. (Baker 2005: 231)

The thought is that the numbers being *prime* plays some explanatory role. Here is Baker's (2009: 614) formalization of the argument (the numbering is, again, mine):

(33) Having a life-cycle period that minimizes intersection with other (nearby/lower) periods is evolutionarily advantageous (*biological law*).
(34) Prime periods minimize intersection (compared to non-prime periods). (*number theoretic theorem*).
(35) Hence organisms with periodic life cycles are likely to evolve periods that are prime (*'mixed' biological/mathematical law*).
(36) Cicadas in ecosystem-type E are limited by biological constraints to periods from 14–18 years. (*ecological constraint*).
(37) Hence cicadas in ecosystem-type E are likely to evolve 17-year periods.

If this argument of Baker's is satisfactory, then it would seem that we have a *genuine* explanatory role that would be fulfilled by a putative mathematical object.

It seems as if this is a good a candidate as any for being a situation in which a putative mathematical object *does* play an explanatory role. In relatively straightforward terms, the reason that the 'primeness' of the number plays such an explanatory role is that prime numbers are divisible (without remainder) only by 1 and themselves. It is precisely this feature that permits us to explain why prime life cycles are of benefit to the cicada: (taking the predator case) predators with *other* life cycles *will not appear* at the same time as the cicada – at least, not on a regular basis. This gives the 17-year cicada an evolutionary advantage; but it is that the life cycle is *prime* that explains why this is so.

Of course, there appears to be an obvious nominalist strategy in the offing. Although we declared ourselves a little uncertain as to how a traditional nominalist paraphrase strategy will help defuse the enhanced indispensability argument, what seems apparent is that the nominalist can simply provide some paraphrase of the claim that 'the number of years of the life cycle of the cicada is prime'. If we can provide a simple nominalistic paraphrase, then it will not be at all clear why we ought to think that what's doing the explanatory work is a putative mathematical object. After all, if we can paraphrase away the commitment to primehood in 'the number of years of the life cycle of the cicada is prime', then whatever we replace primehood *with* can surely play the requisite explanatory role.

The trouble for the nominalist is that sentences of the form 'the number of F's is prime' are not at all easy to paraphrase. Where we might paraphrase away commitment to numbers in sentences like 'the number of cats is two' by saying (crudely):

(38) $\exists x \exists y$ x is a cat & y is a cat and x and y are identical.

It's rather harder to see how we can paraphrase away commitment to primes in the sentence 'the number of cats is prime', using only first order logic and identity. The reason for this, as Baker (2009: 619) points out is that there is an infinite number of ways in which a number could be prime. Thus, consider:

(39) The number of cats is prime.

Any paraphrase of (39) would require us to say that there were two cats, or three cats, or five cats, or seven cats, or eleven cats, or . . . and so on, *ad infinitum*. If the paraphrase required is infinite, then it cannot be completed, and we have no way of completing a paraphrase of sentences like (39).

Since we *have* apparently pointed to a situation in which an explanatory role is played by the primeness of number, so it might seem that Hofweber's strategy will fail in this context. After all, Hofweber's claim is simply that we can explain away why particular sentences appear to entail others and that we can do so without thinking that numbers exist. The enhanced indispensability argument appears to show that it is the very *primeness* of particular numbers that plays an explanatory role in a given theory. Without the property of primeness, as it applies to numbers, we have no explanation of the duration of the life cycle of the periodic cicada. Thus, the Platonist may say, we should think that numbers exist.

# §3.10 Fiction

However, one position that we've yet to consider in detail is prepared to treat all mathematical talk as *literally* false. The view is known as mathematical fictionalism and states, in essence, that mathematical propositions are false, but 'true *according to the fiction of mathematics*'. The point is worth exploring, a little. We might, at least initially, be inclined to say that it is, *strictly* speaking, false that <Hobbits are quite short>. There are, after all, no such things as Hobbits. However, we are most likely prepared to accept the claim that *according to the fiction* 'The Lord of the Rings', it's true that <Hobbits are quite short>. In the same way, although it's strictly speaking false to say that <Sherlock Holmes was a detective> it's nonetheless a proposition that is true *according to the fiction* written by Sir Arthur Conan Doyle.

Thus, when it comes to 'number talk' we might allow that it's *strictly speaking* false to say that, for instance, <2+2=4>, but that it's true *according to the fiction of mathematics*. Although we will move to look at some downsides of this particular move in just a moment, it does seem to be one that has a good deal to recommend it. To begin, we can do away with commitment to mathematical entities. We need simply say that all mathematical truths are true *according to a fiction*. Thus, to say that a given number 'is prime' is simply to say that 'according to the fictions of mathematics, particular numbers are primes: specifically, those that are greater than 1 and are divisible, without remainder, only by themselves and 1'.

How will this bear on the enhanced indispensability argument? Presumably the thought will be that we do still have a 'primeness' of number playing an explanatory role. The explanatory role is not quite the same as we thought. We are, after all, offering an explanation in terms of mathematics, where mathematics is a mere fiction. But can that really be right? It might seem that we've come full circle. At the very start of the chapter we noticed that we might simply respond to the arguments seeming to show that mathematical objects exist by flat-out denying that there are mathematical truths. In a sense, that is what we're now conceding. There are no *genuine* mathematical truths; there are merely mathematical truths *according to the fiction of mathematics*. But what originally moved us to think that such a line was implausible was that mathematics seems to be a discipline in which we make genuine progress; where evidence for the truth of mathematics is given in terms of its success as a component part of the sciences, where progress in the sciences is taken to be indicative of the truth of science and the various components employed in the process of scientific inquiry. In other words: because mathematics is indispensable to science, and because science has made so much progress, we think that both science and mathematics must be true.

Now although that line appears tempting, it seems as if the mathematical fictionalist must resist it, and by resisting it perhaps they do enough to block the enhanced indispensability argument (though I shall leave the drawing of conclusions on this matter to the reader). The best way for the fictionalist to respond is to claim that mathematics can be instrumentally useful, while still being false. The fictionalist should ask, 'what evidence do you have for the claim that mathematics has, historically, tended towards truth?' The natural answer is that such theories have been successful – either simply internally consistent, or perhaps also useful in the sciences. But, in that case, replies the fictionalist, all that you, my Platonist opponent, can assert, is that mathematics has been *successful* in the past. The point, though, is that we have not shown that success *is* a guide to truth – in mathematics, at least. As a consequence, the preceding argument is of no force at all. At least, so claims the fictionalist. In that case, perhaps the explanatory power and success of mathematics in the sciences can be explained away without the need to posit abstract objects – even those such as the property of primeness for which we thought we had found a genuinely explanatory role.

# §3.11 Concluding remarks

Ultimately, I leave it to the reader to determine which of these arguments they think has most force. In helping to decide this, it will be worth pursuing a number of questions. For instance, has the fictionalist really done enough?

After all, the most natural position in the philosophy of science seems to be scientific realism – the view that the successes of science are a good indicator that science approximates truth. If we can then show that mathematical explanations play a *genuine* part of scientific explanations, then does that not suggest that offering up a *mere fiction* as a part of that explanation is woefully inadequate? I suspect that most of us would deny that fictions can play many *genuinely* explanatory roles: none of us think, for instance, that a fictional tale of how we the world came into being actually explains how the world *did* come into being. That being the case, and given the case study from Baker, do we not need something rather more substantive than a merely fictional account of mathematics?

# Recommended reading

### Indispensability and Platonism

Baker, A. 2005. 'Are there Genuine Mathematical Explanations of Physical Phenomena?', *Mind*, 114, 223–38.

Baker, A. 2009. 'Mathematical Explanation in Science', *British Journal for the Philosophy of Science*, 60, 611–33.

Colyvan, M. 2001. *The Indispensability of Mathematics*. Oxford: OUP.

Liggins, D. 2010. 'Epistemological Objections to Platonism', *Philosophy Compass*, 5, 67–77.

Melia, J. 2000. 'Weaseling Away the Indispensability Argument', *Mind*, 109, 455–80.

### Nominalism and paraphrase

Colyvan, M. 2010. 'There's no Easy Road to Nominalism', *Mind*, 119, 285–306.

Field, H. 1980. *Science without Numbers*. Oxford: Blackwell.

Hofweber, T. 2007. 'Innocent Statements and their Metaphysically Loaded Counterparts', *Philosophers' Imprint*, 7. http://www.philosophersimprint.org/007001/

Lewis, D. 1991. *Parts of Classes*. Oxford: Basil Blackwell.

Melia, J. 1995. 'On what there's not', *Analysis*, 55, 223–9.

Salmon, N. 2008. 'Numbers versus Nominalists', *Analysis*, 68, 177–82.

### On the abstract/concrete distinction

Lewis, D. 1986a. *On the Plurality of Worlds*. Oxford: OUP, 81–6.

Lowe, E. J. 2002. *A Survey of Metaphysics*. Oxford: OUP, 366–75.

Swoyer, C. 2008. 'Abstract Entities', in Sider, T., Hawthorne, J. and Zimmerman, D. eds. *Contemporary Debates in Metaphysics*, 12–31.

### Mathematical fictionalism

Burgess, J. and Rosen, G. 1997. *A Subject with no Object*. Oxford: Clarendon.

Daly, C. 2008. 'Mathematical Fictionalism – no Comedy of Errors', *Analysis*, 66, 208–16.

Dorr, C. 2008. 'There are no Abstract Objects', Sider, T., Hawthorne, J. and Zimmerman, D. eds. *Contemporary Debates in Metaphysics*, 32–63.

Field, H. 1980. *Science without Numbers*. Oxford: Blackwell.

Lewis, D. 1991. *Parts of Classes*. Oxford: Basil Blackwell, 57–9.

Yablo, S. 2005. 'The Myth of the Seven', in Kalderon, M. ed. *Fictionalism in Metaphysics*. Oxford: OUP, 88–115.

## Study questions

1) Summarize each of the views that were covered in the chapter. Which view do you prefer: why?
2) Mathematical Fictionalism appears committed to saying that the claims of mathematicians (and scientists) are false. Do you think that's something we should be prepared to endorse?
3) How do you think we should understand the idea of an 'abstract object'?
4) What do you think is the role of paraphrase? Do you think that it is successful? Why?

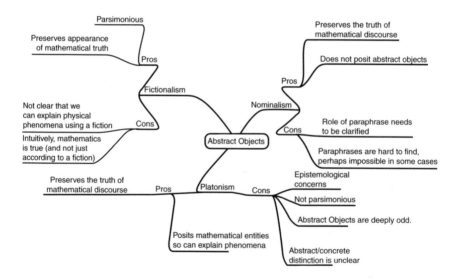

# 4

# Modality

## Chapter Outline

As with the previous chapters, let us begin with some sentences that appear in need of truth-makers.

    (1) There could have been blue ducks.
    (2) The chicken might not have crossed the road.
    (3) Necessarily, no contradiction is true.

Though the contents of (1)–(3) are clearly diverse, they share a common element: each of them expresses a modal proposition. That is, each of the propositions expressed is about not merely how the world *is*, but how it *could* be or how it *must* be. Thus, each of the propositions expressed by the sentences is about what is possible or necessary. Modal logicians have introduced particular symbolism to represent these modalities and it will assist in wider reading to have a grasp of these: the operator '□' states that 'it is necessary that . . .'; the operator '◊' states that 'it is possible that . . .'. To give an example: '◊p' translates into English as 'it's possible that p'.

So, what might we offer up as truth-makers for the propositions expressed in (1)–(3)? Concentrating our attention on (1) it might be tempting to think that ordinary ducks, that are brown in colour, make it true. After all, it seems that when I make the judgement that the ducks 'could have been blue', I'm making a judgement about those brown ducks – that they could be blue.

But if we're to preserve the truth of (1) then we might need to revise that judgement. Clearly, if the ducks are *actually* brown, then their being brown doesn't obviously make it true that they *could be* blue, at all. It's hard to see how being brown will serve as the basis of an ontological ground of 'being possibly blue'. A duck's being brown certainly makes it true that <there is a brown duck>, but it's rather harder to see how we get from there to the result that there *could have been* blue ducks.

The view with which we will begin, and focus a good deal of our attention upon, is that of Lewis (1986a). Lewis argues that what makes true our modal talk – talk of what is necessary and what is possible – are possible worlds. A possible world is a way that the world could be. Each possible world is spatio-temporally distinct from all other worlds and is just as 'real', and just as 'concrete' as our own world. According to Lewis, to say that 'there could have been blue ducks' is just to say that at least one world contains blue ducks.

The previous paragraph packs in a lot of information that we'll spend some time getting better acquainted with in the following sections, before then going on to see quite why Lewis thinks that we should believe in these worlds. In brief, however, the reason that Lewis gives for believing in such worlds is that this gives us the best cost–benefit analysis when it comes to thinking about modality.

# §4.1 Lewis on worlds: Genuine modal realism

As stated, Lewis thinks that worlds are spatio-temporally isolated from one another. This enables Lewis to give a useful definition of what it is to exist at a given possible world, *w*. To exist at *w* is to be spatio-temporally related to all other members of *w*. Thus, a world is a maximal set of spatio-temporally related entities – everything that is spatio-temporally related to an object, x, is a part of the same world as x. Likewise, to say that you're a part of the same possible world as x, is to say that you're spatio-temporally related to x (Lewis (1986a: 71)). So Mars and Julius Caesar are both members of the same possible world that I am. I stand in spatio-temporal relations to both of them. However, blue ducks are no part of the same possible world as me for there is no blue duck that stands in a spatio-temporal relation to me.

It's worth stressing that Lewis *really* thought that all of these worlds existed. Talk of 'possible worlds' is intended not merely as a useful way of talking. Possible worlds exist, according to Lewis. It's also worth noting that, because worlds other than our own are not spatio-temporally related to us, we cannot travel to them, nor can we make any observations of their contents. These worlds are seemingly completely closed off to us.

One obvious commitment that this view carries is that we, too, are members of a possible world. Of course, our world is actual (more of which in a moment); but that does not prevent it from being possible. Being actual and being possible are not mutually exclusive. When we think about it that sounds like the right thing to say: our world must be possible since it's actual; it's hard to imagine that something could be actual but not possible. Were it not possible for me to have £5 in my pocket, then presumably I would not actually have £5 in my pocket. But, since I do actually have £5 in my pocket, so it is possible for me to do so.

When describing possible worlds as concrete, above, I put the term in parentheses: why? The answer is that Lewis himself objects to the description. The reason that Lewis gives for objecting to the classification of worlds as 'concrete' is that he is uncertain as to what, precisely, the term is supposed to signify (1986a: 81–2). However, Lewis *is* prepared to allow that there is no fundamental difference between occupants of this possible world and occupants of any other. Thus, a possible mouse, which is merely a mouse that exists at another possible world, is not obviously any different to a mouse that exists at our world. Worlds and individuals do not exist in a less substantial sense simply by being possible-and-not-actual. Possible mice, just like actual mice, drink milk, eat cheese and live in perpetual fear of cats.

Bricker (2008: 112–13) develops this interpretation of what 'concreteness' amounts to.

(C1) Worlds (typically) have parts that are paradigmatically concrete, such as donkeys, and protons, and stars.

(C2) Worlds are particulars, not universals; they are individuals, not sets.[1]

(C3) Worlds (typically) have parts that stand in spatiotemporal relations and causal relations to one another.

(C4) Worlds are fully determinate; they are not abstractions from anything else.

We will treat Bricker's C1–C4 as our definition of what it is to be 'concrete'.

By offering this account of possibility, Lewis is, in fact, offering us a reduction of the modal. In more detail: we are trying to understand the concept of modality via notions that themselves make no mention of possibility and necessity. When we say that 'it's possible for there to be blue ducks' we are, according to Lewis, making a true claim about the content of one or more possible worlds. The claim that we are making is that 'there exists at least one world, distinct from our own, that includes talking donkeys'. This interpretation of our modal talk does not, itself, use a modal notion. We are thus giving a reductive analysis of what it is to be possible.

As we noted in the first chapter, we typically want to reduce the number of theoretical primitives that are contained in our theory. All things being equal we might then want to rid ourselves of modal primitives and offer some analysis of what it is to be possible and necessary. It looks like Lewis might be able to get us that reduction. To say of some state of affairs, x, that 'x is possible', is simply to say that x exists in at least one world. Since the locution 'exists in at least one world' itself includes no modal notion (it does not deploy the concepts of possibility or necessity) so it seems as if we're being offered a reduction of modality. This is a powerful idea.

But with this idea in mind, we now need to revisit something we said earlier. As we've seen, Lewis commits to the view that every way that a world could be is a way that some world is. However, since Lewis thinks that 'a way that a world could be' is to be reductively analysed as 'a way that some world is' the definition that he has given now says nothing more than 'every way that a world is, is a way that some world is'. That, of course, is nothing more than a truism. If I said to you that there are as many cars in the car park as there are cars in the car park, then I've told you nothing of interest at all. There could be no cars in the car park; five cars in the car park; a thousand cars in the car park; and so on. What Lewis will need, in order to specify the range of possibilities, and so the extent of possibility itself, is a way of expressing the claim that we took 'every way that a world could be is a way that some world is' to make. So, how can Lewis generate as many possible worlds as we think there are possibilities?

To find a way to express the limits of possibility given his reductive analysis of possibility, Lewis appeals to what he describes as a Humean denial of necessary connections. As he has it,

[t]o express the plenitude of possible worlds, I require a *principle of recombination* according to which patching together parts of different possible worlds yields another possible world. Roughly speaking, the principle is that anything can coexist with anything else, at least provided they occupy distinct spatiotemporal positions. (Lewis 1986a: 87–8)[2]

Thus, to give an example: our world contains people and lions. That being the case, and given this principle of recombination, there is a world where the top half of a person is attached to the bottom half of a lion. This follows simply from the fact that there exist lions and people. Given the principle of recombination, and the contents of our own world, Person-lions are possible and so exist at some other world(s).

## §4.2 Why believe it?

We now know a little more about Lewis' view of modality. But why did he hold it and why might we be tempted to do the same?

As stated above, this is another instance of considering the weights and balances involved. We must, in other words, look to see whether or not the costs of endorsing Lewis' view are outweighed by the benefits. Indeed this is perhaps one of the most fully developed cost–benefit analyses in modern philosophy.

If every way that a world could be is a way that some world is, then there are a lot of worlds; plausibly an infinite number. That, although not burden for *qualitative* parsimony, is certainly a heavy *quantitative* burden. That is, although the view is economical with respect to the various types of primitive concepts that are posited and perhaps also primitive with the different *kinds* of entity that it posits, the view is not at all parsimonious when it comes to how many *things* it posits.

Lewis doesn't think that this is too much of a problem. The first explanation for this is that Lewis does not value quantitative parsimony *at all*.

I subscribe to the general view that qualitative parsimony is good in a philosophical or empirical hypothesis; but I recognise no presumption whatever in favour of quantitative parsimony. (Lewis (1973: 87))

The second reason that Lewis thinks that the brute number of worlds is not a problem, is that the pay-off for positing the worlds is considerable.

We have only to believe in the vast real of possibilia and there we find what we need to advance our endeavours. We find the wherewithal to reduce the diversity

> of notions we must accept as primitive, and thereby to improve the unity and economy of the theory that is our professional concern – total theory, the whole of what we take to be true. What price paradise? If we want the theoretical benefits that talk of *possibilia* brings, the most straightforward way to gain honest title to them is to accept such talk as the literal truth . . . *The benefits are worth the ontological cost.* Modal realism is fruitful; that gives us good reason to believe that it is true. (1986a: 4, my italics)

A natural thing for us to explore in more detail, then, is precisely what these benefits are supposed to be.

The first, and arguably most powerful, is the reduction of the modal to the non-modal. The retention of primitive modality is a high price to pay. To see this, simply think about how we would try to understand the *nature* of possibility. What *is it*? Although we are all perfectly capable of using the concept of possibility, it seems a far harder task to specify what possibility *really is*. Suppose, then, that we just treat modality as primitive. In that case, we are conceding ignorance as to the nature of a useful and pervasive concept. That seems a high price to pay. It would be far, far better to not have to pay it.

Other benefits of Lewis' theory abound, too. As we will see in later chapters, Lewis thinks that we can make use of possible worlds to give analyses of both properties and causation. This further strengthens the case in favour of possible worlds; it means that our account of modality can be deployed to analyse a great number of other concepts thus reducing even further the number of primitive concepts that we are required to posit.

But, even supposing that the reduction can be achieved, we might still ask why Lewis thinks that all other worlds must be concrete – just like our world. For instance, perhaps we're prepared to go as far as conceding that there are all of these worlds. It nonetheless seems plausible that there ought to be some difference between our world – that is, after all, the actual world – and those other, merely possible worlds. That *surely* seems intuitive. In the words of Bricker (2008: 123–4), 'I, for one, could not endorse the thesis of a plurality of concrete worlds if I did not hold that there was a fundamental ontological difference between the actual and the merely possible'.

Why does Lewis deny that there is any such difference? Lewis gives us two reasons. First, a sceptical argument (1986a: 93–4). We claim to know that we inhabit the actual world. However, it seems equally likely that occupants of *merely possible* worlds will also claim similarly. Why should we expect them to believe anything else? That being the case, everyone, at all of the different worlds, believes that they are actual. And, or so it seems, everyone has the same evidence for their claims. It will not appear to an occupant of a *merely possible* world that they are the occupant of a *merely possible world*. Just like us, occupants of merely possible worlds will think that they are members of the actual world. Thus, we have the basis for a sceptical induction. Of all of the trillions upon trillions of merely possible and non-actual individuals, only we lucky few billion that inhabit this world, are correct that our world is actual. What luck! So here is the problem: what possible reason can we have for thinking that we are so lucky in our judgements when everyone else is deceived? It seems that the proper conclusion to reach would be that we are not at the actual world ourselves; it is more likely that we're deceived than it is that all of those others are deceived. But we *know* that our world is actual. Absent a good reason we should not think that our world is in any way special; we should not think that there is an ontological difference between our world and the merely possible worlds. We will return to what it is for a world to be actual, for Lewis, below.

Second, Lewis offers us a more metaphysically loaded argument. It is surely a contingent matter which world is actual. That is, although we think that our world is the actual world, this is not necessarily true. It could have turned out that other worlds were actual. That is surely what we mean when we say that other states of affairs are possible, after all. But, to say that something is contingent is to say that it is not necessary: whatever is supposed to be contingent is not the case *at all worlds*. But each world *is* actual, at itself, for every possibility is possibly actual. Thus, each world will have to qualify, in some sense or other, as actual. And so each world will end up being the same and will be of a kind with all of the others. Thus Lewis thinks that we might have some grounds for thinking that there is no ontological difference between any of the worlds. Since our world is concrete, so too all other worlds are concrete.

# §4.3 Actuality

This seems to present us with two objections to Lewis' view. First, at the outset of the chapter we were keen to find truth-makers for a particular group of sentences. But it now appears that, although we might have succeeded in this regard, we now have truth-makers for sentences that ought to be false! For instance, we do not think that the sentence 'there are unicorns' is true, although we certainly *do* think that it's possible for there to be unicorns and, thus, that 'it's possible for there to be unicorns' is true. But, if there simply exist unicorns, at possible worlds other than our own, it would appear that 'there are unicorns' *is* true. Is that not a commitment too far? Are we not committed to thinking such sentences false, simply in light of our current linguistic practices?

Lewis thinks that we can circumvent the objection. As we noted in Chapter 2, in our discussion of unrestricted mereological composition, it seems that we frequently restrict the domain of quantification when we're engaged in everyday conversation. We saw in Chapter 2 that this could be used to explain how it is that there might exist table-pens and Eiffel-tower-dolphins, even if we never normally talk about them.

Precisely the same strategy can be deployed, here. The Lewisian will say that although there do in fact exist such entities as unicorns, when we typically utter sentences about them, we mean to restrict our quantifiers to the *actual world*. Thus, when we use the sentence 'there are no unicorns', the proposition we express says something like <there are no unicorns at the actual world>. That proposition is clearly true. So although there exist all of these merely possible objects, they are non-threatening (claims the Lewisian). Provided you accept that particular sentences have an implicit ' . . . in the actual world' operator, then we can explain away these threatening sentences. Only when we engage in metaphysics, and we lift all of the restrictions on our discourse, does it turns out that sentences like 'there are dinosaurs' are used to express true propositions.

This brings us on to the second objection. If there is nothing special about our world, then in virtue of what is it true to say that our world is the actual world and that all of the other worlds are *merely possible*? There must be some way of marking that distinction, for we surely cannot deny that our world is the actual world.

The way in which Lewis responds to this line of thought is to treat 'actually' as an indexical term. We're familiar with indexical terms in other contexts. Terms such as 'I', 'here' and 'now' are all indexicals. One of the important features of indexical terms is the contribution they make to the truth-conditions of a sentence. Imagine, for instance, that I tell you that 'it is raining here'. Said in Nottingham, that is true. But were I to utter the self-same sentence in Abu Dabi, then (or so I will assume) the sentence is false. Similar effects can be generated by use of the term 'I'. 'I am hungry' said by me, is true. But the very same sentence, said by someone who has just finished a large meal, is false. What these terms have in common, then, is that they seem to play the role of picking out some particular feature of the context in which they are uttered. In the case of 'here', the term picks out the spatial context; in the case of 'now', the term picks out the temporal context; in the case of 'I' the term picks out the context with respect to who uttered the term.

Lewis thinks, 'actually' functions in the same way and that the context that it picks out is the world at which it is uttered. So where 'now' picks out the time at which it is uttered, and 'here' picks out the spatial location at which it is uttered, 'actually' picks out the world at which it is uttered. That means, of course, that the sentence 'our world is actual' is true. In fact, it would be true at whichever world it is uttered. So this solves the problem. The problem, remember, was that we wanted to preserve the claim that our world is the actual world. That result is easily preserved. 'Actually', whenever we use the term, simply serves to pick out the world at which we utter it: *this* possible world. Thus, our world is the actual world.

Of course, this does nothing to mitigate the cost of denying that our world – the actual world – is substantially different in kind from merely possible worlds. This was the concern that we raised towards the end of §4.2. Ultimately, whether or not we think we should endorse Lewis' view will require us to give a *complete* analysis of his view. It is with that in mind that we must now turn to a consideration of how Lewis deals with particular sorts of modal truths.

# §4.4 Counterparts

So far we've been focusing our attention on modal claims about entities that don't exist and considering what makes these true (for instance <there could be blue ducks>). But now consider a different sort of claim, a claim about what it is possible for some existing thing to do.

(4) Jonathan could have been a lawyer.

This is a claim about me (I am Jonathan!), and what I might have done. Had I chosen to read law, rather than philosophy, been lucky with various career breaks and done well enough in my studies, I might have made it as a lawyer. So, (4) looks to express a true proposition.

Consider another case:

(5) Jonathan could have had three fingers and a thumb on his left hand.

Once more, this looks true. Suppose that, contra the actual series of events that unfolded, I slipped one day while chopping vegetables in the kitchen, and severed one of my fingers from my hand. It is certainly conceivable that I could have slipped in such a situation, and so we have reason to think it possible.

Let's consider how to analyse (5). According to the Lewisian view, this requires that there exists a possible world at which Jonathan exists and has only three fingers and a thumb on his left hand. That looks to generate a very odd result when combined with the fact that Jonathan in fact has four fingers and a thumb on his left hand. The following claims look to be true:

(6) Jonathan has three fingers and a thumb on his left hand.
(7) Jonathan has four fingers and a thumb on his left hand.

(7) follows from the fact that (at least at the time of writing) I have four fingers and a thumb on my left hand. It is an actual truth. (6) follows from the fact that I exist in another possible world and I have only three fingers and a thumb on my left hand. But, the natural thought goes, the Jonathan that exists in this world and that is strictly identical to the Jonathan that exists in the other world, cannot have both three and only three fingers on its left hand, and four and only four fingers on its left hand. That would be a contradiction.

Something has got to give. But what is it? We could deny that these two Jonathans are strictly identical, but then we have a very odd claim on our hands. I exist in this world and have four fingers and a thumb on my left hand. At some *other* world, an entity *other* than me has only three fingers and a thumb on its left hand *but* that entity still suffices to make it true that <Jonathan could have three fingers and a thumb on his left hand>. How can something *not identical to me* suffice to ground truths about how it's possible for *me* to be?

Lewis is prepared to confront this oddity head on. What make true these sorts of modal claims are *counterparts*. Thus, (5) is true iff there exists a counterpart of mine, at some possible world, where that counterpart of mine has three fingers and a thumb on his left hand.

What, then, is a counterpart? Roughly speaking a counterpart of mine is an entity that exists at another possible world and that is *sufficiently similar to me* to ground the truth of modal claims about me. Thus, if there is an object at some other world that has the appearance of being the same as me, with the exception of having three fingers and a thumb on its left hand, *then* it's possible for me to have three fingers and a thumb on my left hand. Likewise, it's possible for me to have blonde hair iff there exists an entity at some other possible world that's similar to me in many respects, but that has blonde hair. This *is* a denial of the claim that Jonathan-at-our-world and Jonathan-at-another-world are strictly identical. It *is* a little odd. But that oddness may be worth the cost. After all, it would seem to be better to endorse counterpart theory that to endorse the contradiction entailed by the conjunction of (6) and (7).

We can now go some way to summarizing the Lewisian view of modality. Possibility and necessity are to be reductively analysed in terms of possible worlds. A state of affairs is possible iff it obtains at *some* possible worlds; a state of affairs is necessary iff it obtains at *all* possible worlds. A possible world is a spatio-temporally related collection of concrete objects. It is possible for an object in our world to be different to the way that it in fact is if and only if there is a counterpart of that object at a distinct world and the counterpart is qualitatively different from the object in our world.

With this summary in mind one point is abundantly clear. Lewis is committed to the existence of an enormous number of concrete possible worlds with a huge array of objects at each. This bears repetition: each of these worlds *is just like ours*. This is, quite simply, a staggering proposal. The very *idea* of there being so many worlds simply seems absurd. Surely, this is too vast a realm of objects to take seriously, let alone countenance as a genuine metaphysical position.

This last paragraph reflects a natural predisposition to find Lewis' ontology unbelievable and Lewis himself describes this kind of reaction to his view as an objection called the 'incredulous stare'. How seriously to take the incredulous stare as an objection to Lewis' position is unclear. What seems apparent, at least so far, is that Lewis' position offers us a reductive account of modality: a theory that reduces the number of primitive notions that we are obliged to accept, and offers us ontological ground for our modal truths. What seems most appropriate, then, is to determine whether or not there are ways of avoiding the incredulous stare that manage to do all of the work done for us by Lewis' view. Following Lewis, call this the quest for paradise on the cheap.

# §4.5 Ersatzism

Perhaps we might take the view that the most serious stumbling block for the Lewisian view is treating all of the possible worlds as concrete. If that's right, then we could try to secure the results Lewis achieves, but without positing the vast menagerie of concrete objects. One particularly popular stripe of views that have been offered in an attempt to do exactly this are Ersatzer theories of modality. The word 'ersatz' is usually taken to mean 'imitation' or 'substitute'.

Theories of ersatz worlds offer us substitutes for genuine possible worlds, and try to achieve the same results without having to posit concrete possible worlds. These theories are sometimes described as 'actualist' views of modality, for they posit only the *actual* world as a concrete entity, and each of the other 'worlds' that exist are, in a sense to be made clear in a moment, only *representations* of possible worlds. There are a variety of sub-categories of ersatzer views of modality, but a shared trait of such views is that they assent to the claim that:

(8) <◊P> is true, iff there is a possible world according to which P.

But if worlds are not concrete, spatio-temporally distinct collections of objects, then what *are* they? In what follows we focus our attention on two specific accounts: linguistic ersatzism and 'magical' or 'propositional' ersatzism.

## §4.5.1 Linguistic erstazism

> For the linguistic ersatzer, worlds are a kind of *book*: they represent by containing sentences of an interpreted language. (Melia 2008: 137)

A few words about this proposal are in order. First, and easiest, is the issue of representation. We are reasonably familiar with the ways in which books can represent things to us. The words and sentences within books represent stories, pictures, ideas and concepts (and so on), to us all of the time.

What is slightly less obvious is the sense in which a book can be a possible world. We can begin to understand the idea better via consideration of a problem that faces the linguistic ersatzer.

It appears as if the possibilities will outstrip the content of any written book. No matter how long the book that is written down, it still seems as if we could imagine *just one more* possibility. If you don't believe me, just try writing the book. In any case, borrowing from Melia (2008: 137) it seems at least possible that for any natural number, $n$, there is a corresponding collection of space–time points. Since there are infinitely many natural numbers, so there seems nothing conceptually prohibitive about there being an infinite number of space–time points at a possible world. Thus, to accommodate this, we will need an infinite number of worlds: one world for each value of $n$.[3] It looks like no ordinary book will be sufficiently expressively rich to describe all of the details at such a world, so what should we say? We should be prepared to rethink our understanding of a book, and the language that comprises it. Indeed, an ersatz world is not being thought of as *literally* being a book.

The idea that the linguistic ersatzer will make use of is that just about anything can function as an *interpretable* language. Pixels on the screen can count as a language; a collection of '1's' and '0's' can count as a language; objects can count as a language – provided we can suitably interpret them.

So, the thought is, allow that each property *is* its own name. Thus, the property of redness 'names itself' in our world-making language; the property of charge 'names itself' in our world making language – and so on. These properties are, once more, to be treated *as* their own names. With all of these properties in hand, we now have an extensive language – and one that we know how to interpret: each property names itself. We can use these properties to represent our requisite possibilities. The 'book' is simply the actual world. We can use this 'book' in conjunction with the principle of recombination to represent all of the possibilities that there are. Thus, it is possible for there to be a red car iff the book of the world includes the name of the property 'red' and the name of the property being a 'car'. Since both of those 'names' appear – because both properties are in the world and properties are their own names – so it is possible for there to be a red car.

An obvious benefit of this ersatzer proposal is that it very much appears that we already believe in the entities required. We already believe that there are properties (or at least, we might: see Chapter 6). Since these are acting as their own names, and hence give us the world-making language, so this is a sizeable boon.

## §4.5.2 Aliens

But there's an immediate worry with such a view. Intuitively, it seems that there could have been properties that there are not. Granted, this might leave us with a possible world very different to our own, but there seems to be nothing prohibitive about supposing that a world could be so very different. How will we model such a possibility? If we're linguistic ersatzers, then we will have to generate possible worlds from our existing language – which is a language in which every property names itself. The trouble, of course, is that the property that we wish to name *does not exist*. This alien property, which does not exist, but could have, is not present at the actual world. If the property is not present, then it cannot be its own name, and so it does not appear in our world-making language. If the property does not appear in the world-making language, then we cannot construct a possible world that includes it. Thus, it appears, given linguistic ersatzism it is not possible for there to be alien properties. But this seems very odd. Certainly, it *seems* possible to me that the world could have been other than it is and that thought seems to extend to alien properties. What should we say?

We could modify linguistic ersatzism. We could augment our world-making language with quantifiers and identity; that would permit us to generate the claim that there exists some entity that is not identical with any of the actual properties. Allow that a, b, c are the names of all of the properties that in fact exist. To then specify the existence of a non-actual property, we simply say something of the form: $\exists x \neg(x=a)$ & $\neg(x=b)$ & $\neg(x=c)$ & x is a property. In words: there exists a property that is not identical to a, b or c.

The trouble with this move is that we may well end up conflating apparently distinct possibilities. Suppose that we wanted to describe a state of affairs including *two* alien properties, F and G, and two putative bearers, d and e. Notice, that all that we're committing to with regards to these alien properties is that they exist; that they are not identical to any actual property and that they are not identical to each other. But, in that case, there is no obvious difference between the situation in which Fd and Ge, and Gd and Fe obtain. Simply, although we *have been* told that these alien properties are not identical to one another, we haven't been told enough to be able to distinguish the possibility of Fd and Ge from the possibility of Gd and Fe. Since these are, plausibly, different states of affairs, so, we might worry, linguistic ersatzism lacks the required expressive power.

## §4.5.3 Propositional ersatzism

One way in which we might avoid such problems is to endorse what Lewis calls 'magical' ersatzism, but is perhaps more generously called 'propositional' ersatzism. As with all forms of ersatzism, the propositional ersatzer endorses the bi-conditional expressed in (8). As a reminder,

(8) <◊P> is true iff there is a possible world according to which P.

However, for the propositional ersatzer a possible world is a set of propositions. Propositions are supposedly abstract objects and, as we have already seen, propositions are taken to be the contents of sentences. Possible worlds would, thus, be abstract objects, or collections of abstract objects, that exist at the actual world. Having spent a while discussing abstract objects in Chapter 3, I won't reiterate material concerning the problematic nature of abstract objects. Nonetheless, there are putative advantages to adopting a propositional ersatzism that are worth mentioning here.

Although abstract objects might not be the sorts of entity that we're *naturally* tempted to posit, it might appear that we're already committed to something *like* propositions by our thoughts on everyday discourse. It seems, for example, that when one person claims that 'it is raining' and another claims that 'il pleut', that they are *saying the same thing*. In slightly more philosophically adept language, the two sentences express the *same proposition*.

We can use this to argue in favour of propositional ersatzism ahead of linguistic ersatzisms. We allowed, above, that the way in which sentences represent is familiar to us. But, on inspection, is that really correct? For, although we might allow that sentences *do* represent ideas and concepts to us, the manner in which they do so is somewhat opaque. How does a sentence represent an idea? It would be good to have some account of how this occurs. We can agree that two sentences 'it is raining' and 'il pleut' *say the same thing*; but how, exactly do the two sentences express this? In virtue of what is it true that 'it is raining' and 'il pleut' *express the same content*?

In contrast, a proposition *just is* the representation of some claim or other. It is taken to be the content of that which is expressed by a sentence. That is, a sentence is used to express a proposition, where a proposition *is* the content of what is said. We might then say that 'il pleut' and 'it is raining' express the same content because they both express the proposition <it is raining>. Cast in that light propositions might seem a very natural vehicle for the representation of ideas and concepts.

Notice also that there is no obvious shortage of propositions in the way that we had a shortage of sentences. There is an obvious limit to the length of a book, but no such analogous imposition on the number of propositions there can be. Indeed, one might be tempted to the view that there are as many different propositions as there are thoughts that could be thought and sentences that could be uttered. On the assumption that we *could* think about and could speak about alien properties, so there will be sufficient propositions to provide the truth-makers for talk about alien properties. Thus, propositional ersatzism might be preferred to linguistic ersatzism.

# §4.6 Reduction?

But aside from the fact that a propositional ersatzism would commit us to the existence of abstract objects, it remains to be seen whether or not this rendering of possible worlds compares favourably with the Lewisian account. It might seem obvious that the ersatzisms surveyed are obviously preferable, for they posit a difference between the merely possible and the actual, and they do not posit an infinite number of concrete possible worlds. But it appears, upon closer inspection, that in at least one sense the Lewisian analysis is preferable.

We saw, above, that Lewis is able to reductively analyse modality. Possibility is to be understood in terms of worlds that are spatio-temporally distinct from our own. But, crucially, there are no modal notions used in the analysis of what it is to be a possible world. This does not seem to be the case for the propositional or linguistic ersatzer.

To see why, consider which sorts of propositions (or sentences) will go together to generate possible worlds. We will not, I assume, want to say that the proposition <all grass is green> is to go together with <it is not the case that all grass is green> to generate a possible world. Those two propositions contradict one another, and since contradictions are not typically thought to be possible, so this describes an *impossible* state of affairs.

This means that we must describe some constraints on our possible worlds. Intuitively, only *consistent* sets of propositions (or sentences) can generate a possible world. We do not think that it is possible for <the table is brown> and <it is not the case that the table is brown> to both be true together, for they are inconsistent propositions. So how will we define 'consistency'? The most natural thing to say is that two propositions are consistent iff they do not *entail* a contradiction. But entailment is a modal notion. To say that 'P entails Q' is to say that 'Q is *necessary*, given P'; or that it is '*impossible* for P to be true and Q false'. Possibility and necessity, then, are cropping up in our definition of what it is for something to be possible. We have failed to reduce modality if part of our definition of what it is to be a possible world itself deploys a modal notion.

So at least given this cursory inspection it appears that propositional and linguistic ersatzism cannot give us a *reductive* analysis of modality. To clarify, let us work through matters once more. We began wanting an analysis of possibility. We attempted this by saying that a state of affairs is possible if and only if it occurs at some possible world. When pressed as to the nature of a possible world, we say that they are collections of propositions or sentences. But, as we saw, we needed to say slightly more than that to avoid including *impossible* worlds as possible worlds. Thus we defined a possible world as a *consistent* set of propositions or sentences. In turn, we then required a notion of consistency – and our notion of consistency seems to make use of a modal concept; that of entailment. So our account of what a world is relies on a modal notion, and if we are after a *reduction* of the modal to the non-modal, then we cannot use modal concepts in our analysis. Thus, the propositional and linguistic ersatzer fares less well than Lewis in analysing possibility: possibility remains a primitive notion for the ersatzer.

# §4.7 Combinatorialism

A slightly different view to the forgoing is due to David Armstrong. According to Armstrong, the world consists of various states of affairs (see Chapter 6), which in turn include individuals and simple universals (see Chapter 5). We are then to think of the possibilities as rearrangements of what there is.

To illustrate, I borrow some discussion from Armstrong (1989a: 45). Begin with the claim that there exists an individual a that has the property F, and an individual b that has the property G. Armstrong's thought, then, is that a and G are the truth-makers for 'it's possible that a is G', because the property and the simple individual are *compossible*. Any simple can be combined with any property. And because any simple can be combined with any property, so the existence of both a and G is sufficient for the truth of <it is possible for a to be G>. Given Armstrong's proposal the truth-makers for our modal claims are nothing more than the ordinary elements of our ontology.

From an intuitive point of view, there is something to be recommended about Armstrong's approach. The views of modality that have concerned us so far have seemed to make modality about something other than those entities that occupy our concrete world. When I say that 'it's possible for Barack Obama to win a second term', it appears to me as if I make a claim that is about Barack Obama; it does not appear to me that I make a claim about some counterpart of his (in line with Lewis), and it certainly does not appear to me to be a claim about some merely abstract object or sentence (in line with the linguistic or propositional ersatzer). Since Armstrong is analysing the possibility of some object, a, having some property G *in terms of a and G*, so it seems that his view will mesh more naturally with our preconceptions of what modal claims are about.

Notice, also, that Armstrong's account lays legitimate claim to being a purely naturalistic conception of modality. There are no abstract objects present in his account of modality; this might give us some reason to prefer Armstrong's combinatorial theory to the propositional ersatzer view. Since Armstrong does not posit the vast realm of concrete possible worlds, a la Lewis, this might also give us some reason to prefer his account to that of Lewis. Considerations of parsimony appear to militate in Armstrong's favour.

But there are problems for the combinatorial view. First, it appears that Armstrong has not successfully been able to *reduce* modality. After all, the claim being made here is that a state of affairs is possible iff simple elements of being *can* be combined: <it's possible that a is G> is true iff we *can* combine a and G. 'Can' is plainly a modal notion – if we say that 'Tom *can* reach the top shelf' then we are saying that 'it is possible for Tom to reach the top shelf'. No reduction of modality is affected if we deploy 'can' talk in our definition of what it is to be possible.

Second, it is not immediately apparent that Armstrong can deal with the possibility of alien properties. Truths about possibilities, recall, are made true by existing elements of being. Thus 'it's possible that a is G' is made true by the existence of a and G. If one of a and G do not exist, then it is unclear as to what the truth-maker for such a claim will be. As we saw above, the possibility of alien properties is taken to be the possibility of properties that *do not in fact exist*. It is unclear how Armstrong's combinatorialism can generate the possibility of such actually non-existent entities from its stock of actually existing entities, simply by recombining what actually exists. Since it appears pretty plausible that 'there could have been properties that there are not', so this looks a substantial defect of Armstrong's view.

## §4.8 The problems reconsidered

So far in our reasoning two particular problems have seemed especially pressing, so it's worth reviewing, now, how seriously we ought to take them. First, we've found it difficult to provide truth-makers for alien possibilities. Second, we've found it hard to give a reductive theory of modality. Indeed, so far only Lewis' view has been able to cope with both of these problems. For Lewis, an alien possibility is simply a property that exists at some other world (and not at our own) and we can reductively analyse possibility and necessity in terms of the concrete worlds.

So how much should we worry about the alien properties objection? In some ways, it's tempting to not view this objection as too pressing; it seems largely a matter of modal intuition that we think alien properties possible. If all this objection comes down to is a modal *intuition*, then perhaps we ought to be prepared to swallow the cost of denying the intuition in order to rid ourselves of a commitment to Lewis' plurality of worlds. Is there any way of making this objection more pressing?

One way in which we might attempt to make the alien properties objection more robust is by consideration of scientific practice. During the development and refinement of physical theories, scientists typically consider a range of options and then select the one that appears to match the data most accurately. In doing so, it very much appears that they take seriously the *possibility* that there exist a whole range of entities, only one of which exists. By way of example, in the 1960s physicists took the view that the quarks that we now think of as being 'up' and 'down' quarks were in fact to be identified as 'partons'. That is, physicists took seriously the possibility that there exists a distinct particle, the parton, in addition to quarks.

Now, as a matter of fact, no such particles exist: there are merely the 'up' and 'down' quarks. But an important part of the reasoning process that went into the development of the physical theory concerned the *possibility* that these new particles were partons and that these were a distinct type of entity. It seems, then, that scientific practice gives us at least some reason to take seriously the *possibility* of alien properties.

How much should we then worry about not, so far, being able to give a reductive theory of modality (unless we endorse Lewis' view)? This, I think, is less clear. There is certainly a sense in which we should try to reduce the number of primitive notions that we commit to in our theories. Sider (2003: 185) is right, I think, when he claims that,

> The metaphysician prefers desert landscapes when she can get them; when it is possible to reduce, we should. Of course the reduction might fail; parsimony gives us reason to search but does not guarantee success.

Reduction is to be preferred where all else is equal. Whether or not it is enough to warrant *all of those worlds*: that's a tough question.

The most natural thing for the anti-Lewisian to try to do is to demonstrate that Lewis' view doesn't actually succeed in its reductive ambitions. Can we do that? Perhaps. I shall not pursue the matter here, however, for there are other views that require exposition. In the further readings I suggest material that may be of interest to the reader.

# §4.9 Conventionalism

It looks as if a partial defence of ersatzism might be available, one that permits a reductive analysis. It might not get us alien properties, but perhaps we can let that slide for now. A line that has been developed by Sider (2003) and Cameron (2009a) runs as follows.

What we required, in order to avoid the charge of primitive modality, is some means of differentiating the consistent sets of sentences from the inconsistent ones; what we need is a non-modal way of describing that difference.

To begin, consider the necessarily true proposition <2+2=4>. This proposition, Sider thinks, along with many others, is necessarily true: that it is necessarily true is a matter of convention. That is, we have a convention to describe this proposition as necessarily true and it is because of this convention that the proposition *is* necessarily true.

Caution is required: Sider is not saying that the proposition is *true* in virtue of convention. Far from it. Sider is committed to the claim that whether or not the proposition is true is a matter quite separate from convention. But what makes this proposition, *necessarily* true, is our *convention* to describe (for instance) mathematical truths as necessary truths. Likewise, we have a convention to describe logical truths as necessarily true, natural kind identity truths, as necessarily true and so on. So, because <2+2=4> is a mathematical truth, and we have a convention to treat mathematical truths as necessary truths, so this is a necessary truth.

Cameron thinks that we can develop this line of thinking in order to draw a sharp distinction between the possible and impossible worlds. Consider all of the putative sets of sentences of the linguistic ersatzer; those that include contradictions, as well as those that do not. What is it about the sets of sentences that entail contradictions that make them impossible? According to Cameron, merely that we treat them as such. Here is Cameron (2009a: 14) in his own words.

> We are asked: what makes these worlds possible and these worlds impossible? I answer: just that the first are possible. By this I mean that there is nothing more to the distinction between the worlds than that the first group are the ones we single out as the possible worlds.

This has the feeling of being a 'mind-dependent' account of modality, for it appears that Cameron is making our modal truths depend upon what we're inclined to pick out as possible and as necessary.

But Cameron is at pains to stress that this is not the case. Our interests simply serve to delineate some of the sets of sentences as the sets that are the possible worlds; others as the impossible worlds. Here is Cameron, again:

> Suppose I am presented with a group of people and I point to a sub-group of them and call them the Fs, with the remaining members of the group being the non-Fs. If you ask me in virtue of what a non- F is a non-F the answer is obviously just that they weren't in the group I singled out as the Fs; there is nothing more to be said. Likewise, if I single out a sub-group of all the worlds, not by pointing to them explicitly but by mentioning certain features of them – such as representing the mathematical truths as true, not making false actually true kind identities, etc – and I call the worlds in this sub-group the possible worlds, there is nothing more to be said about why they are the possible worlds than that they are in the group I singled out to be called that. Explanation stops there. (Cameron (2009a: 15))

Can we agree with Cameron that this gives us a proper account of the distinction between the possible and the impossible? Making a decision here is difficult, but for at least one reason we ought to pause. It is unclear that we really do single out particular states as possible and others as impossible in the kind of way that Cameron and Sider argue.

Return, once more, to the discussion of the necessary truths and Sider's claim that which truths are necessary truths is a matter of convention. We are, in endorsing this strategy, allowing that a truth can be labelled 'necessary' iff it is a mathematical truth, or a logical truth, or a true-kind-identity, or . . . etc. But *why* are we fixing upon these truths when there is, in point of fact, *no agreed convention* concerning which truths are the necessary truths. There are those who defend the view that truths of mathematics are only contingently true (Rosen 2002); there are those who defend the view that not all identity statements are necessary truths (Lowe 1982); there is debate about the status of laws (Sidelle (2002)). It's hard to see why to prefer any one view of which truths are to be admitted as necessary by way of convention, without the view collapsing into an *ad hoc* stipulation that some truths are necessary truths and others are not. I take it that such a theory would be undesirable in the extreme.

Perhaps Sider and Cameron can find the resources with which to respond to this accusation. For the time being, though, we might want to note this as a problem that requires more attention.

# §4.10 Fictionalism

Let us now turn our attention to a view that has received much attention: modal fictionalism. There are two ways of interpreting the idea that modality is a fiction. The first is to deny that there are modal truths, but describe talk of what's possible and necessary as a useful fiction – in much the same way that we saw that the mereological Nihilist might argue that we treat talk of composite objects as a useful fiction. I shan't pursue this project, here. The second sort of modal fictionalism that we might countenance is one that attempts to ground the truth of modal talk in fictional works.

We are familiar enough with fictional works, already, and we are also familiar with mathematical fictionalism. As a reminder, suppose that we were talking about Sherlock Holmes. It is, I assume, true to say that Sherlock Holmes lived at 221b Baker Street. Of course, it's *only* true *according to the fiction* written by Sir Arthur Conan Doyle. But, nonetheless, we can give the truth-conditions in terms of the operator: 'according to the fiction that . . .'. To spell this out more clearly:

'Sherlock Holmes lived at 221b Baker Street' is true iff according to the fiction written by Sir Arthur Conan Doyle, the character Sherlock Holmes is described as living at 221b Baker Street.

Or, if we schematize a little:

(9) '<p>' is true iff according to the fiction written by A, p*.

If we are to use a similar strategy to ground the truth of modal talk, then we would have to find a suitable fiction.

One fiction that presents itself fairly naturally is the extensive work on modality by Lewis. Since Lewis has sketched a theory of possibility in enormous detail, so it might seem most apt to insert his work on modality as our work of fiction. Thus,

(10) ◊p is true iff according to the fiction written by Lewis, at some world, p*.
(11) □p is true iff according to the fiction written by Lewis, at all worlds, p*.

To give an example: suppose we think that it's possible that there are blue ducks. If that's right, then it has to be a part of the fiction that *there exist blue ducks at some other world*. Does that give us the right result; does the fiction yield the right result? Intuitively, it does. As we saw above, Lewis thinks that the possible worlds are exhaustive and that for every way that a world could be, some world is. Thus, one of the worlds will contain a blue duck. That means that, according to the Lewisian fiction, there exists a world including a blue duck, and so it is possible that there are blue ducks. On this cursory inspection, it seems as if modal fictionalism will deliver the right kinds of result.

# §4.11 Traditional problems for fictionalism

I do not attempt to cover all of the problems that have been raised for fictionalism, but rest content with discussing two of the traditional problems associated with the view.

The first 'traditional' problem is the Brock-Rosen problem. As we saw just a moment ago, the fictionalist will try to give the truth-conditions for modal claims in terms of fictions. But it seems, then, that we have a modal sentence that is true, and that using this analysis, in conjunction with particular modal sentences, can be made to entail the *existence* of possible worlds. Thus,

(12) Necessarily, there is a plurality of worlds iff according to the Lewisian fiction, at all worlds, there is a plurality of worlds.
(13) According to GMR, at all worlds, there is a plurality of worlds.
(14) Necessarily, there is a plurality of worlds.
(15) There is a plurality of worlds.

Let's work through this a little. To begin, notice that (12) is a modal sentence; thus, we are to give its truth-conditions in terms of the Lewisian fiction. Our sentence 'necessarily there is a plurality of worlds', is true, iff according to the Lewisian fiction there exists a plurality of worlds. According to the Lewisian fiction, of course, at all worlds *there is a plurality of worlds*, so it appears that necessarily, there is a plurality of worlds. If it's necessary that there is a plurality of worlds, then there *is* a plurality of worlds. And so it is that we end up with the conclusion that there is a plurality of worlds. There have been a variety of suggested responses to this problem, and I point in the direction of some of these in the recommended reading.

The second substantial problem for the modal fictionalist is the problem of incompleteness. The Lewisian fiction, as it stands, is pretty sparse. Lewis tells us that every way a world could be is a way some world *is*: but if we're going to use fictionalism as a reductive account of *modality*, then we need to hear something about the *contents* of these fictions. For instance, is it possible that there are talking bears? Is it possible that dogs can fly? Is it possible for me to write coherent notes? What we need is some account of that content.

But here's the worry. Lewis doesn't give us the content. Lewis does not systematically list the content of all of the possible worlds. The natural thing to do is to say that the Lewisian fiction *implies* or entails some content, in the following way. For every way a world could be, there is a world: so any way that something *could* be, is implied as a part of the fiction. So analogously (and here's Nolan's (1997) example) although in *Lord of the Rings* we're never told that Shelob is a giant spider, we're told it by implication. Thus, it's implied (we might say) within the fiction, that Shelob is a spider and, in the same way, it's implied within the Lewisian fiction that (for instance) it's possible that dogs fly.

But this strategy won't work. Implication is a modal notion and the fiction is supposed to reductively analyse the claim that 'x is possible'. We now need the fiction to *entail* or *imply* that x, where entailment and implication are modal notions. Thus, since entailment and implication are modal notions, so they cannot be used in a reductive analysis of modality.

# §4.12 Powers and modality

In the penultimate section of this chapter I want to briefly introduce a theory of modality that, although not as popular in the mainstream literature, is worth noting. I won't comment on it in any great detail since it presupposes some material that we will not cover until Chapter 5. Suppose that we were to ask whether or not it is possible for a horse to not be an animal. The answer is obvious: it is not possible for a horse to not be an animal. Indeed, it is necessary that all horses are animals. Now, let us ask why we think this necessary. Presumably, we think it necessary because it is simply not possible to have some object have the property of being a horse, without also having the property of being an animal. It's a fact about the two properties that they can't be separated.

But now consider the Lewisian story. Indeed, consider *any* of the above accounts that postulate worlds. According to a theory of possible worlds, this inseparability is just a fact about what exists at all of the worlds. Jubien (2007: 105) objects:

> The fundamental problem is that in world theory what passes for 'necessity' is in effect just a bunch of parallel 'contingencies'. The theory provides no basis for understanding why these contingencies repeat unremittingly across the board (while others do not). As a result, it provides no genuine analysis of necessity. What looks superficially like an analysis is really just a trivial consequence of the intuitive notion: *of course* if something is necessary, *and* there are all these

'possible worlds', then something that is necessary will be true in each of them. But that doesn't tell us what forces it to be true in each of them, in other words, what its necessity consists in.

The thought, I take it, is that although we can use these worlds to *model* what is necessary, it seems to be the fact that it is impossible for us to separate the property 'horse' from the property 'animal' that leads us to make the claim that, in no possible world do the two properties come apart.

But this suggests that the source of necessity (and also possibility) is not so much the worlds, as the properties themselves. Let us call this an 'aboutness' worry. It seems that our modal discourse is about what's possible and necessary. And, although we can use possible worlds to *model* that, it nonetheless seems that what leads us to posit the sorts of worlds that we do are the various different ways in which we think it is possible for us to rearrange the various different properties.

This kind of idea is picked up by Jacobs (2009). Jacobs adopts a theory of properties that treats them as *powers*. The idea that is exploited is that powers are something like *dispositions*. Thus, the property of solubility is best thought of as the property 'would dissolve if placed in water'. Thus,

> Properties, . . . , are powers *for something*. They point beyond themselves. Electric charge is the power to repel other negatively charged particles. . . . Their having the power does not involve being related to some mere possibilia, say, the unac-tualised state of affairs of *this* electron being repelled with such-and-such a force. Such possibilities are, rather, metaphorically written into the nature of negative charge. (2009: 236)

This then leads us to what we might think of as a far more intuitive theory of modality. To say that some state of affairs, p, is possible is, simply to say that there is some instantiated property that is a power for some other property that would make true, <p>. Thus, to say that it's possible for me to throw my cup against the wall is simply to say that the properties I instantiate, my *powers*, are such that it is within their capacity to bring it about that the cup is thrown against the wall. Of course, whether or not we find this theory plausible will depend upon the nature of these dispositional properties. We must wait for the next chapter to see whether or not they turn out to be the kinds of entities that we are prepared to posit. We might also worry that such a theory cannot obviously account for alien properties. If our account of what is possible is based on actually existing properties then it is not entirely clear how we will generate the possibility of there existing properties that do not actually exist; what power will make true <there could be a power that does not in fact exist>?

# §4.13 Conclusion

There are a number of issues not explored in this chapter that, were space no issue, it would be interesting to consider. For one thing, we saw in the previous chapter that when positing abstract objects to ground mathematical truths, that we face particular epistemic concerns. Since at least some of the theories of modality that we've considered posit abstract objects, it would be interesting to consider whether or not these sorts of epistemic concerns will carry over to our preference of a theory of possible worlds. We have also not said very much about theories that try to *do away* with possible worlds altogether – I point to some of these in the further reading. Both omissions are somewhat regrettable.

However, the intention behind this chapter is to give the reader a flavour of what I take to be a sizeable portion of the mainstream view of modality. Since possible worlds have played so great a role in that enterprise, as have reductive theories thereof, so they have occupied our attention, here. In the further reading, I list some sources that might be of interest to those who are not persuaded by the need for possible world talk.

# Recommended reading by topic

Lewis' genuine modal realism

Bricker, P. 2008. 'Concrete Possible Worlds', in Sider, T., Hawthorne, J. and Zimmerman, D. eds. *Contemporary Debates in Metaphysics*. Oxford: Blackwell, 111–34.

Lewis, D. 1986a. *On the Plurality of Worlds*. Oxford: Blackwell.

Nolan, D. 2005. *David Lewis*. Chesham: Acumen, esp. chapter 3.

Pruss, A. 2002. 'The Actual and the Possible', in Gale, R. ed. *The Blackwell Guide to Metaphysics*, 317–33.

Linguistic ersatzism

Lewis, D. 1986a. *On the Plurality of Worlds*. Oxford: Blackwell, 136–41.

Melia, J. 2008. 'Ersatz Possible Worlds', in Sider, T., Hawthorne, J. and Zimmerman, D. eds. *Contemporary Debates in Metaphysics*, 135–51.

Nolan, D. 2002. *Topics in the Philosophy of Possible Worlds*. New York: Routledge, esp. chapter 5.

Sider, T. 2002. 'The ersatz Pluriverse', *Journal of Philosophy*, 99, 279–315.

## Fictionalism

Liggins, D. 2006b. 'Modal Fictionalism and Possible-worlds Discourse', *Philosophical Studies*, 138, 151–60.

Nolan, D. 1997. 'Three Problems for "Strong" Modal Fictionalism', *Philosophical Studies*, 87, 259–75.

Rosen, G. 1990. 'Modal Fictionalism', *Mind*, 99, 327–35.

Woodward, R. 2009. 'Why Modal Fictionalism is not Self-Defeating', *Philosophical Studies*, 139, 273–88.

## Magical/Propositional ersatzism

Denby, D. 2006. 'In Defence of "Magical" Ersatzism', *Philosophical Quarterly*, 56, 161–7.

Lewis, D. 1986a. *On the Plurality of Worlds*. Oxford: Blackwell, 174–91.

Plantinga, A. 1974. *The Nature of Necessity*. Oxford: OUP.

Stalnaker, R. 1976. 'Possible Worlds', *Nous*, 10, 65–75.

Van Inwagen, P. 1980. 'Indexicality and Actuality', *Philosophical Review,* 89, 403–26.

## Against possible worlds

Armstrong, D. 1989a. *A Combinatorial Theory of Possibility*. Cambridge: CUP.

Jacobs, J. 2009. 'A Powers Theory of Modality: or, How I Learned to Stop Worrying and Reject Possible Worlds', *Philosophical Studies*, 151, 227–48.

Jubien, M. 2007. 'Analyzing Modality', *Oxford Studies in Metaphysics*, 3, 99–139.

Tallant, J. 2009. 'Ontological Cheats Might Just Prosper', *Analysis*, 69, 422–30.

## Is the Lewisian reduction successful?

Cameron, R. forthcoming, b. 'Why Lewis's Analysis of Modality Succeeds in its Reductive Ambitions', *Philosophers' Imprint*.

Divers, J. and Melia, J. 2002. 'The Analytic Limit of Genuine Modal Realism', *Mind*, 111, 15–36.

Lycan, W. G. 1988. 'Review of On the Plurality of Worlds', *Journal of Philosophy*, LXXXV, 42–7.

Shalkowski, S. 1994. 'The Ontological Ground of the Alethic Modality', *The Philosophical Review*, 103, 669–88.

## Study questions

1) Write out a brief outline of each theory covered here. Which theory do you think is best? Why did you opt for that theory?
2) How important do you think it is that our theory of modality is reductive?
3) How serious do you think the objection from Alien properties?
4) How pressing do you think the 'aboutness' worry raised in §4.12
5) What is the most serious problem you can think of for fictionalism? How would you try to respond to the objection?

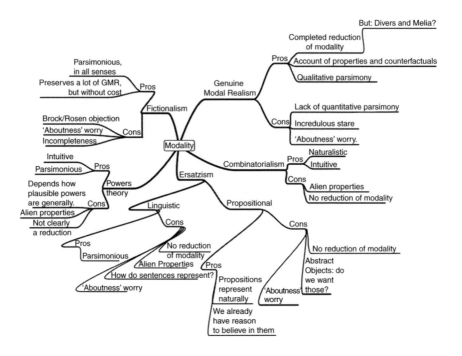

# 5

# Properties

Imagine, if you will, three London buses. Imagine that they are in front of you right now. If your imagination is anything like mine, I think that you'll assent to the truth of the following sentences.

(1) The three buses are the same colour.
(2) The three buses have something in common.
(3) The three buses resemble one another with respect to their colour.

I'm going to assume that you agree with each of (1)–(3) because you've imagined some red, double-decker buses, and, if you didn't imagine these, imagine them now! Each of (1)–(3) seem, intuitively at least, to be true. Each of the buses in question is red.

Similarly, if slightly more technically, suppose that we have three electrons before us. Each of these sub-atomic particles has a negative charge. We would,

I assume, be prepared to assert each of the following:

(4) The three electrons have the same charge.
(5) The three electrons have something in common.
(6) The three electrons resemble one another with respect to their charge.

Both of these cases, the case of the buses and the case of the electrons, appear to be cases with a common structure. We have a particular (the bus, the electron) which we will characterize crudely as a *thing* or *entity*, and we have a property of that particular (the colour, the negative charge). Our concern in this chapter is properties and sentences similar to those in each of (1)–(6). Assuming that sentences like (1)–(6) are true, what sorts of things *are* properties, such that they make true these various sentences?

Before we proceed, it's perhaps worthwhile deploying a little terminology. We identified cases in which particulars had properties. Throughout the chapter I will assume that we can identify a particular as x, y or z, or a, b or c, and that we can identify properties using the letters F, G and H. This will enable us to say things like 'x is F' (perhaps as a way of saying that 'the bus is red'), or that 'y is G' (perhaps as a way of saying that 'the electron has a negative charge').

# §5.1 Universals

One thought, and a very natural one at that, is that when we have true sentences of the form 'x is F' and 'y is F' that there is some property – the entity, F – that both x and y have in common. In the buses case, introduced above, this would amount to our saying that there is some entity 'being red', that is shared by both x and y (the two buses, for instance). On first inspection, that doesn't seem all that implausible. We will call these repeatable entities 'universals'.

There are many important distinctions that we will need to draw in our discussion of properties; here is the first. Universals are repeatable properties and may be thought to be either transcendent or immanent. To say of a universal that it is transcendent is to say that it exists over and above its instances. It is an abstract entity. So, although we might say that each of the buses is red, the colour red *itself* exists independently of each of the instances of red objects. Thus, even were no red object in the world it would still be the case that the colour red existed. This view is Platonic – in that it has its roots in the work of Plato. In contrast, the view of universals as immanent treats them as existing *only at their instances.* Thus, were it to be the case that no red objects exist, then the colour red would not exist. This view is broadly Aristotelian.

It is worth pausing a moment to consider why we might be tempted towards Platonism about universals, for the view appears to commit us to properties as existing outside space and time and, thus, to abstracta. And, as we have already seen (in Chapter 3), there are substantial concerns with positing abstract entities. So we had better have some good reason for thinking that properties exist outside space and time.

Here is Russell (2001) on the matter. To begin, note that Edinburgh is to the north of London. Notice, also, that 'to the north of' seems to be something that is repeatable. Edinburgh is to the north of London, as are Sheffield, Nottingham, Leeds, Durham and Peterhead. We might think, therefore, that there is a universal 'north of'. Then,

> 'north of' does not seem to *exist* in the same sense in which Edinburgh and London exist. If we ask 'Where and when does this relation exist?' the answer must be 'Nowhere and nowhen'. There is no place or time where we can find the relation 'north of'. It does not exist in Edinburgh any more than in London, for it relates the two and is neutral between them. Nor can we say that it exists at any particular time. Now everything that can be apprehended by the senses or by introspection exists at some particular time. Hence the relation 'north of' is radically different from such things. It is neither in space nor in time, neither material nor mental; yet it is something. (2001: 18)

Thus, if the relation exists, but is in neither space nor time, then the universal must exist quite apart from its instances that appear in the world.

The first point worth making is one of clarification. Russell's claim that 'to the north of' exists in a different sense to Edinburgh is, on at least one reading, plausibly false. Merely that the relation does not exist in space and time does not establish that the way in which it exists is any different to Edinburgh, so much that *where and when* it exists differs from where and when Edinburgh exists. We certainly do not need to see this as an argument for the conclusion that there is more than one sort of existence, as Russell appears to imply.

Second, there might well be a reply to Russell. It *seems* to make perfect sense to say of properties and relations that they exist whenever their instances do. Thus, although there is no sense in which the relational property 'to the north of' exists at some place and time to the exclusion of all others, it is nonetheless something that exists in space and time by virtue of 'being to the north of' being something that is instantiated by concrete particulars –

Edinburgh and London. Certainly, this seems to be the sort of position that Lowe (2006: 25) is endorsing when he claims in connection with properties, 'that its manner of existing is, in a perfectly good sense, "immanent" . . . , inasmuch as it exists only "in" or "through" its particular instances, precisely insofar as they instantiate it'. This would be one way in which we might respond to the Russellian argument for the claim that properties and relations exist outside space and time. When we also factor in concerns about parsimony – it is clearly preferable to avoid positing universals as *distinct* from their instances, in addition to their existing at their instances – and concerns about what it actually means to exist 'outside space and time', it becomes apparent that we have substantial reason to prefer an Aristotelian view of universals – that they are immanent. From now on, then, I shall assume the view that universals are immanent.

# §5.2 Predicates and properties

The next point we must note is that not every predicate denotes a property. To demonstrate that this must be so, consider the following sentence and keep in mind that the sky is, of course, blue in colour.

(7) The sky is not green.

This sentence is true. Here 'not green' seems to perform as a predicate: this being so, it makes sense to ask whether we need a further universal of 'not green' that the sky need instantiate? After all, the sentence is true, and we have said that predicates denote properties.

This would seem an odd claim to make in connection with (7). It would seem far more natural to think that the truth-maker for (7) is the sky's being blue, rather than the sky's instantiating some further property 'being not green'. It would therefore be natural to think that sentences like (7) show us, not that there are properties such as 'being not green', but that not every predicate denotes a universal.

But one might still be tempted, even given that this is a slightly odd result, to think that sentences like (7) give us good reason to think that the property of 'being not green' exists. After all, we accept similar sorts of argument when it comes to what we might think of as *positive* predicates (e.g. is red, is charged, is green, etc.). We allow that these sorts of predicates point to universals, so why not accept that negative predicates (e.g. is not red, is not charged, is not green etc.) point to universals, too? What is the difference between these two sorts of cases, such that one *does* show that there are properties and the other does not? Despite the view being odd, I have not yet shown that we *must* endorse the view that not all predicates denote properties.

The crunch comes when we consider the following sorts of predicates:

(8)  x is non-self-exemplifying.

To begin, let's try and get a grip on what 'is non-self-exemplifying' means. It clearly applies to certain entities: George Bush, for instance, does not exemplify himself: the number 2 does not exemplify itself since it is a single number (though the number 1 does). Nottingham Castle doesn't exemplify itself. By way of contrast, the property, 'being incorporeal' *does* exemplify itself, since the property 'being incorporeal' is, itself, incorporeal (it lacks a physical body). Likewise, the property (if there is such a property) as 'being self-identical' exemplifies itself; since being self-identical is a property that is identical with itself!

So here is why the predicate 'is non-self-exemplifying' cannot denote a property. Suppose, for a moment, the property 'non-self-exemplifying' exemplified itself; then, in virtue of being the property 'non-self-exemplifying' it would have to not be self-exemplifying. In other words, it the property 'non-self-exemplifying' self-exemplifies, then it non-self-exemplifies. Contradiction! If, on the other hand, it does not self-exemplify, then it self-exemplifies itself since it is purportedly the property of being 'non-self-exemplifying'. Contradiction ensues either way and so it seems safe to assume that no such property can exist. Thus it seems right to infer that not every grammatically well-formed predicate can denote a property.

All of this raises an interesting and important question. We began with the idea that many of the predicate terms with which we are familiar, predicates like 'is red', denote properties. However, since we are now supposing that not all predicates denote properties, we must then ask 'which ones do'?

One very intuitive thought is that we should restrict our account of which predicates denote universals to only those properties that (a) make a causal difference or, (b) those that make a difference to what is true. After all, if a property does not make a causal difference, and does not make a difference to what is true, then it is hard to see why we should want to posit it.

To see these principles in action consider the case we might make against disjunctive universals; that is, properties that correspond in their structure to instances of disjunctive predication:

> (9) x is red or blue.
> (10) y has mass m or mass m*.

Consider (10). If y has mass m, then (10) is true (that's inimical to the nature of a disjunction – it's true if either disjunct is true). In that instance, (10) would be true. So do we then need to think of y as instantiating a disjunctive *universal*?

Two reasons to think not, that draw on the principles just specified: first, y being m makes a causal difference (were it not of mass m, y would not (for instance) depress a scale as much as it otherwise would; m would not exert the same gravitational force – and so-on). But y being m *or m\** doesn't make the slightest contribution to the causal powers of y. The disjunctive 'property' would make no discernible contribution to the causal powers of y; all of the work is done by the property m.

Second, if y instantiates the universal *m*, then y and *m* make true the proposition <y is m or m*>. Given that this is so we can preserve the truth of (10) without recourse to including any disjunctive *universals* in our ontology. Similar considerations as these can obviously be brought against 'negative' universals, too. If an object has the property of having a mass of 50KG, then no further causal or truth-making work would be done by it also positing the property of 'not having mass 49KG'.

This kind of thinking reaches its apotheosis in Lewis' distinction between the sparse and abundant properties. The abundant properties are such that there is a property for every descriptive condition that you care to give. Our disjunctive properties could go on this list, as could nearly any other predicate that you specify. So, for Lewis, there is an abundant property of 'being a banana or a cat'; a property of 'being square ad yellow' and so on.

But the predicates just used are not the *interesting* predicates; these are not the ones that denote what Lewis calls the 'sparse' properties.

> Physics has its short list of 'fundamental physical properties': the charges and masses of particles, also their so-called 'spins' and 'colours' and 'flavours', and maybe a few more that have yet to be discovered. . . . What physics has undertaken, whether or not ours is a world where the undertaking will succeed, is an inventory of the *sparse* properties. (Lewis 1986a: 60)

These sparse properties will be relatively few – only those properties that are posited by our ultimate and best physical theory. These properties – the ones uncovered by our best physics – may also be called 'natural'. Thus, we have the abundant properties and we have the sparse, natural properties. Lewis' thought is that the predicates that denote *natural properties* are in fact denoting universals (or tropes – a distinct theory of properties that we shall come on to in a moment).

So here is the picture: predicates denoting the posits of our best and final physics are, in fact, denoting universals; all other predicates are denoting parts of the world that are constructed *out of* the various natural properties. Thus, the seat upon which I am sitting satisfies the predicate 'is white' and so there is a property of being white. But the property is not perfectly natural (and so is not a universal). Instead, 'the chair is white' is to be understood as made true by a particular construction of natural properties (properties of mass, charge, spin etc.).

Lewis' picture is undeniably intuitive. The idea being mined is that the fundamental properties of physics can be used to explain how the world appears to us. Thus, once we understand how charge, mass, spin (etc.) must be arranged in order to generate something that is white, so we understand what it is for something to be white. And, in that case, there is no obvious need to posit a distinct property of 'being white'; we can understand what it is to be white in terms of the structure and arrangement of the fundamental properties. Thus, it is only the sparse, natural properties that are immanent universals: all other properties are, in some way, derivative.

But, although it is certainly intuitive to think that there is a distinction between the universals and the mere properties, and this account also helps us to specify which predicates denote universals (something that we were previously uncertain of), there are also other reasons that Lewis thinks that we should endorse the distinction between sparse/natural properties and the abundant properties. We will consider one such reason here.

# §5.3 Intrinsic and extrinsic properties

It is very plausible that there is some distinction between the intrinsic properties and the extrinsic properties. The idea to be explicated is that there are some properties that appear to be such that an object can have them quite independently of what else exists. Thus, the mass of a particular object is not dependent on anything else. I have the mass that I do regardless of whether or not anything else exists. However, some properties appear different. For example, the weight of an object is in part dependent upon the intensity of the gravitational force being exerted on the object in question. Thus, my mass is intrinsic to me; I have the same mass regardless of where I find myself. My weight, on the other hand, we may describe as extrinsic. My weight depends upon the force exerted upon me.

But as intuitive as the distinction may seem, it is rather hard to cash out the *precise* distinction between intrinsic and extrinsic properties. The gloss that I gave above will fail if subjected to any serious scrutiny. For instance, we may suppose that, were it not the case that the earth existed, then I would not have reached my current mass – had the earth not existed then the nutritional resources to which I would have had access would have been very different, thus leading to my having a different mass. In that case, it appears that my mass is, in a sense, dependent upon what exists – the earth – despite my mass intuitively being intrinsic.

The way in which Lewis uses the distinction between the natural and abundant properties to generate a distinction between the intrinsic and extrinsic properties is as follows. Let us begin with the observation that all of the natural properties are intrinsic; the charge, mass, spin (etc.) of an object will not depend (in the relevant sense) upon the existence of any other object. However, not all of the intrinsic properties will be natural: the property of 'having a mass *and* having a charge' is intrinsic, but is not natural.

Keep that in mind. Now we need to add to the mixture the notion of a 'duplicate'. We can call two things 'duplicates' iff (i) they have the same perfectly natural properties, and (ii) their parts can be put into correspondence in such a way that the corresponding parts have the same perfectly natural properties. Consider an example: two quarks are duplicates of one another iff they have the same mass, charge, spin (etc.) and the parts of the quarks have the same mass, charge, spin (etc.). If, however, one of our two quarks had a different spin, then the two quarks would not be duplicates of one another.

Using the concept of what it is to be a duplicate, we can then define what it is to be intrinsic: a property, F, is intrinsic iff F can never vary across two duplicates.

I think it's worth pausing just a moment to show how this definition would rule mass intrinsic and weight extrinsic. Suppose that we have two duplicates of one another: two people, Elizabeth and Verity. Suppose, further, that the two people are duplicates of one another, right down to the last detail (in terms of their natural properties). Let us also suppose that Verity is on Jupiter;

Elizabeth is on Earth. It is clear that, although both may have a mass of 55Kg, they will have very different weights. Formally, we allow that the weight of an object is equal to its mass multiplied by the gravitational force. We typically treat the gravitational force on earth as equal to '1'. Thus, Elizabeth's 'weight' is 55Kg. Verity's 'weight' on the other hand is 130Kg.

What cases like this reveal is that two duplicates can have different weight in different circumstances. Given our definition, above, that means that weight cannot be intrinsic. Mass, on the other hand, does not vary across these scenarios and so is intrinsic. Verity and Elizabeth would have the same mass in all possible situations, provided Verity and Elizabeth are duplicates of one another.[1] We can thus see that there is a putative advantage to drawing the distinction that Lewis does between the natural and abundant properties. The advantage is, quite simply, that we can use the distinction between the natural and abundant properties to help us draw a distinction between the extrinsic and intrinsic properties – that is an important theoretical advance.

# §5.4 Tropes

Thus far we've concentrated our attention on a theory of properties that treats them as universals: entities that can, quite literally, be repeated. But there are other theories of properties available to us. The view that we shall consider next is trope theory. The idea, here, is that properties are particularized. It is, therefore, false to say that 'redness' is a repeatable entity. Rather, although properties exist, they are to be treated as properties *of* some entity or other. Each of the London buses that we considered at the outset are red, but they are each red *in virtue of* each bus having a different property of redness.

The case is perhaps made more vivid by considering a stock example from the literature.

(11) Plato is wise.
(12) Socrates is wise.

What makes (11) and (12) true is that both Plato and Socrates bear properties. However, the properties are different. (11) is made true by Plato and the property of *Plato's wisdom*. (12) is made true by Socrates and the property of *Socrates' wisdom*. Further, it's not the case that *Plato's wisdom = Socrates' wisdom*. Platonic-wisdom and Socratic-wisdom are *not* the same property. We have two different properties: Platonic wisdom and Socratic wisdom. This is different from theories that posit universals. A universal *is* the same property at every point at which it is instantiated. If we thought that properties were universals, and not tropes, then (11) and (12) would be true because Plato and Socrates instantiated *the very same property* of wisdom.

Likewise, consider the following pair of sentences:

(13) Electron $e_1$ has a negative charge.
(14) Electron $e_2$ has a negative charge.

Both of these sentences are true. But, according to trope theory, what makes it true that $e_1$ has a negative charge is the trope *$e_1$'s negative charge*; what makes it true that $e_2$ has a negative charge is the trope *$e_2$'s negative charge*. These are distinct properties.

Indeed, we can generalize. A trope theorist will claim that, in any case where we attribute the same property, F, to two (or more) distinct particulars x and y, the properties they bear are not literally identical. Rather, what we will have is x's F-ness, and y's F-ness.

A good question then arises. It seems to us as if Plato and Socrates have something in common. They *share* some property – that of being wise. But on the analysis we've just offered, a trope analysis, that's false. There is no property of wisdom that is shared by both Plato and Socrates; no property that is shared by $e_1$ and $e_2$. So what makes it true that:

(15) Plato and Socrates share a property: wisdom.
(16) Electrons $e_1$ and $e_2$ share a property: negative charge.

Well, if trope theory is true, then nothing makes these sentences true. (15) and (16) are both false if we endorse trope theory. The trope theorist will not think this too much of a problem. The trope theorist denies that there is any such property that is shared.

Imagine, then, someone responding, against the trope theorist, in the following way:

> Look, we all agree that Plato and Socrates resemble one another in a particular respect: they are both wise. According to your trope theory, they don't actually share a property, so they don't resemble one another in the way that we all agree that they are. So, trope theory fails to preserve the surely obvious fact that Plato and Socrates resemble one another and that $e_1$ and $e_2$ also resemble one another.

The objection, as stated, appears compelling. But it contains what the trope theorist will claim is a faulty inference: the inference from there being no shared property to the two particulars not resembling one another.

The trope theorist will claim that Socrates' wisdom resembles Plato's wisdom; that $e_1$'s charge resembles $e_2$'s charge. And, because of this, we *can* say that the particulars (Socrates and Plato; $e_1$ and $e_2$) resemble one another. Now in the objection there was an implication (in the second sentence) that if objects don't share a property, then they don't resemble one another. But we have not been given any reason to believe that. And the trope theorist will claim that we are not likely to be given such a reason, either. The trope theorist will simply deny that we require the sharing of properties for a resemblance.

But this reply from the trope theorist is only partly satisfying, for we have not been told what resemblance *is*. And, at first blush, it might well seem that whatever account of resemblance we give, there is going to be a problem. Resemblance appears to be a relation. Moreover, it appears to be a repeatable relation. Consider all of the electrons that make up the earth. Each of these has a charge. Thus, each electron resembles each other electron. To put things more formally: each electron stands in the relation of resemblance to every other. It therefore appears that there is a *repeatable* relation of resemblance that stands between each electron and every other. And, as we know, repeatable relations are not tropes, but universals. So at a first pass it would appear that the trope theorist is committed to the existence of universals. That is not a good result.

One solution available to the trope theorist is to deny that resemblance is a relation – contra appearances. According to the trope theorist, resemblance may just be a primitive feature of our theory. So, yes, (15) and (16) are both false, and, yes, all instances of wisdom and negative charge resemble one another: but that they resemble one another is not something we can further analyse. It is just a primitive feature of reality that wisdom tropes and charge tropes resemble one another.

Of course, we might think that this is for the trope theorist to take an unfair way out. It appeared that what we were trying to do was to analyse predication. That's what we started out trying to do with our opening sentences. We had sentences that we agreed were true, and we tried to analyse what it was about the world that meant that not only did the subject term of the sentence refer to an object in the world, but the predicate *also* served to pick out some element of reality. It now appears that we're denying that some predicates can be analysed at all. That might be taken to be a sizeable disadvantage of trope theory, for it appears that there are predicates that can be deployed in sentences where we cannot locate an appropriate truth-maker. It is *just true* that some objects resemble one another (though see §5.8).

The final theory that I want to consider (though it comes in a variety of flavours) is nominalism.

# §5.5 Nominalism[2]

According to the nominalist, there are no properties at all. We will begin our survey of the 'nominalisms' available with consideration of Ostrich nominalism

> Ostrich nominalism: The truth of the sentence 'a is *F*' does not require of us any property, *F*. We merely require that a falls under the predicate 'is *F*'.

So, consider an example:

> (17) Socrates is wise.

The sort analysis of this sentence *seems* to suggest is that there is some *thing*, wise, that Socrates *is*. Or, at least, that there is some way of being, wise, that Socrates instantiates. The reply from the Ostrich nominalist is that there are only particulars. In this case, there is only Socrates. The Ostrich nominalist will deal with claim that (17) is, in part, brute and unanalysable: it's just a matter of fact that there is some particular, Socrates, that is wise. We can't analyse this any further than saying that there's some particular, Socrates, of whom it's correct to predicate wisdom. We have, if you will, reached ontological bedrock with such an explanation.

The idea, then, will be that talk about wisdom is nothing more than talk about wise objects. This is crucial. The obvious advantage of this strategy is parsimony: we have only one *sort of thing* in the world – namely, particulars.

Let us consider some problems with Ostrich nominalism, so-called due to remarks of David Armstrong's. Armstrong's thought runs thus. Suppose that we are presented with two sentences: one says that a is *F*, the other says that b is *F*. The natural question, then, is what it is that makes both a and b, are F. Now it appears, when we are considering Ostrich nominalism, that we are ignoring this question. Thus, when pressed as to why both a and b are F, we simply claim that both a and b fall under the predicate, F. To the further question: *in virtue of what do they both fall under the predicate F?* We simply reply: in virtue of a's falling under F, and b's falling under F. Thus,

we have nothing more to say about what makes a *F*, it just *is F*; that is a basic and inexplicable fact about the universe. (Devitt (1997: 97))

This raises an important question for us. What reason could we have for insisting that there is more to be said? If there is no reason to think that there is anything more to be said, then there would appear to not be an interesting objection in the vicinity.

Armstrong (1997a: 103) responds. He begins with a quote from Quine, who is, here, being treated as an Ostrich nominalist.

. . . what does Quine offer us? He simply says:

That the houses and roses and sunsets are all of them red may be taken as ultimate and irreducible. (p. 81)

. . . It is natural to interpret him instead as saying that, although these tokens are all of the same type, yet we have no need to consider what sameness of type is . . . If this is the way to interpret Quine, then is he not an Ostrich about types? Like an Oxford philosopher of yore, he keeps on saying that he does not deny that many different objects are all of them red, but what this ostensible sameness is he refuses to explain (except to say that it is ultimate and irreducible).[3]

Armstrong's objection to Ostrich nominalism (on this matter, at least) comes down to a question of 'sameness'. There is a need to explain, according to Armstrong, what, precisely, the sameness of two red objects consists in. Saying that 'both objects are red' does not give us an explanation of their being the same; it simply tells us that they *are* same. So here is one problem for the Ostrich nominalist: explain the sameness of all things F.

The second tranche of problems is more complex and concerns the way in which Ostrich nominalists will deal with sentences that seem to say that all objects of one sort have some other property, thus:

(18) Courage is a moral virtue.

Remember, the Ostrich nominalist thinks that the way in which to conceive of predication is as something that applies to particulars and does so simply as a matter of brute fact. The obvious interpretation of (18), then, is something like:

(19) Courageous individuals are morally virtuous.

But there are at least two problems with this. First, it seems reasonable to think that (18) would be true even in the absence of anyone who was courageous. So, suppose that we lived in a world where all of the courageous people had been wiped out. (18) still seems like it's true. But if that's right then it can't be correctly paraphrased by (19), for were there no people then (19) would appear to be false.

The second problem is this. Suppose that it were true, and well known, that all tall people were morally virtuous. Now, the way in which the Ostrich nominalist dealt with (18) was to say that we could paraphrase the meaning of (18) by recourse to (19) and so do away with any unwanted ontological commitment to the property of courage (see Chapter 3 for a discussion of nominalism and paraphrase).

As a product of the fact that we're considering a case where all tall people are morally virtuous it turns out that (20) is true.

(20) Tall individuals are morally virtuous.

So now consider the Ostrich nominalist's strategy. (20) is of the same form as (19). Notice, though, that (19) entailed that 'Courage is a moral virtue'. And, in that case, (20) should be taken to entail that 'Tallness is a moral virtue'. (20) entails this for the same reasons that the Ostrich nominalist thinks that 'courageous individuals are morally virtuous' entails that 'courage is a moral virtue'. But that, surely, is ridiculous. In the case we are considering we are not, I assume, supposing that it is the tallness of the individuals concerned that is a moral virtue. Rather, by some accident, it turns out that tall people *just so happen* to be virtuous people.

It thus seems that Ostrich nominalism faces a number of problems – I leave it to the reader to determine whether or not these are soluble. Let us then move on to look at another form of nominalism.

# §5.6 Class nominalism

Class nominalism: The truth of the sentence 'a is *F*' does not require any property, F. We merely require that there is a class of objects that are all F and that a is one of the objects that is in the class.

According to class nominalism Socrates and Plato are both wise because they are both members of the class of wise objects; our London buses are red because the particular buses, x, y are all members of the class of red objects; two electrons have the same charge because they are members of the same class of objects.

However, a problem lies in wait for the class nominalist. To say of a particular that it has a given property, F, is simply to say that it falls within a particular class of objects. That means that we can identify two particular properties as being the same as one another iff the classes are co-extensive – that is, iff the classes contain exactly the same objects. That suggests a recipe for providing a counterexample to class nominalism: find two properties that are different from one another, but whereby all objects in one class, are also in another.

Are there such cases? There are. Consider the properties ' . . . is cordate', and ' . . . is renate'. The former is the property of having a heart; the latter, the property of having a kidney. These are clearly different properties. But notice, although the properties are clearly distinct, all creatures that are cordate are renate. All members of the class of cordate creatures are members of the class of renate creatures. Thus, given class nominalism, the two properties are the same. Class nominalism is, therefore, false.

In Chapter 4 we considered, among other things, Lewis' genuine modal realism. Notice that the problem under consideration will disappear if we endorse genuine modal realism for the class of objects that are renate and the class of objects that are renate will differ in *possible* extension. That is, there are possible worlds at which creatures are renate but not cordate, and worlds at which there are creatures that are cordate but not renate. Provided that we then allow that, properly considered, the class of objects that we consider include all of the objects that exist at worlds other than our own, then we will not face the problem of accidentally co-extensive classes of object. This might then give us another reason to prefer Lewis' theory of modality.

However, in a final twist in the tail, we might do well just to note that there *appears* to be a counterexample to even this version of class nominalism. Recall that we provided a counterexample previously by giving an example of two distinct properties which were identified as the same property given class nominalism. To do that in this case, we would need to find two obviously distinct properties that were, necessarily, born by the same particulars. A case that may be considered, here, is that of the properties of trilaterality and triangularity. The former is the property of having three sides; the latter as the property of having three internal angles. Now, clearly, as a matter of necessity every object that is triangular is trilateral. Thus, necessarily, every particular that is within the class of trilateral objects is a member of the class of triangular objects. It follows, given class nominalism, that these two seemingly distinct properties are the same. Time, then, to consider another form of nominalism.[4]

# §5.7 Resemblance nominalism

Resemblance nominalism: The truth of the sentence 'a is F' does not require any property, F. We merely require that there an object, a, that is F. We can then specify that any object that resembles a, is F.

To see how the theory works, consider the following three sentences:

(21) The sapphire, x, is blue.
(22) The sapphire, y, is blue.
(23) x is the same colour as y.

What makes each of these true is that x and y are both a part of the class of objects that resemble one another. Thus, x is blue because x is a member of the class of objects that fall under the predicate 'is blue' by virtue of resembling some paradigmatically blue object; y is blue because it falls under the predicate 'is blue' by virtue of resembling some paradigmatically blue object, and the two are the same colour because they are a part of the same resemblance class. This isn't to say, of course, that the proponent of resemblance is committed to the existence of *properties*: it's just to say that there are two objects, x and y, and that x and y resemble one another. No mention of properties! What we have is a putative paraphrase of colour property talk in terms of talk about classes of objects that resemble one another.

There are a number of points to be raised here. To begin with, it looks like just insisting upon resemblance between x and y might fail. Suppose, first, I have three objects: a small sapphire, a small grey stone and a large blue monkey. According to the account just canvassed, we can call objects 'blue' iff they resemble the sapphire. So, which object resembles the sapphire more closely: a blue monkey or a small grey stone? My money is on the small grey stone here. Small grey stones seem to me to resemble sapphires much more closely than do large blue monkeys.

That's a problem, for we said that anything that resembles the sapphire is blue, but we also said that the stone, that is grey, resembles the sapphire. So it must be the case that the stone, which is grey, is blue. That's the wrong result.

Intuitively, what has gone wrong is that we've ignored what it is that the resemblance is supposed to be *with respect to*. If we are trying to identify what it is to be blue by resemblance to the sapphire, we don't mean the sapphire considered as a whole, we mean that an object is blue iff it resembles the sapphire *with respect to its colour*. Clearly, the monkey resembles the sapphire with respect to its colour; the stone does not. Thus we have no problems here.

The trouble with this reply is that the resemblance has to consist in resemblance with respect to a colour. Colours would, if they existed, be properties. If you're a Resemblance nominalist then, strictly speaking, there are no such *things* as colours as there are no properties. For the Resemblance nominalist there are simply concrete particulars that resemble one another. So this solution, intuitive as it is, won't work.

Here's the second worry. We said, above, that the Resemblance nominalist requires that the two blue objects resemble one another, in order for them both to be considered blue. So, consider the following sentences and suppose them true:

(24) The sapphire resembles the monkey.
(25) The monkey resembles a bottle.

(suppose that, in both cases, the resemblance is colour based).

Clearly, (24) and (25) entail:

(26) Resemblance is something that the monkey and the sapphire and the monkey and the bottle have in common.

In order for (26) to be true it looks as if there will have to be a resemblance relation, in which the sapphire stands to the monkey and the monkey stands to the bottle. Now that wouldn't be a problem, other than for the fact that it seems to be the same relation in both instances: namely, resemblance. When it comes to spelling out their view, it looks like the Resemblance nominalist will have to say that objects are (for instance) of the same colour, precisely because they *resemble one another*. That resemblance, in turn, is best understood as a relation in which things stand to one another. Of course, the relation, if it can be multiply instantiated, will have to be a universal. But, of course, if we're going to introduce universals, then why bother with the resemblance nominalism in the first place?

There's a potential solution to the problem though it throws up some interesting dialectical concerns. The proponent of Resemblance nominalist might just suggest that the relation of resemblance is a *brute fact*: it's just a primitive part of Resemblance nominalism that objects resemble one another. That isn't to say, obviously, that there's a *universal* in play, here: rather, resembling one another is just something that objects *do*.

So here's a classic weights and balance situation: the proponent of universals can explain resemblance (the instantiation of the very same universal) but because they posit particulars *and* properties, so the proponent of universals looks to have the more complex ontology. The nominalist, on the other hand, has a far simpler ontology consisting of only particulars, but must posit nothing more than a *brute fact* (primitive) to explain resemblance. In between these theories we find trope theory, that does posit genuine properties, but takes the resemblance between them to be a primitive matter. We must then weigh these competing theories and try to decide which theory is best.

# §5.8 Primitive predication

At this stage it is tempting to think that the proponent of universals will fare better in this debate, even if they have the more richly populated ontology. For, given any predicate, the proponent of universals can offer an analysis. If the predicate is one that appears to point to a property that is a part of our best physics, then the property is natural and so is a universal. If, on the other hand, the predicate is not one that plays an important role in our best physics, then the property is less than perfectly natural. In that case the predicate is to be analysed via the various different perfectly natural properties. We can use this against the nominalist and the trope theorist. Both posit unexplained predication; both require some notion of resemblance to be primitive.

The trouble with this line of argument is that it seems false to say that the proponent of universals can complete an analysis of predication. Consider, for instance, the sentence:

(27) The particular, a, instantiates the universal F.

In this sentence, we appear to have a particular predicate: 'instantiates the universal F'. With what element of ontology could we analyse this predicate? Well, let us suppose that we deployed a relation 'instantiation' such that the relation in some as yet unspecified way connected a to F. That would analyse the predicate. But, then, that would permit us a further construction:

(28) The particular a, instantiates the relation of instantiation to the universal, F.

Once more, if we are to complete our analysis of predication we will have to offer some element of ontology with which to analyse the predicate 'instantiates the relation of instantiation to the universal, F', and, whatever we then use to analyse *this*, will then seemingly require us to posit some further instantiation, which, in turn, will need to be analysed. It is easy to see that if we proceed down this road we will have to posit an infinitely large ontology in order to comprehensively analyse predication. This problem of analysing predication is sometimes referred to as Bradley's regress and it is a problem to which we will return in Chapter 6.

But that gives us a response to the proponent of universals who claims that their theory is preferable to the trope theory and nominalism on the grounds that it does not admit of primitive predication. Here's Lewis (1983: 354)

'Neither do predications of instantiates' fall under Armstrong's general analysis of (otherwise unanalyzed) predication. . . . So let all who have felt the bite of Armstrong's relation regress rise up and cry '*Tu quoque*!'

If this line of argument is correct, then it becomes much harder to choose between the competing theories for even the proponent of universals will have to allow that not all predication can be analysed.

# §5.9 Properties as dispositions?

For the time being let us suppose that there are properties (that the nominalisms we surveyed are false). There has, of late, been renewed interest in the idea that properties are dispositional in character. Here we pick up on the theory of properties as powers/dispositions that was mentioned in §4.12. To see what is meant, consider the following.

(29) The cup is fragile.

The predicate 'is fragile' seems to describe some way that the cup *is*. But what do we mean when we say that the cup 'is fragile'? One plausible interpretation of the meaning of the claim is that we mean that the cup is *disposed* to break in particular circumstances. Thus, properly speaking, what 'is fragile' means is that were we to drop the cup, it would shatter.

We have, I take it, a rough and ready concept to hand as to what it means for a property to be dispositional. It is also natural to see some properties (such as fragility) as dispositional. Other properties seem not to be, however. For instance, being triangular does not, on first inspection at least, appear to be dispositional in character. Call these non-dispositional properties 'categorical'. Someone who endorses this kind of view – that there is a distinction between dispositional properties and categorical properties – is a property dualist: they commit to there being more than one sort of property. Someone who thinks that all properties are either categorical or that all properties are dispositional is a property Monist.

One way to make the distinction between the categorical properties and the dispositional properties sharp, has been proposed by Mumford (1998:77).

> Dispositional properties *are ascriptions of properties that occupy a particular functional role as a matter of conceptual necessity and have particular shape or structure characterizations only a posteriori.*
>
> Categorical ascriptions *are ascriptions of shapes and structures which have particular functional properties only a posteriori*[5]

To help us get a little clearer on these, let us return to our examples. Consider the property of fragility. It seems that if we describe an object as fragile then we are ascribing to it a particular role of necessity: if I call an object fragile then I commit to the view that, of necessity, were it to be dropped onto a hard surface, then it would break. It is inconceivable that a fragile object would not shatter if dropped onto such a surface. Likewise, we may say that the three buses we mentioned at the outset of the chapter are red because they are disposed to reflect light at a given wavelength.

Other properties do not *seem* to behave in such a way. For instance, I can conceive of the property of triangularity without immediately conceiving of it playing any functional role. Certainly, I can conceive of an object being triangular without thinking that it *has* to behave in any particular way as a matter of conceptual necessity.

There is, however, a potential problem for proponents of the view that properties are dispositional: either all properties, or just some. These cases are known as 'finks'. Here is an example of one. Consider the sentence:

(28) The wire is live.

This sentence appears to make a dispositional ascription. The sentence seems to describe the wire as being such that, were a conductive material to come into contact with the wire, then the electrical current would flow from the wire to the conductor. It is, we might think, a conceptual necessity that, if we think of something's *being live* that we think of it as *being such that electricity will flow from it, if it is brought into contact with a conductive material*. We thus satisfy the above description of what it is for a property to be dispositional. We can formalize this particular case in the following conditional:

> (29) Were the wire to be brought into contact with a conducive material, then electricity would flow from wire to the conductive material.

So far, so good.

But suppose that the wire were connected to a machine called an 'electro-fink'. The machine detects whether or not the wire is about to be touched by a conductive material. If it is, then the machine renders an otherwise live wire, dead, and an otherwise dead wire, live.

The effect of the machine is this. Suppose that the wire is in fact dead and not touched by anyone. In that case, it appears to be true that 'were the wire brought into contact with a conductive material, then electricity will flow from it'. Were this to be the case, we would find that the property of 'being live', as analysed by (29), would be had by a dead wire. That's a bad result.

Notice, also, that given (29) a live wire is not live! Suppose that the wire were live and touched by some conductive material. In that case, the Electro-fink will kill the flow of electricity, and no current will flow from the wire to the conductive material.

There is a seemingly obvious way in which to respond to objections such as this one. In the 'Electro-fink' counterexample we have introduced a means of blocking the disposition from being manifested. All that we must do, then, is rule out such blocks. To do this, we must simply say that dispositions to behave in particular ways, are only dispositions to behave in that way *in particular circumstances*.

Of course, we must then specify what the 'particular circumstances' are. Let's go back to the case of fragility since it is a little easier to consider. When we say that the cup is fragile, we mean to say that if it were dropped then it would break. But, that's not quite right. Someone could catch the cup, thus preventing it from dropping to the floor; the floor could, in fact, have a very soft and deep rug on it, cushioning the cup's fall and stopping it from breaking; the cup could be dropped from only a few millimetres above the floor, thus meaning it would not break.

As these cases make plain, we're going to have to rule out an awful lot of putative counterexample cases. But the worry then becomes this: in order to rule out all of the cases in question, we must specify that the conditions are (what is sometimes known as) ideal. One way to proscribe these is simply to say that:

> (30) 'The cup is fragile' means that, were the cup dropped in circumstances where it would break, then it would break.

But, plainly, the conditional is a tautology. It says little more than 'were the cup to break, then it would break'. That cannot be used as an analysis of what it is to be the property of fragility.

One way in which proponents of dispositional theories of properties have tried to respond is by giving a different account of the conditions in question. In direct response to the Electro-fink case, Mumford (1998:89) thinks that we should make use of 'normal' conditions. Here is what he says, at length:

> To say something is soluble is to say that it will dissolve, in liquid, in a context relative to the ascription. The ascription in the actual world is relative to actual world conditions. It is also relative to actual world conditions that can vaguely be understood as 'normal'. Disposition ascriptions are made for a reason. The ideal conditions that facilitate the manifestation of the disposition are thus expected to be ones which are not realized only in exceptional circumstances . . . In making an appropriate and useful disposition ascription I am saying that, in ordinary conditions for the present context, if a particular antecedent is realized, a particular manifestation usually follows.

This, Mumford thinks, will suffice to explain away the Electro-fink case. Clearly, the case there is anything *but* normal. Electro-finks are not the sorts of object that we expect to encounter in the actual world.

It is, I think, unclear as to whether or not this will do. One natural avenue to explore in response to Mumford is whether or not the specification of 'ordinary conditions' is actually useful to us. Have we really done enough in calling upon these conditions to rigorously specify an analysis of a property? We might think that this rather vague and imprecise resort to 'normal circumstances' is not especially availing when it comes to giving a sharp and thorough analysis of what it is to be a particular property.

# §5.10 The distinction between property and particular

So far in this chapter we have been working on the assumption that there is a genuine distinction between property and particular. The legitimacy of the distinction has been attacked (by Ramsey (1925), among others), and it is worth spending a while looking at why. After all, we have, so far, simply assumed the veracity of the distinction.

In a number of places in the chapter we have used the following example:

(31) Socrates is wise.

The crude way in which we might then think of the distinction between particular and property is that the particular is that which is referred to by the term in the subject position in the sentence. Thus, Socrates is a particular (rather than a property) because 'Socrates' – the term that refers to Socrates – plays the role of subject in the sentence. For similar reasons, we might think that the term 'is wise' refers to a property: 'is wise' plays the role of predicate.

But this won't do. Consider the following sentence:

(32) Wisdom is Socratic.

In (32) wisdom plays the grammatical role of subject; 'is Socratic' the role of predicate. (32) is also perfectly meaningful. Thus, if we thought that the grammatical structure of the sentence revealed its ontological commitments, then we would be committed to Wisdom as a particular, as well as a property.

But this plainly makes no sense. We do not think of wisdom as a particular. Rather, it is a property. It seems, therefore, that we require a rather more sophisticated means of distinguishing between property and particular. For the time being, however, we should simply note that any theory positing an ontological distinction between particular and property would do well to provide us with some account of the distinction between the two.

# §5.11 Conclusions

In this chapter we have surveyed the main theories of properties. The dialectic seems to leave us with a choice: one the one hand, we have proponents of universals. Universals seem to afford us a slightly more straightforward analysis and explanation of similarity and resemblance. However, they carry with them a steeper ontological cost than their opponents. The various stripes of nominalism have a lesser ontological cost, but seem to struggle slightly more with the explanatory burden. Sandwiched neatly in between is trope theory. We have also considered whether or not, if there are such things as properties, they ought to be considered dispositional.

# Recommended reading

### General

Armstrong, D. 1989b. *Universals: An Opinionated Introduction.* Boulder: Westview Press.

Lewis, D. 1986a. *On the Plurality of Worlds.* Oxford: Blackwell, 50–69.

Mellor, D. H. and Oliver, A. eds. 1997. *Properties.* Oxford: OUP.

Oliver, A. 1996. 'The Metaphysics of Properties', *Mind*, 105, 1–80.

### Universals

Aune, B. 2003. 'Universals and Predication', in Gale, R. ed. *The Blackwell Guide to Metaphysics.* Oxford: Blackwell, 131–50.

Loux, M. J. 1998. *Metaphysics: A Contemporary Introduction.* London: Routledge, 20–47.

Lowe, E. J. 2006. *The Four Category Ontology.* Oxford: OUP, 87–98.

Russell, B. 1912. *The Problems of Philosophy.* Oxford: OUP, 88–100 (reprinted in Van Inwagen, P. and Zimmerman, D. eds. 2008. *Metaphysics: The Big Questions* 2nd *edition.* Oxford: Blackwell, 53–9.

### Nominalism

Hochberg, H. 1988. 'A Refutation of Moderate Nominalism', *Australasian Journal of Philosophy*, 66, 188–207.

Lowe, E. J. 2002. *A Survey of Metaphysics.* Oxford: OUP, 347–60.

Rodriguez-Pereyra, G. 2002. *Resemblance Nominalism: A Solution to the Problem of Universals.* Oxford: OUP.

### Trope theory

Campbell, K. 1990. *Abstract Particulars.* Oxford: Blackwell.

Daly, C. 1997. 'Tropes', in Mellor, D. and Oliver, A. eds. *Properties.* Oxford: OUP, 140–59.

Williams, C. D. 1953. 'On the Elements of Being', *Review of Metaphysics*, 7, 3–18, 171–92.

### Dispositions

Molnar, G. 2003. *Powers: A Study in Metaphysics.* Oxford: OUP (edited by Stephen Mumford).

Mumford, S. 1998. *Dispositions.* Oxford: OUP.

## Study questions

1) Write out each of the theories of properties that have been covered. Which theory do you find most convincing? Why do you find that theory the most convincing?
2) A lot of weight has been put on the idea that we must 'analyse predication'. How do you think we should understand this idea? Do you think that it's important that we succeed in our ambition to analyse predication?
3) Theories of universals seem to be more ontologically costly than the nominalisms covered (they posit property *and* particular). Do you think that this additional ontology is worth it?
4) We considered the claim that at least some properties are dispositional. How convincing do you find the idea? How convincing do you think the idea that *all* properties are dispositional?

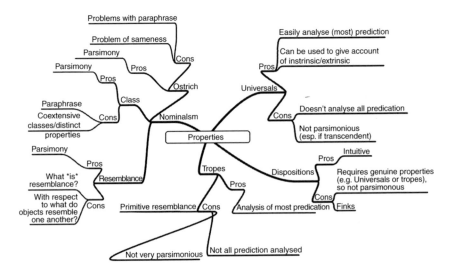

# 6

# Substratum and Other Theories

Consider the following three sentences.

(1) The table in my office is made from wood.
(2) The table in my office is brown.
(3) The table in my office is flat.
(4) There is a table in my office.

We discussed, in the previous chapter, what sort of ontology we might call upon such as to ensure that our discourse about properties is true. But one question we did not ask is what sorts of entity were being referred to by the subject term in the sentence. It seems, or so it would be natural to think, that the term 'the table' is picking something out and so the referent of the term is a part of the truth-maker for the propositions expressed by each of (1)–(4).

The idea with which we'll begin is that it appears that there is something common to each of (1)–(4); something that is picked out by the term 'the table'. Let's think about this in some more detail. Each of (1)–(3) seems to ascribe some properties *to* the table. The natural thought, then, is that the table itself is distinct from those properties. Thus, there is a *table* and the table has all of the properties described above.

# §6.1 Substance

This idea of a substance is well represented in the work of Locke (*An Essay Concerning Human Understanding* (II, XXIII, IV).

> when we talk or think of any particular sort of corporeal substances, such as horse, stone etc., though the idea we have of either of them be but the complication or collection of those several simple ideas of sensible qualities, which we used to find united in the thing called horse or stone; yet, because we cannot conceive how they should subsist alone, nor one in another, we suppose them existing in and supported by some common subject; which support we denote by the name substance, though it be certain we have no clear idea of that thing we suppose a support

Thus the table that we were speaking of a moment ago is a *substance*. Drawing on the above quote, this substance *unites* properties (the table's properties), even though we do not yet have too clear an idea of what this 'substance' is.

The first point to make clear is that the way in which the term 'substance' is deployed in this debate differs from the way in which we might deploy the term in more everyday situations. It is, I think, more common for us to imagine 'substance' as meaning some particular chemical kind of matter – such as gold, silver, lead, etc. Or, perhaps, to think that term 'substance' is even less specific – as in, 'there was an odd looking substance on the pavement'. To be clear, then, the term 'substance' as we shall use it here is a term of art (a technical term), and one of the issues that we shall pursue is quite how we are to understand the term 'substance' and whether or not we can give it an adequate definition. For the time being, we will use Locke's definition. It is that which unites and supports properties.

Also contained in the quotation above are two arguments (or the outline of two arguments) for the existence of substance. This is good. For we have said little (if anything) so far that would motivate us to believe in the existence of substance.

The first argument runs thus: we think that ordinary objects (tables, horses, stones, etc.) have properties. Moreover, it seems to us as if these properties are united in some way. This suggests that there *is* something that plays the role of uniting the disparate properties. This is substance.

The second argument is similar. Consider the properties of ordinary objects. We cannot conceive of these properties just *being* in the world. More precisely, I cannot simply imagine some redness, or some flat-ness; if I can imagine these properties at all, then it is only as they are instantiated *by some entity or other*. Whatever it is that plays the role, then, of *having* these properties ('supporting' is Locke's term here) is that which we will call 'substance'.[1] Since the substance itself plays the role of 'having' or 'supporting' properties, we shall assume that the substance itself is property-less. It is the role of the substance, that which itself has no properties, to bear properties.

So we now have two arguments in favour of substance. We need something to play the role of *uniting* disparate properties; we need something to *bear* properties. This is substance. Now although we have so far said little about the *nature* of substance, these two arguments just surveyed seem suggestive. It seems that substance must be such as to *bear* and support properties: *that* is its nature. The key feature of substance, through which we shall try to define it, is that it bears and unites properties. Although it might be good to say rather more than this, we at least have some idea of what substance is supposed to be.

There also seems to be another role being performed by substance. We have said that the table is brown, flat and so on. Now, suppose that the table is in a room full of other tables, each of which has the same properties as our original table. If all of the tables have precisely the same properties (universals, perhaps: §5.1), then it is unclear what it is that makes it true that we have *many* tables: after all, what we have is simply *the same* properties, repeated many times over. If we can call upon substance, then it appears that we have a ready explanation. Substances individuate. Thus, the table in my office is different from all other tables *because it is a different substance*. It is the uniqueness of substances that plays the requisite role in individuating objects from one another.

# §6.2 Substantial problems

There are (at least) two problems for the sorts of theory of substance that I have just outlined. The first sort of problem that we will tackle is metaphysical and concerns the nature of the substances itself.

To see the thrust of the objection I want to re-consider the nature of substance as it was introduced above. We said that substance is that which, in a sense, lacks properties: it is intended to be that which bears properties and is itself property-less. But, in another sense, it seems pretty clear that substance, by *bearing* properties, *has properties!* Thus, substance both has properties and does not have properties. This seems a contradiction.

Let's unpack that argument a little. Consider a particular table. Suppose that it is brown. We can say that 'the table is brown'. We are also supposing that the table is a substance. That seems to entail that 'the substance is brown'. Thus the substance has a property. How, then, can we deny that substances have properties? To make plain the contradiction, compare:

(5) Substance is that which itself has no properties.
(6) Substance has properties.

Since (5) and (6) are plainly contradictory, we surely cannot hold onto them both. How are we to then understand 'substance'?

This problem is readily solved for there is plainly an ambiguity between the way in which we use the term 'has' in (5) and (6). What we wanted to say, when we said that a substance is that which does not have properties, is that substance is that which *bears* properties; is that which *grounds* properties; is *independent* of its properties. But the substance itself does not *have* any of those properties.

One crude metaphor for this idea is that of a pin-cushion. Suppose that properties are represented by pins and that the pin-cushion represents substance. A pin-cushion itself *has no properties* in that it is not a pin. But, in another sense, it *does* 'have properties' because many pins are to be found sticking out of it. This kind of 'support' that the pin-cushion lends to the pins might be thought to be analogous to the way in which substance supports properties.

This suggests a way in which to make more perspicuous the nature of substance. We might agree that *all* substances *support* properties. But, although we agree that all substance support properties, we might go on to say that none of the properties that a substance has are *essential* to it. Just as you could remove any one of the pins, yet the pin-cushion would remain, a table that is brown, might have been yellow, or green; rather than being flat it might have been scratched, and so on.

Thus,

(7) None of the properties of a substance belongs to its essence.

Plainly, (7) does not contradict (6) and so we have circumvented the initial problem.

But at what cost have we avoided the problem? Look hard at (7); it commits us to the idea that substrata have *no* essential properties. Is that *really* true? Look back at what we said above concerning what a substance had to do: substances *had* to differentiate and individuate. So it's essential to a particular substance that it individuates itself from all other substances. Isn't it also essential to a substance that it bear properties? It seems impossible to conceive of a substance without a property. But, since it is of the nature of substance to bear some properties, it would be impossible for a substance to exist in the absence of it bearing at least some properties even if it is not the case that an individual substance had to bear any *particular* property.

So it would *appear* that substance has essential properties: it is of the essence of substance that it individuates, and it is of the essence of substance that it bears properties.

Well, so what? We might concede all of this and simply describe substance as being that which has the essential properties mentioned, but no other properties.

The problem is that it appears as if we are off on a regress. One of the reasons we posited substance was in order to ground properties. We said that it seemed that we *needed* substance to *unite* properties, and to be that which, in some sense or other, *bears* properties. But we have now said that, far from being that which has no properties, substance itself is propertied; and, in that case, we might think that we need something to support, or bear, these essential properties. Now suppose that we do posit some further ontology to bear and support these properties: call it schmubstance. Presumably, schmubstance will also have some essential properties (however we define schmubstance, the way in which we define it will presumably describe some things that it *must* do; these will be its essential properties). Thus, we will need some more ontology to support these properties, and so on and so on. It is hard to see how to block this regress.

The second sort of problem with a substance view is epistemic (see §1.5), which is to say that it concerns how we would come to know about this substance. Substances themselves don't have any properties. So, it's not true to say that the *substance* that is the table is brown, or is flat or is made from wood. Rather, these are properties that are instantiated, but are not *literally* properties *of* the substance itself. That means, then, that we cannot, in fact, perceive substances. After all, although I perceive the tables' flat-ness, brown-ness and so on, it isn't at all obvious that I also then perceive some property-less property bearer that *is* the substance. If we cannot perceive substances, then it is unclear how we can come to have knowledge about them.

Now we need to be careful, here. The substance theorist has an obvious reply. Since substances are what individuate objects, so by experiencing objects themselves, we are, albeit indirectly, experiencing substances. Dialectically the thought would be that because the substances are objects, so because we experience objects as distinct we must be indirectly experiencing the individual substances.

What this shows us, then, is that we need to be more careful in the way that we phrase the objection to substance theory. One way to try and develop this line of argument would be to note that the substance theorist owes us a more detailed explanation of how it is that we individuate so reliably. In more detail and drawing on the argument against mathematical Platonism (§3.5), we might offer the following argument. For the most part, if people agree that p is an individual, then p is an individual. We're good at individuating particulars. Where we have such a reliable process, we ought to have some explanation of *why* the process is so reliable; an explanation of how it is that the presence of a substance leads us to detect it and individuate it from others so reliably. But, of course, because we do not think that substance *itself has* properties, so we cannot think that we are perceiving the substance itself directly and that means that we have no explanation of the reliability of our judgements about individuals. It remains then a complete mystery, therefore, as to how we are able to perceive substances.

The final objection to substance, and one that although perhaps less philosophically technical sometimes seems to exert a greater power over the mind, is that for all that's been said about substance, the notion remains rather opaque. Substance is (complications aside) that which bears properties, but does not have any properties essentially. But what *is* it? It seems that our characterization of the concept is very thin. Very little of any (forgive the pun) substance has been said. All that we have really done is specify a *role* that is to be played: the bearing of properties and individuating. That is not a terribly informative analysis.

With that in mind it may pay dividends to see whether or not there are other theories available to us that will do the work of substance without any of the attendant complications.

# §6.3 Bundle Theory

The problems that we identified with substance theory seemed to be with substance itself. It seemed difficult to explain how we could experience it; how to understand its nature and how to describe it. The natural thought, then, is to drop it from our ontology all together. Of course, we still have our original sentences to consider. But perhaps we made a wrong turn. At the outset I suggested that the obvious inference was that because there appeared some *thing* in common in each of (1)–(3), that was not identical to the properties, we should posit a thing; a substance. That *thing* has caused the problems; so let's just say that objects are bundles of properties. This, obviously, forces a choice upon us: what theory of properties shall we opt for? Let's start off with (Aristotelian) universals. A table just *is* a bundle of properties. This, unimaginatively, we shall call Bundle Theory (BT).

It's pretty obvious that the BT will avoid the problems associated with substance theory, for all of the problems we hit upon were problems with the nature of substance and we are now denying that there is any such thing. What will concern us is then whether or not BT brings with it any other problems. As we shall see, it appears that there are challenges in the offing.

It will help us in what follows to have an example to hand. Let's consider the case of a ball. Let's suppose that the ball is red, round, has a mass of 1kg and is 30cm in diameter. The first point to make, then, is that the following sentence appears to be analytic, given BT:

(8) The ball is red.

Why is this analytic and why is that a problem? For our purposes it will suffice to say that a truth is analytic iff it is true in virtue of the meanings of the terms involved. Thus we may say that 'all unmarried men are bachelors' expresses an analytic truth. That this sentence is true is simply guaranteed by the meanings of the terms. We must now look to see why to think that (8) *is* analytic, given BT.

Begin by considering what the term 'the ball' refers to. It refers to a collection of properties: specifically, it refers to the properties 'is red; is round; is 1kg in mass; is 30cm in diameter'. In some sense or other, the term 'the ball' is simply picking out that collection of properties. In that case, of course, another way to express the content of (8) is:

(9) The bundle of the properties 'is red'; 'is round'; 'is 1kg in mass'; 'is 30cm in diameter', is, itself, red.

But this amounts to saying that the bundle of properties 'is red. . . . , is, itself, red'. Plainly, saying that 'something that is red, is red', is an analytic truth. And so it seems that sentences like (8) turn out to be analytic. After all, a sentence that says that 'something that is red, is red' is a sentence that is true in virtue of the meaning of the words used. That's a surprising result since we're trying to talk about the ball and some of its properties. Sentences like 'the ball is red' really don't look analytic; if any truth is a candidate for being *not* analytic then it is a subject–predicate sentence such as (8). It looks like an intuitive cost of BT that it denies that this is so. We do naturally think of sentences like (8) expressing more than a tautology.[2]

The second problem is plausibly more severe. Suppose that someone asks 'what *is* the ball?' Given BT, the correct response is 'the bundle of properties: "is red", "is round", "mass 1kg"; "diameter 30cm"'. So then: if that's *all* that there is to our ball, then it seems that if we have something that is all of those things, then we have our ball.

Now consider the following principle:

> Identity of Indiscernibles (IoI): necessarily, if, for every property *F*, object *x* has *F* if and only if object *y* has *F*, then *x* is identical to *y*.

The principle appears a little complex at first, but the idea is pretty straightforward. Let's make the case a little more obvious. Suppose that I tell you that 'my wife has brown hair if and only if Katherine has brown hair'. What do you think that you now know? What new piece of information have you been able to infer? I take it that you have inferred from my claim that my wife is Katherine – and you'd be right. But notice how you reasoned: you moved from the claim that 'Katherine has a property iff my wife has a property', to the claim that 'Katherine is identical to my wife'. In fact, you used IoI in your reasoning, without knowing it! That's quite a striking idea, and one that we'll return to.

The next step of the argument requires us to *seemingly* change tack a little. I'd like you to try and conceive of the following: a possible world that includes only two objects – two red, round, balls; both with mass 1kg and both with a diameter of 30cm. According to the Bundle Theorist, what you have conceived of is as follows:

> Ball 1: red; round; 30cm in diameter; 1kg in mass
> Ball 2: red; round; 30cm in diameter; 1kg in mass

With that description in mind, have a look at IoI once more. Notice, in particular, that, for any property you care to name, Ball 1 has a particular property if and only if Ball 2 has a particular property. Thus, both are red; both are round and so on.

According to IoI, where we have that (where x has a property iff y has a property), we have, in fact, a single entity (x=y). But that seems very odd indeed. I asked you to conceive of *two* objects, both with all of the same properties. And you managed; at least, it certainly seemed conceivable that there could be such a thing. What we have just found, however, is that you were wrong, and that it's impossible for there to be such a thing as the two red balls described. That looks *extremely* odd and, plausibly, gives us a reason to not believe BT.

The natural first move would be to say that IoI is false. But that looks problematic for at least two reasons. First, we agreed above that it's highly intuitive and a principle that we ought not to want to give up. Indeed, it seems the sort of principle that we endorse and deploy without even realizing (as I tried to demonstrate).

Second, it doesn't seem that the proponent of BT *can* deny IoI. One way to express IoI, using logic, will help us to see why. Allow the following to express IoI – where 'F' stands for properties.

$$\forall F(Fx \leftrightarrow Fy) \rightarrow x=y.$$

We know from logic that this principle is false only if we can find a way for the antecedent to be true, but the consequent, false. (In other words, what we would need to find is a situation in which two objects shared *all of the same properties*, but are not identical.) But, if we're Bundle Theorists, then we are committed to the view that an object is *nothing more than a collection of properties*. So, to have a true antecedent in the above, we would need to have it turn out that there exist x, and y, and that they have the same properties. But since x and y are *nothing more than a collection of properties*, if they 'have the same properties', then they are the same thing. Thus we cannot generate a false consequent while preserving a true antecedent.

The final objection to BT is perhaps the simplest. Suppose that we have all of these collections of properties. Why don't they just float apart? The world is nothing more than collections, bundles, of properties. That being the case, at some point we would expect a particular property to just float away. After all, if there's nothing tying these bundles together, then *at some point, surely* they ought to come apart. But they have never done so. Properties have never simply floated away from one another. Now, what explains that? Moreover, it *seems* impossible for them to do so; it doesn't just seem to be the case that, as a matter of fact they do not: so what explains *this*? If we simply endorse BT as is, then there is no obvious way in which to answer this question. That looks like an explanatory deficiency.

# §6.4 Responding

At the current time, it's hard to see which theory to prefer. We've seen that there are some problems for theories of substance, but there are also some sizeable problems for BT. Let's see, first, whether or not we can find a way in which to respond to the objections facing BT.

The first problem that I'll consider, here, is the problem of floating properties. One obvious way in which to respond to this problem is to posit some sort of relation that binds the properties together and keeps them present. Call this a 'compresence' relation. Of course, one might object to the compresence relation that, although it might be enough to bind together the properties, there is nothing to bind the compresence relation *to* the properties, and so no reason for *them* to not float away. However, such an objection seems a little unfair; it certainly seems that the proponent of substance cannot make such an objection, for we may just as easily ask them what it is that keeps substances together with properties. Granted, substances are what bind properties together, but what binds properties to substances?

Another thought may be worth raising in connection with the compresence relation. The function of the relation is simply to bind properties together. Thus, aside from 'binding' the relation *has* no properties. Is this so very different to substance? After all, this is reminiscent of the way in which we defined substance (its sole roles were to bear properties, and to individuate). If we thought that one of the problems with substance is that it is too thin a notion for us to understand, then it seems likely that we will object to the compresence relation in a similar fashion.

Of course, unless we suppose that the compresence relation plays the role of individuating the bundles from one another – and then it appears to come even closer to our model of substance – then we still have no way of differentiating one bundle of properties from another and will still face the objection from the IoI.

However, there is a route open to us that is suggested by our consideration of properties in the previous chapter. There, we considered a theory of properties that we called trope theory; the idea was that a property is *particularized*, such that rather than saying that there is literally a single property, wisdom, shared by both Socrates and Plato, properly speaking we should say that what we have is two properties: Socrates' wisdom, and Plato's wisdom. A trope metaphysic might help us here.

Consider the case of Ball 1 and Ball 2, again. If we adopted a trope metaphysic, then what we would have is the following:

Ball 1: Ball 1-redness; Ball 1-roundness; Ball 1-1kg; Ball 1-30cm-in-diameter

Ball 2: Ball 2-redness; Ball 2-roundness; Ball 2-1kg; Ball 2-30cm-in-diameter

Now clearly these are distinct lists of property. No property that appears on the Ball 1 list appears on the Ball 2 list. And since the original problem that we faced with the IoI was that the two lists contained all and only the same properties, it seems as if we have done enough to circumvent the objection.

Notice two points, however. First, we have had to endorse a trope metaphysic. As we saw in the previous chapter, such a metaphysic may well carry with it various *other* problems. So, whether or not you're prepared to endorse this as a solution will require you to think carefully about the independent plausibility of a trope theory of properties.

Second, suppose that we added to that list comprence relations to prevent the tropes from drifting away from one another. Relations are simply tropes. So what we would have to add to the list on Ball 1's side is a Ball 1-comprence trope; on Ball 2's side we would have to add a Ball 2-comprence trope. This, even more than before, looks like substance: this relation is both what binds all of the tropes together and, because it is *unique* to this particular object, is fully sufficient to individuate every object from any other. Of course, that needn't be a problem. But it should give us pause for thought: how different do we think that these posits really are? How different are the attendant theories?

# §6.5 States of affairs

With these two theories in mind let us see what else is on the market. Let's begin this exploration with an objection. I'll cast this as an objection against bundle theory, though (as I hope is clear) the objection could just as easily be made to substance theory.

Let us suppose that we have two particulars – two objects: in this case, the table in my office and the door to my office. Let us also suppose that the door is to the north of my desk. The following sentence would then look to be true:

(10) The office door is to the north of the office desk.

Let's think about what makes true (10). We're going to assume Bundle Theory, so we'll need a bundle of properties that is to be identified as the table, and a further bundle of properties that is the desk; we'll also require a relation – to the north of – that stands between the two bundles. We needn't commit ourselves to any particular view of properties, for the time being. That collection of entities (both bundles and the relation), or so it would seem, is the truthmaker for (10).

But appearances may be deceptive. Consider the list of entities once again. We have two bundles and a relation 'to the north of'. Those three entities, on their own, don't obviously generate the result that the office door is to the north of the office desk. The list of entities (the office desk, the relation 'to the north of' and the office door) makes no mention of the ways in which the entities on the list are arranged with respect to one another. Those three entities mentioned, then, could make true (9); they could make true (11).

(11) The office desk is to the north of the office door.

Indeed, those three entities (desk, door and relation) look to be just as good as a truth-maker for (11) as they do for (10). It will all come down to how we arrange them with respect to one another.

Now, clearly, that's a problem. What makes it true that the office door is to the north of the office desk, can't also make it true that the office desk is to the north of the office door! Sentences (10) and (11), though similar, will clearly require different truth-makers.

We can express this a little more formally, and doing so we can generalize the problem. Suppose that we allow 'R' to stand for any relational term (such as 'to the north of') and that we let 'a' and 'b' stand for any two particulars. What we want is to have different truth-makers for the expressions Rab and

Rba. At the moment, however, we seem to be lacking that. At the moment all that we have as truth-makers are the particulars, a and b, and the relation R. We need something more. Here's Armstrong (1993) making the point:

> Let a love b, and b love a. The two states of affairs are presumably independent. Either could have occurred without the other.
>
> Yet the two different states of affairs involve exactly the same constituents. How are they to be differentiated? (1993: 430–1)

The 'something more' that I mentioned is, David Armstrong claims, what the 'world of state of affairs' give us. The world is actually, most fundamentally, a world that is a collection of states of affairs.

We need to be cautious. We might, in common parlance, be inclined to talk of 'states of affairs', in order to describe the way that something is with respect to its primary attribute(s). Thus, we might wonder, with respect to gender inequality, 'how it is that this state of affairs has come about'. What *we* need to be clear on, however, is that 'state of affairs' has a very particular, metaphysical, commitment when we use the term.

The role that Armstrong gives to states of affairs is very similar to that which Russell called 'facts':

> The first truism to which I wish to draw your attention . . . is that the world contains *facts*, which are what they are whatever we may choose to think about them, and that there are also *beliefs*, which have reference to facts, and by reference to facts are either true or false. . . . If I say 'It is raining', what I say is true in a certain condition of weather and is false in other conditions. The condition of weather that makes my statement true (or false as the case may be), is what I should call a 'fact.' (Russell 1956: 182)

Armstrong prefers the term 'state of affairs', however, though for reasons that are simply stylistic. So, how should we understand a 'state of affairs?' This question will require us to take on board some new terminology. Here is our definition, to be further unpacked.

> A state of affairs exists if and only if a particular has a property, or a relation holds between two or more particular. (1993: 429)

Thus, a state of affairs has two constituents. A thin particular, and either a property or relation.[3] We must now try to make sense of what a 'thin particular', or as it appears in the quotation 'particular', is.

Armstrong (1993: 433–4) characterizes a 'thin particular' in the following way:

> The thin particular is the particular considered in abstraction from all its properties. Although not bare, it is very thin indeed. (But you can be thin without being bare.) For me, all thin particulars, although numerically different, are, as it were, indistinguishably different. Particulars . . . have no mysterious inner and particularized essence that marks off one from another and accounts for their numerical difference. The secret of numerical difference is simply numerical difference. . . . Notice, however, that it is not hidden, as Locke had it hidden. Even in our most basic, most elementary, perceptions we are aware of particulars, though of course particulars as having certain properties and relations, that is: particulars in states of affairs.

So, a thin particular is a particular – such as a table, Barack Obama, a rabbit – considered 'in abstraction from all its properties'. An example of a thin particular might be something like a table considered in abstraction from all of its properties. Nothing *accounts* for the numerical difference and distinctness of thin particulars; rather, they *are* numerically different and distinct. We can, through perception, become aware of particulars, through seeing them in states of affairs. That, at least, is Armstrong's claim.

It's important to notice that, because of the reasoning Armstrong gives, a thin particular will not be a substance. Recall that a substance is such that *it* accounts for numerical difference: two tables will be distinct from one another iff they are distinct substances, where the substance has, in some sense, the essential property of *being that particular substance*. Armstrong simply denies that there is any such property involved.

Notice, however, that I said that states of affairs have constituents – I did not say that they have parts. According to Armstrong, there are (at least) two different senses of 'part' available to us. The first of these is what he dubs 'mereological parthood'. This is the sense in which (e.g.) the Universalist (see Chapter 2) will talk about parthood. Clearly, the fusion of any particulars a, b and c, is identical to the fusion of b, c and a.

However, the second sense of 'parthood' – Armstrong's sense of the term – is a non-mereological parthood. So why must this second type of parthood occur and what is it? Let's start with what it is. Suppose that we have three particulars, a, b and c. Imagine that they are parts of an object in the mereological sense of parthood. There is, as we have said, no difference between a + b + c and b + c + a. We get the same fusion composed out of a + b + c and b + c + a. However, as we've already seen, there *is* a difference between the state of affairs Rab and Rba, despite the fact that both states of affairs have very same elements as constituents. Thus, whatever sort of composition *is* involved in states of affairs, it is not the same sort of composition that is involved when we think about mereological fusions. This 'non-mereological sense' of parthood is one where the way in which we arrange the constituents *does* matter to what is composed.

So here is one way to think about the difference. Suppose that we have an object composed from a, b, and c; a, b and c, are mereological parts of an fusion O and they are the only parts. O is identical to the fusion O* that is composed from c, b and a. However, suppose that we have a state of affairs, S, which has as its non-mereological parts, the relation R, and the particulars a and b, and that they form the state of affairs, Rab. The state of affairs S is *not* identical to the state of affairs, Q, that includes the same constituents, but that is non-mereologically composed such that Rba.

Armstrong, however, does not say that much about what, exactly, non-mereological composition is. It is, in some senses, a primitive of his theory and it leads some, Lewis (1992: 213) in particular, to give the idea pretty short shrift.

> To me, it is mysterious how a state of affairs is made out of its particular and universal constituents. . . . It is some sort of unmereological composition, and to my mind, that is a contradiction in terms.

Whether or not this is quite fair to Armstrong is something that we might wonder about. There is a sense after all in which I seem to be able to understand what is being said when we say that the state of affairs Rab is different from the state of affairs Rba, despite their containing the very same elements. And, since Armstrong thinks that, for instance, London's being to the south of Nottingham, just *is* a state of affairs, and we can understand that, it's not entirely clear that the objection is fair. Additionally, we might also think, Armstrong is, just as any theorist is, entitled to some primitive terms. Is there a particularly strong reason for thinking that the non-mereological composition is any more mysterious than any other primitive?

# §6.6 Bradley's regress

In the previous chapter we saw that there is a problem with supposing that all predication can be analysed: the problem to which I alluded is known as Bradley's regress. The idea, in a nutshell, was that if all predicates require analysis via ontology, then we will need some element of our ontology to make true the claim that 'a is F'; a, F and the connection between them – call that connection, C. But, then, we have a, F, and C; 'a's being connected to F'. But, in addition, it is true that 'a is connected to C and F is connected to C'. These additional predications also require ontology; an additional relation to connect these disparate elements of our metaphysics. Call this E. Thus, we now have a, F, C, and E. But, in addition, it is true that a is connected to E. . . . The regress here looks to be infinite.

Here is Armstrong's (1993: 432) presentation of the problem:

> States of affairs are thought to labour under a certain further difficulty, though. It is a difficulty most usually articulated for the particular case of an ontology of particulars and universals, but seems to be a general one. It is the difficulty of predication, the difficulty of the nexus of instantiation (as they say in Iowa), the difficulty of the non-relational tie (W.E. Johnson and P.F. Strawson), the difficulty of the formal distinction (as Scotus put it), the difficulty of participation (as Plato had it). Is not bringing the constituents of a state of affairs, the particulars, the properties and the relations, together into states of affairs, a further relation in which all the constituents stand? But then the new relation is just a further element which requires to be integrated along with the other constituents. Most contemporary opponents of universals take comfort from this argument. Often it seems to be the only argument they have to set against the multifarious difficulties facing their particular variety of Nominalism.

But Armstrong thinks that proponents of states of affairs have a way of sidestepping the objection.

> Well, those of us who accept states of affairs do have to accept what one might think of as an operator that takes constituents of states of affairs to states of affairs (and, in thought, to merely possible states of affairs). But I think that we are under no compulsion to take this 'formation' of states of affairs as a further constituent, something on the same level as the original constituents. One reason for this, I suggest, is that once the putative states of affairs are reached, all further 'relations' in the regress that our Nominalist friends say that we must accept supervene upon the states of affairs. That a state of affairs having certain constituents exists, is, I take it, a contingent matter. But all the alleged further relations in the regress flow necessarily from the structure of the state of affairs. So I suggest that this supervenience is a sign that these 'extra' relations do not have to be taken seriously ontologically.

It's worth spending a moment unpicking Armstrong's claim for his view. The thought seems to be that because we have a state of affairs, such as *a*'s being

*F*, we do not need any further 'tie' or connection. One way to think of this that can be instructive is to think of this in terms of the state of affairs, though constituted by both a and F, being itself an entity. Thus, we should not think of a and F as two entities, in need of connection to one another (and then in need of connection to their connector, and so on), but think of *a*'s being F as an entity. If *a*'s being F is itself an entity, then it seems rather more obvious why there would not need to be any further connection involved. All that we require, which is *a*'s being connected to F, is given to us by the entity that *is* *a*'s being F.

How plausible is that as a response? Opinions on this will vary. There may well be the temptation to say that in insisting that a is connected to F by virtue of there being a state of affairs that *is* *a*'s being F, we haven't avoided the problem, so much as stated what the problem is: we all agree that a is F, what needs to be explained is how that gets to be the case. Simply insisting that it is so by virtue of *a*'s being F doesn't seem terribly edifying. However, there may be a certain intuitive plausibility to what Armstrong says. The state of affairs of *a*'s being F is perfectly comprehensible (perhaps); the thin particular and the property are both involved in constituting this state of affairs, but it is the state of affairs that is the fundamental entity here; it is the state of affairs of *a*'s being *F* that is the reason that a is F.

# §6.7 Return to substance

With this view of states of affairs in hand we should now return our attention to substance. For there are contemporary theories of substance that seek to try and deal with the problems that face substance theories. If successful such theories would provide us with an important option. I'll proceed, here, by outlining the theory in question before turning to explaining how this might help us circumvent the problems that afflicted the Lockean theorist of substance that we considered earlier on.

In his *The Possibility of Metaphysics*, Lowe (1998) defines substance in the following way:

> (T7) x is a substance if and only if x is a particular and there is no particular y such that y is not identical with x and the identity of x depends on the identity of y. (1998: 151)

First, here by 'substance' Lowe has in mind what we call individual substances or concrete particulars – things like you and me and other concrete particular objects. Second, by 'identity dependence' Lowe has the following in mind.

(D3) The identity of x depends upon the identity of y $=_{df}$ Necessarily, there is a function F such that it is a part of the essence of x that x is the F of y. (1998: 149)

It is wrong, Lowe then claims, to think of there being properties that then reside *in* concrete particulars. Properties are *not* entities. Instead, Lowe (2006) thinks, we should schematize reality in the following way:

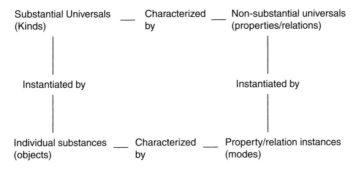

(2006: 22)

Here is the idea: there are substantial universals – for example, being a tomato. This, as a universal, is a property that is repeatable and it is instantiated at least once, but plausibly also many times over in the guise of individual substances. Now what differentiates one substantial universal from another are the non-substantial universals (the properties and relations) that, for example, tomatoes have. Tomatoes, but not potatoes, are red. Particular instances of these non-substantial universals are then exemplified by individual substances – for instance, each tomato exemplifies a particular instance of red.

In any case, Lowe describes the nature of a particular in the following way:

But why shouldn't we say that it is *the thing itself* – the thing that *has* the properties – which provides the ontological support for those properties and which thus occupies the role of 'material substratum'? If we say this, then we are by no means committed, of course, to saying that material substrata are themselves featureless. But if we do say this, we must certainly also say that things and their properties – in the sense of their modes or individual accidents – are items

> belonging to quite different ontological categories, since the former are now
> being conceived of as being ontologically independent entities in contrast with
> the latter: in short, the former – the things which have the properties – are being
> conceived of as *individual substances*. (1998: 193)

Since *I* am a substance, and I am not a bare particular, the idea is that we can circumvent both the epistemological and ontological worries. Because *I* am not a bare particular, rather, I am a person, and it is perfectly obvious that everyone can perceive *me*, so there is no epistemic problem. Further, since we are not, now, conceiving of properties as entities, rather, properties are 'ways that things are', so there is no chance of a regress. It is not the case that properties are distinct *things* that require bonding to their bearers, rather, a property of (say) the table, is simply a way that the table *is*. If properties are not *things*, entities, then there is no reason to think that we will face a problem when it comes to their needing instantiating. Simply, if they aren't existent *things*, they will not require such a bond.

# §6.8 One substance, or many?

The final issue that I want to close this chapter with is the question of how many substances there are. Supposing either a state of affairs metaphysics, or a substance metaphysics, how many substances or states of affairs are there? For the remainder of the chapter I will consider a substance metaphysic, but I think that the case I make could be replicated with a states of affairs metaphysics.

The assumption with which we have been working is that a substance *is* a particular thing. Thus, a rose is a substance; I am a substance; the table is a substance, and so on. However, there is a distinct view available: there is only one substance. This view has been defended, recently, by Jonathan Schaffer (2010a).

Let's begin with an intuition: it seems that both the whole universe, and all of the various parts of the universe, exist. That is, both of the following seem true:

(11) The whole universe exists.
(12) The universe has many parts.

So far, so uncontroversial. Next up we need to consider some cases. Think about a heap of grains of sand. Here, it seems pretty obvious to us that the parts are prior to the whole. What do we mean by this? The heap exists in virtue of the many grains of sand. We do not think, intuitively, that the many grains of sand exist *because* the heap does. That seems to be the wrong way around. Consider, also, a mosaic: again, because of the tiles, the whole picture exists. We do not think that that, because there is a picture, all of the various tiles exist. Now there seems to be something that these cases (and others like them) have in common. It seems to us as if these are cases where the whole exists because the parts do.

However, now consider some other cases. First, consider a circle that's partitioned into entirely arbitrary portions. It *seems* that because the partitioning is entirely arbitrary (and somehow the circle strikes us as unified in some important way) that the circle is prior to the arbitrary portions thereof. In other words, it seems to us that in some very intuitive way the parts of the circle can only exist because the circle does. Next, think about the relation between organs of the body and the person whose organs they are. It strikes us as obvious and intuitive that the parts of the body are there *because* the body is there; that (e.g.) the liver exists *because* it is a part of a functioning body. These cases are ones in which it seems to us that the whole is prior to the parts – cases in which the parts only exist *because* the whole exists.

So, if that's right, and let's assume for the time being that it is, then commonsense takes a remarkably fine-grained view. The thought seems to be that where we have *properly unified* things (the body, the circle) that we think that the whole is prior to the parts: the parts exist because the whole does. But, where we have somehow arbitrary wholes, the parts are prior to the whole: the whole exists because the parts do. What is important to us is that integrated wholes appear to us to be prior to their parts.

The question, then, is whether or not we ought to regard the world (the universe) as prior to its parts, or whether we think that the parts of the world are prior to the world itself. Arguably the most telling thought, here, is that division in the world seems to be arbitrary. So, consider a table and some particle, *e*, that's *pretty much* on the border of the table. Ought we to say, of *e*, that it *is* a part of the table? Ought we to say, of *e*, that it's *not* a part of the table? It doesn't seem that we've any entirely credible way to answer that question. To borrow, again, from Lewis (1999)

> There are always outlying particles, questionably parts of the thing, not definitely included and not definitely not included. So there are always many aggregates, differing by a little bit here and a little bit there, with equal claim to be the thing. (1999: 165)

If we accept that, then it seems that objects *in the world* are only arbitrary partitions of the world. That is, we carve up the world into what we *say* are tables and chairs and so on, but such partitioning seems (perhaps) to be entirely arbitrary.

So here's the thought. The world exists; the world has parts (tables, chairs and so on); the parts are arbitrary portions of the world. If we take seriously the intuition, stated above, that where unified wholes admit of arbitrary partition then the whole is prior, then it seems that in the case of the world and its parts we have reason to suppose that the world is prior. In (still more) other words, it looks true to say that the world is prior to its many parts. If all of the parts of that argument are successful, and it is certainly a large 'if', then we have a successful argument for the conclusion that Schaffer dubs 'Priority Monism':

> Priority Monism: the world is a single unified whole, and is prior to its many parts.

We can contrast this with an explicit statement of Priority Pluralism (the views of (e.g.) Lowe and Armstrong would both fall under this heading, I think)

> Priority Pluralism: the world is a single unified whole whose many parts are prior to the whole.

This is quite a surprising result. For the whole of the chapter up until this point we had been proceeding on the assumption that there were many fundamental 'things'; many substances. But it now turns out that we have an argument that points in the other direction. There is only one substance and it is fundamental and prior to its parts.

Clearly, Priority Monism is compatible with the view that there are such things as chairs, tables and the like (just as states of affairs are compatible with the existence of relations and thin particulars), it just turns out that tables, chairs (you and me) are all parts of a single unified substance (or what have you) that is more fundamental than any of its parts (than any of us). So, should we believe it?

I'll consider two further arguments that Schaffer puts forward, here. The first is an argument that borrows quite heavily from Quantum Mechanics. I'll offer a flavour of the argument that Schaffer gives, but I will hold back on the details simply because of the complexity.

The particular experiment we'll consider is known as the EPR experiment (standing for 'Einstein, Podolsky and Rosen', the names of the three physicists who designed the experiment). Suppose that we have an electron emitter at a location L, that's precisely half-way between L1 and L2. There are particular ways of generating systems of electrons such that if we emitted two entangled electrons from L in the directions of L1 and L2, then, although the measurement we make of E1 at L1 is spatially removed from the measurement we make of E2 at L2, the measurement we make at L1 *seems* to determine the outcome of the findings at L2. So, for instance, probabilistically, if we just measured the spin of E2 at L2 it should come out as 'up' half of the time, and 'down' the other half of the time. However, if we make a measurement at L1 *before* we make the measurement at L2, then 100 per cent of the time, the subsequent measurement we make at L2 will be the opposite of that which we make at L1. So, to give you an example, if we measure the spin of E1 and it turns out to be 'up' then the spin of E2 at L2 will be 'down'.

In other words:

> The outcomes of measurements do sometimes depend non-locally on the outcomes of other, distant, measurements . . . (Albert 1992: 72)

The thought, then, is that it's the *system* that determines the values of the measurements we make. Notice, also, that 'the system' is not identical to, or reducible to, any of the component particles that we are observing.

Moreover, given the way in which quantum particles interact, it appears that, to at least some degree, the whole of the universe is a large entangled state. If we allowed that the universe *is* a single entangled state, then all that we have to do to fix the nature of the universe (including the nature of all of the particles and so on) is fix the nature of that entangled state. This seems to suggest that the whole entangled state is, in some sense, *prior to*, or more fundamental than, the various particles. Thus the Priority Monist thinks that the entangled state is fundamental.

The second argument that Schaffer offers is one that trades on the possibility of gunk. An object can be said to be 'gunky' iff every proper part of that object itself has proper parts. So, imagine a square. We can conceive of halving the square. Of each of those halves, we can conceive of further halves. And halves of them, and halves of them . . . and so on without limit. These halves all seem to have parts. Schaffer then argues that Monism permits the possibility of gunk, whereas pluralism does not, and that because we think that gunk is possible, so we ought to think that Pluralism is false. Let us now turn to the reasoning involved.

Suppose that the one whole is prior (in other words, suppose that Priority Monism is true). In that case, clearly the whole can simply admit of division without end. No trouble there.

But now suppose some kind of pluralism where the *parts* are *prior* (fundamental). The worry is that, if a world is gunky, then there's no *ultimate* level of fundamentality or priority. Each 'entity' is such that it is further divisible, and so no entity can be considered fundamental. At least, it would be arbitrary and ad hoc to pick out any particular level as being the level that is fundamental. Without such a fundamental base, it's hard to see that *anything's* fundamental.

In very metaphorical terms, fundamentality *would* come from the 'bottom-up', but since there is no 'bottom', there's nowhere for the fundamentality to come from given pluralism. That looks like a real worry for the pluralist precisely because the idea of substance that we tried to articulate above, traded explicitly on the idea that a substance is in some sense metaphysically fundamental. In contrast, given pluralism, the whole is fundamental; fundamentality comes from the top-down, and so we face no problems with gunk.

## §6.9 Concluding remarks

Schaffer's Monism seems tempting, though there might remain the nagging suspicion that there is *something* suspect about the world being a single substance. Pursuing that suspicion is something that can be done in the further reading. It is also clear that the topic is closely related to theories of properties. As ever, it is clear that we will require a careful weighing of our options.

## Recommended reading

### Substance

Hoffman, J. and Rozencrantz, G. S. 1994. *Substance among Other Categories*. Cambridge: CUP.

Lowe, E. J. 1998. *The Possibility of Metaphysics*. Oxford: Clarendon, chapters 6 and 7.

Lowe, E. J. 2005. *Locke*. London: Routledge, 59–96.

Lowe, E. J. 2006. *The Four Category Ontology*. Oxford: OUP, chapter 1.

Simons, P. M. 1998. 'Farewell to Substance: A Differentiated Leave-Taking', *Ratio*, 11, 235–52.

### Bundle Theory

Black, M. 1952. 'The Identity of Indiscernibles', *Mind*, 6, 153–64.

Casullo, A. 2001. 'A Fourth Version of the Bundle Theory', in Loux, M. ed. *Metaphysics: Contemporary Readings*. London: Routledge, 134–50.

Simons, P. 1994. 'Particulars in Particular Clothing: Three Trope Theories of Substance', *Philosophy and Phenomenological Research*, 54, 553–75.

Van Cleve, J. 2001. 'Three Versions of the Bundle Theory', in Loux, M. ed. *Metaphysics: Contemporary Readings*. London: Routledge, 121–33.

### States of affairs

Armstrong, D. 1993. 'A World of States of Affairs'. In *Philosophical Perspectives*, 7, 429–40.

Armstrong, D. 1997b. *A World of States of Affairs*. Cambridge: CUP.

Lowe, E. J. 1998. *The Possibility of Metaphysics*. Oxford: Clarendon, 241–3.

### Monism

Cameron, R. 2010. 'From Humean Truthmaker Theory to Priority Monism', *Nous*, 44, 178–98.

Morganatti, M. 2009. 'Ontological Priority, Fundamentality and Monism', *Dialectica*, 63, 271–88.

Schaffer, J. 2010a. 'The Priority of the Whole', *Philosophical Review*, 119, 31–76.

Sider, T. 2009a. 'Against Monism', *Analysis*, 67, 1–7.

## Study questions

1) Write out a brief description of all of the positions outlined in the chapter. Which theory do you find most convincing? Why do you find that theory most convincing?

2) Suppose that you were tempted by a substance view: would you opt for a pluralistic or Monistic account of substance? Why have you opted for that view?

3) An objection to states of affairs is that they require 'non-mereological composition'. How seriously do you think we should take that objection?

4) Do you think that there is an important difference between the compresence relation and substance? What are the philosophical consequences of your view?

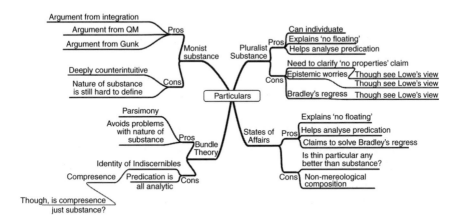

# 7

# Time

Let's begin this chapter with a consideration of two sentences.

(1) The battle of Hastings is earlier than the First World War.
(2) The moon landing is a past event.

As with previous chapters, we must consider what it is that might make the propositions expressed by these two sentences true. (1) *appears* to describe a relation; that is, on first inspection a natural way for the proposition expressed by (1) to be made true is by the existence of two events (the battle of Hastings and the First World War), and the relation 'earlier than', that stands between them. One noteworthy feature of (1) is that it appears to describe an *unchanging* state of affairs. That is, if (1) is true, then that it is true does not change over time. In language that philosophers sometimes use to describe this kind of talk, *(1) is always true, if it is true at all.* It would make sense to suppose, therefore, that the truth-maker for (1) is itself unchanging.

Now (2) doesn't seem to be quite the same. Although we do want to say that (2) is *now* true, there was a time when we would not have wanted to say this. The moon landing occurred in 1969, so we would presumably want to say that in 1969 (2) is false, and at any time earlier than 1969, (2) is false. It would seem therefore that what makes (2) true must change, in some way, in order for (2) itself to change truth-value over time. In contrast, as we have already seen, whatever makes true (1) need not change over time.

A way in which we might attempt to cash this out is via the implantation of a *property* of 'being past'. The moon landing is an event that was once future. It was future in virtue of instantiating the property 'being future'. Then the event lost the property of 'being future', and came to instantiate the property 'being present'. Then the event lost the property of 'being present', and acquired the property 'being past'. All other events will behave in the same way. They will start off bearing the property 'being future', then come to bear the property 'being present', and then, finally, come to bear the property 'being past'.

We then need some nomenclature introduced by John Ellis McTaggart: the 'fixed and permanent' relations that make true propositions expressed by the likes of (1), are described as B-relations. B-relations are the relations 'earlier than', and 'later than'. In contrast, the temporal properties that make true propositions expressed by the likes of (2) are described as 'A-properties'; the properties of 'being past', 'being present' and 'being future'.[1]

Intuitively, at least, these two sets of resources serve to underpin how we think about time. The A-theoretic properties seem to capture the idea that there is something objective about time's flow: events *literally* change from being future, to present to past. The B-relations, on the other hand, serve to capture the sense in which we think that there are unchanging relations among members of the temporal series. Nonetheless, as we shall now see, there are substantial problems in maintaining this pre-theoretically intuitive view.

# §7.1 McTaggart

As well as dividing temporal ontology into the categories of A and B-theoretic resources, McTaggart (infamously) used these resources to argue that time itself must be unreal. Although it's rare to find a philosopher who agrees with McTaggart's conclusion, most contemporary writing on time owes some intellectual debt to McTaggart's 1908 paper 'The Unreality of Time'.

McTaggart argued that both the A- and B-theoretic resources were essential to the reality of time. In outline, McTaggart argued that the A-properties were essential in order for time to be real. However, the A-properties are allegedly contradictory and so cannot be instantiated. That being the case, time cannot be real. Why, then, did McTaggart think that the A-properties were contradictory? The dialectic proceeds here by means of two distinct arguments. First I'll give an argument to show that the A-series is contradictory. Second, I'll present McTaggart's reason for thinking that this means that time is unreal.

Plainly, we do not think that any event can be past, present *and* future. However, notice also that when we described the A-properties above, we said that events are first future, then present and then past. Now we do not, of course, think that any event is past, present and future *at the same time*. But we do think, I take it, that events *have been* present, *have been future* and *are now* past. Take note, then, of the italicized portion of the above: for example *have been* present. Saying that x 'has been' the case, is surely just another way of saying that x 'is past'. And, in that case, to say that x *'has been* present' is to say that x is past-present. Or, if you prefer, present in the past. Since the truth of talk about the present requires a property of presence to be instantiated, and talk about the past requires a property of pastness to be instantiated, so the claim that some state of affairs *has been* present, appears to require that an event in time instantiates both properties and that cannot happen.

In McTaggart's (1908: 468–9) own words:

> What we have done is this – to meet the difficulty that my writing of this article has the characteristics of past, present and future, we say that it is present, has been future, and will be past. But 'has been' is only distinguished from 'is' by being existence in the past and not in the present, and 'will be' is only distinguished from both by being existence in the future. Thus our statement comes to this – that the event in question is present in the present, future in the past, past in the future.

So we see that the A-series involves a contradiction and for that reason we should deny that there are A-properties.

We noted above that no entity can instantiate the properties of both (e.g.) presence and pastness, and so it seems that the A-properties cannot be instantiated. Why though does this lead to the unreality of time? Why not simply think that the B-relations suffice for the reality of time?

Well, as we have already said, the natural thought is that whatever makes true (1) is itself unchanging. But we do not think that time can be real if there is no change. Time, or so it seems, is intricately bound up with change such that in the absence of change there can be no time. Of course, the B-relations themselves do not change, nor do entities change with regards to which other entities they are earlier than and later than. So (we might think) there is no change at a B-theoretic world, and so there could be no time at such a world. In view of this, and the contradictory nature of the A-series, McTaggart concluded that time is unreal.

There are a number of ways in which philosophers have responded. The mainstream view in the philosophy of time is (contra McTaggart) B-theoretic: that is, most philosophers who take an interest in the philosophy of time adopt a metaphysic according to which the 'fixed and permanent' B-relations – 'earlier than' and 'later than' – are fully sufficient for the reality of time. Indeed, it's not uncommon to see such philosophers use McTaggart's argument against the reality of the A-series as an argument *against* there being A-theoretic ontological resources while also claiming that the B-series is sufficient for the reality of time.

## §7.2 B-theory

According to the B-theory of time, as typically described, all events in time exist. That is, the creation of Mars outposts in the year 3029 exists, as does the big bang, the battle of Hastings and all of the events in between. Assuming that the universe comes to an end at some point, then that event exists, too. All of these events are related to one another by 'earlier than' and 'later than' relations. The network of B-relations suffices for the reality of time.

Three projects then look especially pressing for the B-theorist. First, we have denied that there exist A-theoretic ontological resources. That being the case, we now owe an explanation of how it is that sentences like (2) express true propositions. What are the relevant truth-makers? Second, if all times exist and are related by fixed and permanent B-relations, then how are we to explain the passage of time? Third, our experiences of time are such that there seems to be a sense in which we are constantly 'moving' through time: how can the B-theorist explain that sensation of 'movement'? Let's look at the kind of answers that B-theorists have given.

## §7.2.1 Tensed truths

Most, though not all, B-theorists claim that tensed truths are true in virtue of the earlier-than/later than relations. The way in which to make sense of this, they claim, is that tensed sentences have the following truth-conditions:

> For any sentence token, *u*, of the form, 'x is present', *u* is true iff (if and only if) x is simultaneous with *u*.
>
> For any sentence token, *u*, of the form, 'x is past', *u* is true iff x is earlier than *u*.
>
> For any sentence token, *u*, of the form, 'x is future', *u* is true iff x is later than *u*.[2]

Thus, a sentence token of, 'the creation of Mars outposts is future', is true, according to the B-theorist, provided the creation of Mars outposts stands in a B-theoretic 'later than' relation to the time at which the sentence token is tokened.[3] So where we might have thought that tensed sentences require what we might, very crudely, call 'A-theoretic' truth-makers, the B-theorist explicitly denies this, and offers us 'B-theoretic' truth-makers for tensed sentences.

## §7.2.2 The passage of time

As we have seen, the thought that initially motivated McTaggart to posit A-series change as essential to the reality of time was that entities in time that are related by unchanging relations are not, themselves, sufficient to account for the sort of change that goes on in temporal passage. That the battle of Hastings is earlier than the First World War is permanent and unchanging. In contrast, the passage of time seems to require change. The natural worry for us to have, then, is that this is simply not sufficient for the passage of time.

To see the problem more clearly consider the (much cited) example of a poker. A poker may be hot at one end; cold at the other. But that is not to then say that the poker *changes* in any interesting kind of way. Rather, there is simply a variation in the temperature of the poker along its length. This case is analogous to the temporal case. To say that the battle of Hastings is earlier than the First World War is just to say something unchanging. It is simply to say that there is variation in which events exist over time. This is just the same as there being variation in temperature across the length of the poker. Since, or so we might think, *change* rather than mere variation is required for the passage of time, the B-theoretic account of passage simply cannot be right.

There are a number of ways to cash out the B-theorists response, here, and two points in particular seem worth making. First, what is unclear in the forgoing is *exactly what* is supposed to be missing from the account of temporal passage. After all, we're prepared to concede that the battle of Hastings *is* earlier than the First World War and that there is variation in what exists over time. And if that's the case, then *surely* time *is* real. What, *exactly* is supposed to be wrong with saying that temporal change across a duration just is variation in the properties instantiated by objects that exist/persist through a temporal region? Perhaps temporal change *is* like spatial variation. The point is well explained by considering a stick that is bent at one time, and straight at another. The stick is bent at one time and straight at another; it has one property at one time, and another property at a later time. What, exactly, is missing from this account of change? Absent an answer to this question we might well think that the B-theorist has done enough to account for change. So perhaps change over time *is* just like variation across space. It just so happens that there is an intrinsic difference between the nature of time and space. There just isn't anything more that we can say about B-relations, other than they are analogous to spatial relations, but are the relations 'earlier than'/'later than', and so are obviously temporal.

The second point (thought related to the first) concerns the thought that a B-theoretic view of time seems a bit like a 'block'. We might well be tempted to think of B-theoretic time as akin to a dimension. That being the case, the whole of reality might be compared to a block, with one temporal dimension, and three spatial dimensions. Now perhaps it is this mental image that we have that is causing the problem. The time of our experiences seems to be flowing and intimately bound up with what we might insist on calling 'real change'. Clearly, this static image of a block is just not well suited to capturing this sense of change and flow. The block, after all, does not change.

But quite apart from the fact that this notion of 'real change' remains unarticulated, the B-theorist has a reply that they might make to this accusation of 'blockyness'. When we look for change in the 'block', we're making a mistake. We're supposing that the 'block' itself, needs to change, rather than allowing that change occurs *within* the block. What the B-theorist will say is that for there to be a change in the world does not require that the whole of reality changes. We do not require past, present and future entities to undergo a change. Rather, for there to be a change in the world we merely require that objects *within* time vary their properties, over time. Thus, if there is a rod that exists at many different times, and has different properties at those times, then we may say that 'the rod has undergone a change'.

All things considered, then, it's hard to see how the opponent of the B-theorist is to find fault with this. Perhaps they can, but the task looks far from straightforward.

## §7.2.3 Sensing passage

But the final problem might give us pause, for if all of these times *exist*, and *are* related to one another, then, we might ask, how is it that we have a *sensation* of temporal passage? The sensation of temporal passage seems to us as if we're moving through time. It seems, perhaps, as if there is a 'now' of awareness, and that this 'now' – or locus of experience – is constantly traversing time generating what D. C. Williams (1951) memorably described as the 'whoosh and whizz' of the feeling of moving through time. It is notoriously hard to pin down what, exactly, this sensation *is* or what it feels like. But the basic idea that is being exploited, I think, is that there is a sense in which we seem to move through time that is not captured by the B-theorist, who denies that we literally move through time. Rather, according to the B-theorist, we are simply located at many different times.

One route that the B-theorist might take, but on first inspection that they ought to avoid, is to say that our sensation of passage is *illusory*, and that there is no genuine sense in which we experience a 'now' that moves through time. The move looks initially suspect because to say so *might* seem to require of us that our experiences of time are *all* illusory. After all, we might wonder, what does our experience of time consist in if it's not this experience of passage? And, if all of our experiences of time are this *merely illusory* sense of passage, then it's just not clear that we have *any* awareness of time itself. Given our natural reluctance to posit ontology where we're not capable of perceiving said posit (e.g. §1.5), we might then be reluctant to posit B-relations.

The B-theorist may have a reply that they can offer, here. The B-theorist may allow that *some* of our experiences of time are of a 'moving now', but surely *not all of them*. Thus, when I hear the opening bars of a particular piece of music it does not merely appear to me that this particular strain of music occurs now; it also appears to me that particular notes occur earlier than others, and that certain notes occur later than others. Here, then, is a clear sense in which our experiences of time are not illusory if time is B-theoretic. We are experiencing what it is for one event to be earlier than another.

Moreover, our experience of the movement of the now is readily explained. 'Nowness' for the B-theorist does not consist in some mind-independent temporal fact or property. Instead, my experience of nowness simply consists in my experience of a particular state of affairs and *judging* it to be present. My experience of judging particular events to be present *is* what it's like to experience events *as* present. So perhaps the problems of temporal experience can be dealt with.

# §7.3 Doing enough to be special?

Nonetheless, not all philosophers think that the B-theorist does enough in their attempts to answer the preceding. Some, for instance, claim that an asymmetry in our attitudes towards the past and future can be treated as pointing to a serious deficiency in the B-theory.[4] Although both past and future events exist, we only fear those events that are in the future. If all times exist, then that would not be rational. There would be no reason to fear future events but not past events. However, we are perfectly rational to only fear events that are in the future, so the B-theory must be false. Others claim that the account of change given is lacking, and others attempt to point to serious flaws within the semantics of the B-theoretic account of tensed sentences.

But one particular argument against the B-theory interests me here, because it moves us in the direction of a direct competitor to the B-theory: presentism. It appears intuitive to us that there is something special about the present. Quite what that specialness consists in is hard to pin down, but it appears pretty obvious (to some philosophers at any rate) that we think that there *is* something special about the present. Now, obviously, the B-theory fails to respect that intuition; according to the B-theory something's being present is nothing more than it existing simultaneous with us. And there's nothing obviously special about that. So, we might say, it is a black mark against the B-theory that it fails to preserve that intuition. The natural question is whether or not there is a view that successfully preserves that intuition.

There is. Presentism is the view that *only present objects exist*. Plainly, such a view will preserve the intuition that the present is special in some way: after all, the present time is the only time that exists. What could be more 'special' than that? Moreover, we saw above that there was an intuition that the B-theorist does not quite do enough to get 'genuine' change. The presentist can perhaps do better. According to the presentist, all objects are present objects and, from moment to moment, these objects undergo a change. Thus, *the whole of reality* changes from moment to moment. That's quite a claim and perhaps it goes some way to capturing our sense of what genuine change is.

Much of the rest of the chapter revolves around a discussion of presentism. The view itself is certainly a minority position, but the fact that it has been the subject of so much recent literature leads to it having such a prominent place in our discussion here.

# §7.4 Truths about the past

The presentist will face an obvious question: if only the present exists, what makes true our talk about the past?

In fact, there are at least two different, though related, questions that need to be asked of the presentist. First, what makes true our talk about *particular* times, such that 'I was hungry' is true? Second, what is it that makes true our talk about 'spans' of time? So, suppose that the presentist *can* provide the resources to make true our talk about individual times, what will they say about claims like 'there have been two kings called Charles'? After all, if only the present exists, and only the present has *ever* existed, then there is, at any one time, only one king called Charles that has existed. Presentists have attempted answers to these questions, as we shall now see, but how plausible these answers are is something for the reader to decide for themselves.

Let's begin by considering the first sort of truth about the past that was noted above:

(3) I was hungry.

What is it that *makes* the proposition expressed by (3) true? Presumably, we *do* think it's true. I certainly do. I can vividly remember my hunger pangs just prior to lunch today. Here, I'll carve the terrain in two and explore so-called 'properties' solutions and 'ersatz' solutions.

## §7.4.1 Singular times and properties solutions

Bigelow (1996) argues that the best way to ground true talk about the past is to envisage the world instantiating past-tensed properties. Thus, what makes (3) true is that the world instantiates the property of 'having included a hungry Jonathan'. Similarly, consider the proposition <there were dinosaurs>. What will make true this proposition is that the world instantiates the property 'having included dinosaurs'.

It's not uncommon, though, to read of philosophers objecting to these kinds of proposals on the ground that these properties appear to include an irrevocably 'tensed' component, and that this seems to enable them to 'point beyond' what exists. The idea, I take it, is that when we think of normal properties, we typically think of them as making a difference to the nature of the object that instantiates them.[5] To clarify, consider the humble tomato. The property of redness that is instantiated by the tomato makes a difference to the nature of the tomato.[6] But in direct contrast, it appears that the 'tensed' property does *not* make a difference to the nature of the world. For although the 'tensed' property does tell us how the world *was* it does not make any difference to how the world is: more precisely, it does not make a difference to the present intrinsic nature of the world. To illustrate: merely that the world *has included dinosaurs* does not tell us *anything* about how the world *is now*, nor does the property *having included dinosaurs* make any difference to how the world is *now*. Since, according to the presentist, only the *now* exists, so this is a property that makes no difference to the nature of anything that exists. That seems like a strange property – certainly, it appears radically unlike our other properties.

We should now consider the dialectical situation. We presented the presentist with the truth-maker objection; they responded with a 'properties' solution. But the *sort* of properties that the presentist is positing are *utterly* unlike other properties. The only reason the presentist believes in these really weird properties is because of the truth-maker objection. So there is no *positive* reason to believe in these properties. The presentist only postulates them as a defensive manoeuvre. Moreover, they are deeply odd properties. This looks like a poor dialectical situation for the presentist.

One way in which presentists have responded is due to Ross Cameron (forthcoming, c). Cameron claims that the presentist should, instead, appeal to what he calls *distributional properties*. To give a spatial analogue: a domino might have the property of being black in certain regions, and then also have the property of being white in other regions. An alternative *distributional* solution is to say that the surface of the domino instantiates the property of 'being polkadotted'. This property is much like a conjunction of ordinary properties. It's *like* 'being white at region R' and 'being black at region S' and 'being white at region T' . . . and so on. But the property is subtly difference. Rather than being a *conjunction* of properties, the distributional property is a *single* property: being polkadotted.

How does this help the presentist? Cameron thinks that the world might currently instantiate the property of, say,

> Temporal Distributional Property (TDP): Being such to include dinosaurs at t; being such to include me at t*; being such to include martian outposts at t** . . . and so on.

This helps, Cameron thinks, because the TDP *does* make a difference to how things *are now*. After all, Cameron thinks, it is in virtue of the world instantiating the particular TDP that it does, that I now exist. So the TDP *does* make a difference to how the world is. *Granted* it also makes a difference to how the world was, at t, and how it will be, at t**. But that's not the issue. The issue, according to Cameron, is that the 'tensed' property solution due to Bigelow required us to endorse properties that *don't* make a difference to how the world *is*. The TDP solution solves that problem.

There's a lot that could be said about Cameron's proposal, but two things might be worth noting. First, Cameron's property is *not* tensed. The careful reader will already have noted that the language used to describe the TDP is all tenseless. Thus, in order to generate the result that any *one* of these properties is *now* instantiated, Cameron also appeals to a property of age. His claim, then, is that the property of being a particular age, in conjunction with a given TDP suffices for a particular part of the TDP to be instantiated.

Second, it's not in fact clear that Cameron has identified the real problem. The diagnosis of the problem, above, was that we find problematic the claim that there are properties that *don't* make a difference to the nature of their bearers. That sounded plausible.

But what seems equally plausible is that we might find objectionable properties that make a difference to the nature of *non-existent entities*. We might worry, for instance, that it would simply make no sense to say that there could be a world that included four spatial regions, $s_1$, $s_2$, $s_3$, and $s_4$; but have an object at that world instantiate the spatial distributional property: being polkadotted at regions $s_2$–$s_5$. How, after all, could the property that purports to give some nature to a particular region be instantiated if the region does not exist? The very idea seems nonsensical, or so we might think. Similarly, then, simply by saying that an entity *now* has a particular distributional property that makes a difference to how it was and will be seems somehow puzzling: those past and future instances of the entity in question do not exist. And, if they do not exist, it is fairly puzzling to think that the distributional properties can make a difference to them.

## §7.4.2 Ersatzer proposals

As we saw in Chapter 2, *modal* ersatzers think that they can generate an under-standing of what a possible world is; they are sets of consistent sentences (or propositions). Temporal ersatzers make a slightly different claim. Crisp (2007), for instance, proceeds in the following way. Allow that there are sets of max-imally consistent sentences (or propositions). The temporal ersatzer will call these times in much the same way that modal ersatzers will call sets of consist-ent sentences (or propositions) possible worlds. We can then relate these times to one another via an *ersatz* B-relation. This ersatz B-relation is much like an ordinary B-relation, but rather than relating physical times to one another, the ersatz B-relation relates these maximally consistent sets of sentences (or prop-ositions) to one another.

For 'there were dinosaurs' to be true, requires that there is a maximally consistent set of sentences (or propositions) including the (tenseless) sentence (or proposition) 'dinosaurs exist' – call this set 1 – and that this set of sen-tences (or propositions) is ersatz B-related to another set of maximally con-sistent tenseless sentences (or propositions), including the sentence 'there are no dinosaurs' – call this set 2 – such that the set 1 is 'ersatz earlier than' set 2. To the initiate, this may appear confusing, complex and irrelevant. But much of the motivation for endorsing this kind of view can be gleaned from noting the potential explanatory power of ersatzer proposals *in general*. We saw, in Chapter 3, that although linguistic and propositional ersatzisms may face some problems, they are nonetheless powerful and influential views. No sur-prise, then, that a temporal analogue might be considered as a solution to the truth-maker problem for presentism.

Two problems may then arise; the first easily soluble, the second perhaps less so. First, the idea of an 'ersatz' B-relation seems somehow dubious. After all, B-relations are supposed to relate *times*, rather than these abstract entities.

Crisp (2007: 106) replies:

> Why should my *earlier than* relation be any more dubious than the eternalist's B-theoretic *earlier than* relation on times, events and the like? True, my relation links abstract times; hers links concrete times. But why think that a demerit for my relation?

Unless we can then give some reason to think that an *ersatz* B-relation is more dubious than a genuine B-relation, Crisp doesn't see that there is a problem here.

Albeit tentatively, we might attempt to press this problem as follows: to say that something is 'ersatz' is to say that it is a substitution for; an imitation of, or representation of some other thing. In this case, it would seem that we're being invited to think that an ersatz B-relation is an imitation of a B-relation. In what sense, then, does it merely imitate the B-relation? We may grant one difference between the two: that the ersatz B-relation relates abstract times, rather than concrete times. But, of course, to merely say that ersatz B-relations imitate B-relations in the sense that ersatz B-relations only relate abstract times, is not yet to understand the nature of the ersatz B-relation itself.

By way of demonstration, I suppose that we have a sensible grasp of the spatial relation: 'one mile distant'. Suppose, then, that I postulated that spaces other than the 'here' do not really exist, but that, instead, we should understand talk about other places as 'made true by' abstract spaces. These are maximally consistent sets of sentences (or propositions) that are ersatz spatially related to one another. Do I thereby gain any particular insight into the nature of an ersatz spatial relation 'one mile distant' that relates abstract spaces rather than concrete spaces? It's hard to see how. When we moved from saying that the relation related concrete spaces to saying that it related abstract spaces, we moved from my understanding the relation, to my not understanding it. I understood the spatial relation precisely because I understand what spaces are, and I have a grasp of how they relate to one another. By so substantially changing the nature of the relata of the spatial relation, we render the ersatz spatial-relation itself unintelligible.

The same point might apply to the temporal case. By changing relata *so substantially* we change the nature of the relation in such a way that renders it unintelligible. So when we move from saying that the B-relation relates concrete times, to saying that the ersatz B-relation relates abstract times, we change the nature of the relation under consideration *so fundamentally* to render the notion opaque. At least, so we might worry.

The second objection to this style of ersatzism runs thus: at this moment in time, there exists one concrete time (the present); there also exists a collection of ersatz times. Some of these are ersatz B-related to one another. At a later time a different concrete time will exist. It is then possible that, over time, the abstract times that are ersatz B-related to one another will change and that looks deeply problematic.

To illustrate, suppose that when the concrete time that exists is 00:00:00 in January the 1st, 2000, the abstract times that are ersatz B-related to one another are:

A, B, C, D, E, F and G

Suppose that we take time A to represent January 1st, 00:00:00. What is then to *prevent* this changing, so that when the concrete time that exists is 00:00:01 on January the 1st, 2000, which we shall call ersatz time B, the abstract times that are ersatz B-related to one another are:

S, B, T, U, V, W, X and Y

What is to *stop* that? Plainly, something must, else we might find ourselves in a situation where it is true, one minute, that dinosaurs existed, but false the very next second! It's hard to see what the ersatzer can say, here. But they surely owe us some account of why this cannot happen. The ball is very much in the ersatzer's court.

In any case, what has become clear as we've moved through the options is that the presentist has more work to do if they are to find a satisfactory solution to the truth-maker problem for talk about the past.

# §7.5 Spans

Before we move away from presentism and the ground of our temporal talk, we must consider our second problem. Rather than considering true talk about *single* times, we might want to consider parts of our language that at least appear to talk about *many* times. An example of such a sentence is 'there have been two kings of England called "Charles"'. The locution 'have been' clearly serves to pick out more than one single time. How are we to account for this when plainly, since we're assuming presentism, it has never in fact been the case that more than one king called Charles exists? How can this be? The sentence is true, at least we naturally suppose it is, even though the sentence talks about *more than one time*.

One thing that we might do is try to develop a plural quantifier. To begin, assume that we've been able to solve the problem of making true propositions about single times other than the present, discussed immediately above. Then we might say that to say that 'there have been two kings called "Charles"' we simply need it to be the case that 'it has been the case that (there is a king called Charles) and it has been the case that (there is a king called Charles)' (Lewis 2004: 6).

But things will rapidly become more complex. What should we say about claims such as 'there have been several kings called "George"'? In the case where we were definite about the numbers of kings it was easy to see what to say, but it is far less obvious in the case where the number of kings is not specified. Moreover, what should we say about infinitary constructions? What, for instance, should we say about sentences like, 'there have been an infinite number of times'? If we try to construct a plural quantifier then we will have to include an *infinite* number of nested singular quantifiers and, quite simply, we cannot do such a thing. Nor, it seems, should we rule out such a sentence: it's at least metaphysically possible that there is no first moment. Further, *if* time is continuous such that between any two moments in time a further moment occurs, then we will *have* to be able to speak of an infinite number of times. Such a view of time is not unreasonable and it would be odd if presentism were obliged to rule out such a possibility because presentism commits us to a peculiar way of understanding span-talk. Since it at least appears that the presentist cannot speak of an infinite number of times in this way, so there is a remaining problem for presentist to consider.[7]

# §7.6 Cross-time relations

Another problem, similar yet distinct, concerns how we are to ground cross-time relational judgements. By way of example consider the sentence, 'the rain caused the flood'. There are other examples we could consider, such as 'Verity admires Socrates', but the causal case seems especially pressing.

I take it that the proper disambiguation of this is to say that the rain that fell at one time caused the flood at another, later, time. The problem, then, concerns the causal relation that is seemingly described, here, as relating two distinct times.

In the case described, it very much appears as if we have a relation, causation, with two relata: the falling rain, and the flood. If a causal relation is to be said to hold between two distinct events, then we must surely say that both events exist. After all, the relata of a relation must exist in order to be related. To see this in a more obvious case, consider the relation 'to the left of'. How can I be 'to the left of' something, a table (say), if it does not exist? Certainly, it would seem false to say of me that 'I'm to the left of the non-existent table' (in fact that might well sound like nonsense).

At least one presentist has accepted this outcome and argued that there are no truths about cross-time relations. Crisp (2005) has argued that this is so, but that this is not such a great cost for the presentist to bear. He grants, as he surely must, that this is strange: we certainly *think* that there are truths that purport to be about cross-time relations: we *think* that the rain fall caused the flood, for example. But, nonetheless, Crisp doesn't think that the cost is too great to bear.

In support of this judgement, Crisp draws a distinction between truths and Moorean truths. Moorean truths are propositions that we are seemingly *obliged* to accept, as the truth of these proposition seems more probable than *anything* that might appear in the premises of an argument that could be thought of as rejecting the truth of the proposition. Cross-time relational talk is not Moorean, according to Crisp. Sentences like 'I admire Caesar' or that 'the rain caused the flood' are sentences that we certainly believe to be true; but we do not think of them as such that their denial is utterly implausible. Thus, if presentism entails the denial of the truth of such propositions, then so be it. There is nothing more to be said. We simply deny that cross-time relational talk is true and argue that we do not thereby incur much of a cost because we do not think it very pressing to preserve the truth of cross-time relational talk.

Although we might find something appealing in Crisp's move, we might retain a worry regarding a tension between what Crisp claims about these cross-time relational sentences and the general motivation for presentism. Above, we noted that a motivation for presentism is that it preserves our intuition that the present is special in some way. Here, Crisp is inviting us to agree that certain sentences that we would have thought, intuitively, to be true, are in fact false. Even if we grant Crisp that cross-time relational truths are not Moorean, it nonetheless seems that there is some cost to our intuitions in denying that these propositions are true. We might then ask: if what is motivating presentism is the preservation of our intuitions, then can we consistently deny our other intuitions about time? There is a temptation to think that we cannot consistently do so. If that's right, then we ought not to deny that there are cross-time relational truths.

A more promising strategy would be to try and give truth-makers for our cross-time relational talk. One way that we might begin to attempt to do so is to offer the following by way of an analysis of causal talk. The sort of thing that we might offer up is something like this:

> 'X is the cause of Y' is true iff X occurred and Y is occurring, and had X not occurred, then y would not now be occurring.[8]

What is essential to this analysis is that we do not require that X itself exists.

But two points are worth making, here. First, it isn't wholly clear that the counterfactual analysis of causation is to be accepted – as we will see in Chapter 9. So whatever theory of causation that we settle upon had better be amenable to some kind of 'tensed' treatment. Second, the proposal looks like it will help us with causal talk; can it be amended to deal with cases like 'Jonathan admires Socrates'? The natural thought would be to offer a paraphrase of this along the lines of,

Admires: 'x admires y' is true iff x and y both exist and x admires y, or x exists and y has existed, and there both is and was some property, $\varphi$, such that it was the case that '$\varphi$ is instantiated by y' and x now admires the property, $\varphi$.

We can then explain this sort of move in the following way. Suppose that I admire Socrates. Then, we might say, what this really commits us to is that Socrates had some property, wisdom (say), and I admire the property of wisdom. Since the property of wisdom still exists, so I stand in a relation only to an existing property. *This* is what we mean when we talk about cross-time relations obtaining.

Although there may be something to be said for this kind of paraphrase, one immediate and intuitive objection is that the paraphrase simply misidentifies what is going on in the scenario described. What I admire is Socrates; *not* the property of wisdom. Perhaps I do not in general admire wisdom *at all*. Rather, my admiration extends to Socrates because of his actions, his particular properties, and perhaps also that I've been taught that Socrates is an admirable figure: indeed, to focus upon the last concern, is it not plausible that I admire Socrates, even without knowing of any of his properties? Suppose, for instance, that my wife, whose judgements I trust implicitly, informs me that Socrates is admirable. From that moment on, perhaps I then form the belief that Socrates is admirable and, if asked, would assert that 'I admire Socrates'. It seems clear that, *if* the case described is plausible (which is certainly a point worth pressing), then it cannot simply be Socrates' properties that I admire.

At least at the current time, it would appear that there is more that needs to be said.

# §7.7 Growing Block

A distinctive view of time is the so-called Growing Block view of time. According to this view the past and present exist, but the future does not. Naturally, this view offers us a very natural solution to the truth-maker problem for talk about the past: what makes true propositions about the past is the past itself. Thus, <there were dinosaurs> is true because dinosaurs exist in the past – they are a part of the block.

It's worth noting, as well, that the Growing Block view of time permits us to go some way to preserving the intuition that there's something special about the present. Where the past is the body of the block, the present is the last layer of the block that has been added. The present, thus, is at the dividing line between existence (the past) and the as yet non-existent future. So at the moment, at least, things look pretty rosy for the Growing Block theorist. The view has a solution to the grounding problem and also offers us an explanation of the specialness of the present. In fact it gets even better, for at each moment there is a change in the totality of what exists. Thus, in the same way as the presentist, the proponent of Growing Block seems to preserve the idea that there is genuine change.

But at least one problem needs to be mentioned, here, in connection with the preservation of the idea that the present is somehow made special on the Growing Block view. Consider the occupants of the block – not those people who occupy the front edge, but the body of the block itself. Each of those people are, surely, certain that they are present. I take it that *nothing* is more certain to us than the belief that 'I am present'. Each of those people, who occupy the body of the block, will have belief tokens of the form 'I am present'. But their beliefs will be false. To be present, given the Growing Block model, is to reside at the *edge* of the block. And since these people occupy the *body*, rather than the *edge*, of the block, so their beliefs are false. This gives us the basis for a sceptical argument. There are many more people within the body of the block than there are at the edge and we have just as much evidence that we are at the edge of the block as do those people who we think of as residing within the body of the block. Since both we and they have the same evidence for our claim that 'I am present', and we take all of our predecessors to be incorrect in their judgement, so it would seem most rational for us to conclude that we, too, are incorrect, and that we do not exist in the present.

But, on the very plausible assumption that we do not want to give up on the truth of the belief that we are present, so we are seemingly obliged to give up on the Growing Block view of time. This argument is analogous to the argument that Lewis gives in connection with what it is to be actual that we looked at in §4.4.

# §7.8 The special theory of relativity

So far I've said nothing specific about the relationship between our best physics and our metaphysics, but in this context we are obliged to engage in such considerations. According to the special theory of relativity, to say that something is present is really to say that it is present *relative to a frame of reference*. Put as simply as possible (and possibly *too* simply), two objects are members of the same inertial frame of reference iff they are travelling at the same velocity as one another. To illustrate, consider two people, Charles and Elizabeth: Charles stood at the roadside; Elizabeth is driving past in her car. Charles and Elizabeth, we may say, occupy different frames of reference. If Elizabeth is driving at a steady 50 miles per hour, then *relative* to Elizabeth, another car travelling at 50 miles per hour (in the same direction) is in fact stationary. Relative to Charles, of course, the second car is travelling at 50 miles per hour.

Now one phenomena in particular is in need of explanation. Suppose that Charles owns a barn. He stands at the entrance to his barn. Elizabeth has with her a pole. At rest, the pole is marginally longer than the barn. Elizabeth runs very quickly towards the barn (in fact, nearly at the speed of light). What Charles will see is the pole *wholly inside the barn!* Despite the fact that, at rest, the pole is longer than the barn, accelerated relative to Charles, the pole will now appear shorter. By contrast, to Elizabeth the barn will appear even shorter than it did before she got up to speed and so her observations will never record the pole as being wholly within the barn.

Obviously this is a strange state of affairs. But the special theory of relativity, in union with a particular view of time, is able to offer us a sensible explanation of this phenomenon. Rather than asking whose perspective on the pole and the barn *is correct* we should think of them *both* as being correct. By way of comparison, think about spatial perspectives. Hold up a ruler in front of you, so that the longest edge is facing you. Now turn the ruler so that the longest edge is pointing somewhere over your left shoulder. The ruler will appear to be shorter (at least it will no longer seem to span so much distance in the direction left-to-right). Of course, we don't want to say that the ruler has changed length simply because we've turned it! We simply say that the ruler appears shorter than it did before because we're taking a different perspective upon things.

Matters are taken to be similar in the relativistic case. Rather than viewing the length of the pole and barn as fixed, we should view them as a matter of perspective. How long the pole appears to us is simply a matter of which perspective we take of the pole – which is to say, how quickly we're travelling relative to it. Likewise, which events are simultaneous with which others is simply a matter that will *appear* different from frame to frame.

The idea is perhaps best illustrated with the aid of a very simply diagram. Consider two events, d and e, and two inertial frames of reference. One frame is perhaps to be thought of as the one we occupy on the earth; the other occupied by someone travelling past the earth at great velocity.

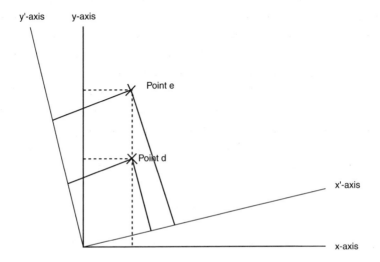

Allow that the x axis is taken to represent our view of which *place* things occur in, and the y axis is taken to represent the time at which things occur. Then, the two crosses (at point d and point e) can be seen as representing, in this case, two distinct events. According to an occupant of this (x, y) frame of reference, the two events will occur at precisely the same point in space, though at different times. Let us suppose that these are the observations made on earth. Notice that in the other frame, the (x', y') frame, the two events are represented as appearing at slightly different points in space, though closer together in time. *This is in fact what an observer travelling past the earth at great velocity will observe.*

Now, notice that on the proposed account what will be viewed as 'simultaneous' will vary from frame to frame. In effect, those events viewed as simultaneous will be those seen as occurring parallel with the x (or x') axis. But this then appears to generate the result that there *is* no such thing as *absolute* simultaneity; rather, what is simultaneous with us will be dependent upon which frame of reference we occupy.

This has been a sizeable digression; what has been the point? The presentist believes that only present objects exist. Presumably, the presentist also thinks that if some entity, *e*, is present, then it exists simultaneously with everything else that exists. It would be strange indeed to say that only the present exists, but that those entities that are present do not exist simultaneously with one another. But we've seen that there is, in fact, no genuine fact of the matter as to which events are simultaneous with others; which events are simultaneous with others is simply dependent upon the frame of reference one occupies. That would seem to suggest that what is present is a frame relative matter. That, in turn, would appear to suggest that what *exists* is a frame relative matter.[9] But surely that cannot be right. For one thing, a frame of reference is nothing more than a co-ordinate system dependent upon one's velocity. For another, there are many *different* frames of reference. So there are *many different* sets of existing things! This appears to then make reality fragmented. What exists changes from frame to frame. Most philosophers will balk at this suggestion. Existence, we think, is a singular, unified, state. It is not fragmented in the way described above.[10] It seems, therefore, that presentism faces substantial problems.

# §7.9 Can the presentist reply?

It seems that the presentists have broadly three options available to them, but it's hard to see how any of these is terribly palatable. First, they might simply choose to ignore the special theory, or at least argue that metaphysical concerns trump concerns from science. The worry with such a line is well put by Sider (2001: 42): 'in cases of science versus metaphysics, historically the smart money has been on science'.

The second option is to offer some revision to our metaphysics in order to make it compatible with our best physics. In particular, it has been suggested that we deny not only the existence of other times, but other spaces as well. This 'here-now-ism' avoids the relativistic problems altogether, for on the here-now model there is no problematic simultaneity as the only thing that exists as the here and now. But there are worries with this line, too. For one thing, the view seems absurdly solipsistic; where we might perhaps be prepared to accept that no times other than the present time exist, the same simply does not seem to be true of space. For another thing, we might have worries that, once again, what exists *is simply dependent on one's frame of reference*. That seemed to lead to a fragmented notion of existence, above, and still seems to here.

The third and final option is to try and make appeal to science *itself* for a plane of absolute simultaneity. Some philosophers have tried to argue that the best interpretations of quantum mechanics will include a preferred frame of reference, and that this can be used to define absolute simultaneity. Others have tried to argue that the General Theory of Relativity implies the existence of an absolute frame of reference and that *this* can be used to determine that there is a plane of absolute simultaneity. I leave to the reader the task of pursuing these concerns.

One point appears clear. The scientific orthodoxy holds that there is no such thing as absolute simultaneity; un-amended presentism entails that there is absolute simultaneity. Thus, un-amended presentism is incompatible with orthodox relativity. B-theory, which does *not* posit a relation (or at least does not *need* to posit a relation) of absolute simultaneity is compatible with orthodox physics. On those grounds, a rejection of presentism may well seem in order.

# §7.10 Conclusion

On balance, it would appear that B-theory has more to recommend it than presentism, but, equally, that presentism is an on-going concern. Indeed, the view is only in its infancy (having only come to light as a fully developed position in the last 20–30 years – though it has its contemporary roots in the work of Arthur Prior (see, e.g., Prior 2003)). Of course, we can only evaluate a view *at* the current time; that being the case, on balance, it would seem that a tentative rejection is in order – even if that rejection is tempered with the observation that future work may yet vindicate presentism, even in light of the objection from relativity.[11]

There are also various issues not touched upon in this section. For instance, there remain those who are sceptical as to whether or not the debate between the presentist and eternalist is well formed. I recommend some reading on this topic below. There also remains the question of whether or not our choice of theory of persistence dictates anything regarding our theory of time (or vice versa). This topic is voluminous, and I defer discussion of it to the next chapter.

# Recommended reading by topic

On McTaggart's paradox

Dummett, Michael A. E. 1960. 'A Defence of McTaggart's Proof of the Unreality of Time', *Philosophical Review*, 69, 497–504.

Lowe, E. J. 1987. 'The Indexical Fallacy in McTaggart's Proof of the Unreality of Time', *Mind*, 96, 62–70.

McTaggart, J. E. 1908. 'The Unreality of Time', *Mind*, 17, 457–74.

Oaklander, L. N. 2004. *The Ontology of Time*. New York: Prometheus Books, Essay 1.

## The truth-maker problem for presentism

Armstrong, D. 2004. *Truth and Truthmakers*. Cambridge: CUP, 145–50.

Bigelow, J. 1996. 'Presentism and Properties', *Philosophical Perspectives*, 10, 35–52.

Bourne, C. 2006. 'A Theory of Presentism', *Canadian Journal of Philosophy*, 36, 1–23.

Cameron, R. forthcoming, c. 'Truthmaking for Presentists', *Oxford Studies in Metaphysics*, 6.

Crisp, T. 2007. 'Presentism and the Grounding Objection', *Nous*, 41, 90–109.

Markosian, N. 2004. 'A Defence of Presentism', in *Oxford Studies in Metaphysics*, 1, 47–82.

## Passage and our experience of time

Oaklander, L. N. and White, A. 2007. 'B-time: A Reply to Tallant', *Analysis*, 67, 332–40.

Olson, E. 2009. 'The Rate of Time's Passage', *Analysis*, 69, 3–9.

Philips, I. 2009. 'Rate Abuse: A Reply to Olson', *Analysis*, 69, 503–50.

Savitt, S. 2002. 'On Absolute Becoming and the Myth of Passage', in Callender, C. ed. *Time, Relativity and Experience*, Cambridge: CUP, 153–68.

Tallant, J. 2007. 'What is B-time?', *Analysis*, 67, 147–56.

Tallant, J. 2010a. 'A Sketch of a Presentist Theory of Passage', *Erkenntnis*, 73,133–40.

## Presentism and relativity

Balashov, Y. and Janssen, M. 2003. 'Presentism and Relativity'. *British Journal for the Philosophy of Science*, 54, 327–46.

Craig, W. L. 2008. 'The Metaphysics of Special Relativity: Three Views', in Craig, W. L. and Smith, Q. eds. *Einstein, Relativity and Absolute Simultaneity*. London: Routledge, 11–49.

Crisp, T. 2008. 'Presentism, Eternalism and Relativity Physics', in Craig, W. L. and Smith, Q. eds. *Einstein, Relativity and Absolute Simultaneity*. London: Routledge, 262–78.

Hawley, K. 2006. 'Science as a Guide to Metaphysics?', *Synthese*, 149, 541–70.

Saunders, S. 2002. 'How Relativity Contradicts Presentism', in Callender, C. ed. *Time, Relativity and Experience*, Cambridge: CUP, 277–92.

## Presentism and cross-time relations

Crisp, T. 2005. 'Presentism and Cross-Time Relations', *American Philosophical Quarterly* 42, 5–17.

De Clerq, R. 2006. 'Presentism and the Problem of Cross-Time Relations', *Philosophy and Phenomenological Research*, 72, 386–402.

## Eternalism and tense

Craig, W. L. 1999. 'On Truth Conditions of Tensed Sentence Types', *Synthese*, 120, 265–70.

Dyke, H. 2002. 'Tokens, Dates and Tenseless Truth Conditions', *Synthese*, 131, 329–51.

Dyke, H. 2003. 'Temporal Language and Temporal Reality', *Philosophical Quarterly*, 53, 380–91.

Mellor, D. H. 1981. *Real Time*. Cambridge: CUP.

Oaklander, L. N. 1991. 'A Defence of the New Tenseless Theory of Time', *Philosophical Quarterly*, 41, 26–38.

## Growing Block

Bourne, C. 2002. 'When am I? A Tense Time for Some Tense Theorists?' *Australian Journal of Philosophy*, 80, 359–71.

Button, T. 2006. 'There's No Time Like the Present', *Analysis*, 66,130–35.

Oaklander, L. N. ed. 2001. *The Importance of Time*. Dordrecht: Kluwer, Section I.

Tallant, J. forthcoming. 'There's No Future in No Futurism', *Erkenntnis*.

Tooley, M. 1997. *Time, Tense and Causation*. Oxford: Clarendon.

## Study Questions

1) Write out a definition of each of presentism, B-theory and Growing Block theory. Which theory do you prefer?
2) What do you think is the most serious problem for B-theory and how do you think we should respond to that problem?
3) How seriously do you think we should take the intuition that there is something 'special' about the present? Do you think that this intuition can be used to motivate presentism?
4) What do you think is the most serious problem with presentism? How do you think the presentist should respond?

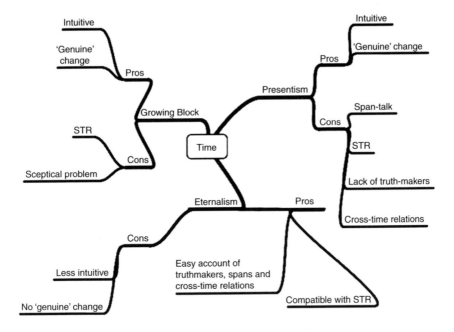

# 8

# Persistence

## Chapter Outline

Suppose we consider two different pairs of sentences.
First,

(1) Jonathan woke up this morning and ate toast for breakfast
(2) Jonathan is now eating pizza for his lunch.

Second,

(3) I am hungry.
(4) I am no longer hungry; I've had something to eat.

These pairs of sentences share a number of features in common. Both pairs
include a sentence about a particular time and a second sentence about a later
time. Another feature that the sentences have in common is that they appear
to refer to the same individual at these different times. If we turn our attention

to the first pair then it seems entirely plausible to think that the individual 'Jonathan' referred to in the first sentence is identical to the individual 'Jonathan' in the second. Likewise, I take it that we can all imagine first uttering sentence (3), and then uttering sentence (4). In these cases, I will assume, we think that what we refer to with the first person pronoun, I, is something that is identical over time.

What the truth of these sentences point to is the seeming truism that objects can persist through time. The pairs that we've discussed actually involve a special type of object, people. But it seems entirely reasonable to expect matters to generalize. I left my house this morning in order to come to work. I did so by opening the front door of my house. When I return to my house in a while, I very much expect it to have the same front door. Unless I've had a visit from a particularly obtuse burglar, or my wife has decided to engage in some surprise DIY, this is indeed what I will find.

So let us then turn our attention to a sentence that encapsulates this.

> (5) The front door through which I return to my house this evening, will be the same front door through which I left the house this morning.

The question that concerns us in this chapter is what it is that makes it true that the front door is *the same*. To get a flavour of the sorts of issues that will concern us, consider two different points. First, we know from physics that the subatomic particles that will constitute the door when I return through it this evening will *not* be the same ones that constituted it this morning. Thus, what we need to know is how the door can stay the same, despite being constituted by very different matter at different times. Second, it's entirely plausible for the door to have undergone some other sorts of changes (changes other than changes to its constitution), but for to still be true to it say of it that it is 'the same front door'. Imagine, for instance, that at around lunchtime my cat scratches the otherwise pristine front door. We would, I shall assume, say that the door in the morning is the same door as the door in the evening, even though the door in the evening is scratched while the door in the morning is not.

What we need is some account of how it is that the door can undergo these various changes, and yet remain the very same door. To make matters even clearer, let us now draw out some of the intuitions that seem to be in play here.[1]

> A1: An object can survive a change.
> A2: A change in an object is understood as the object bearing incompatible properties at different times (e.g. a non-scratch and scratch).

To these, let us now add a further assumption – one that, although not discussed, I hope to be sufficiently intuitive to not warrant further exposition.

> A3: No object can bear incompatible properties: that is, no object can be F and also be ¬F.

These three assumptions will help us to get a sense of the options open to us. If, as per A1, an object can survive a change, and, as per A2, a change requires an object to bear incompatible properties, then we are forced to deny A3. For, if both A1 and A2 are true, then there are objects that can survive change, and so bear incompatible properties. Once more, consider the case of my front door: when I left it was not scratched; when I returned, it was scratched. Thus, my door is both scratched and not scratched.

A3 is a well-enshrined assumption, and is quite so intuitive, that, I suspect, most of us would prefer not to deny A3. To accept A3, after all, is to allow that an object can be both bent and not bent; hot and not hot; charged and not charged: these do not seem like situations that we think genuinely possible.

That leaves us with the choice of denying either A1 or A2. But, at least on first inspection, you might well think that both of these are just as undeniable as A3. Certainly at the outset it is not appealing to have to deny either. However, the metaphysical positions that we shall explore try to get rid of the sense of there being a problem with making such a denial. In the next section I will introduce and explore two positions that, at least in some sense or other, look to deny A1: Exdurantism and Perdurantism. In the section that follows I will look at endurantism; a view that looks to deny A2.

# §8.1 Denying A1: Perdurance and exdurance

The claim made in A1 is that an object can survive a change. The two views that we will outline here look to deny this. On the face of it, that looks absurd. How can we possibly commit to the view that objects do not persist through time? Is it not *obvious* to me that the cup on my desk is the same cup that I drank coffee from earlier this morning? Further, is it not even more obvious that *I* am the same person that I was when I woke up this morning?

The trick to denying A1 lies in properly disambiguating it, and accounting for what is said, and, as ever, engaging in an appraisal of the costs and benefits of endorsing the resulting views.

In §4.4, when considering whether or not it is possible for me to have slipped and severed one of my fingers from my hand, we considered an apparently contradictory pair of sentences. This pair was generated by the fact that, according to the Lewisian analysis of modality, to say that it is possible for me to have three fingers and a thumb on my left hand is just to say that there is a world at which I have three fingers and a thumb on my left hand. Since it is possible that I have three fingers and a thumb on my left and, and also possible that I have four fingers and a thumb on my left hand, so we end up with the following pair:

(6)  Jonathan has three fingers and a thumb on his left hand.
(7)  Jonathan has four fingers and a thumb on his left hand (I preserve the numbering from the original).

Now, as you will recall, the device that we saw Lewis deploy in Chapter 4 was that of a counterpart relation. The idea was that I am not strictly and literally identical to the entity that has three fingers and a thumb on its left hand that exists at another world. Rather, I have four fingers and a thumb on my left hand, and what makes the proposition expressed by (6) true is that a counterpart of mine has three fingers and a thumb on its left hand.

This suggests a way in which we might deny A1. We can allow that when we talk of objects persisting over time we are not talking about the very same object, strictly and literally, existing at lots of different times. Rather, what we are talking about is an object existing at one time, and having counterparts at other times, such that those counterparts make true talk about how the object has been and will be. Here's Sider (2001: 193) describing the view:

> the truth-condition of an utterance 'Ted was once a boy' is this: there exists some person stage x prior to the time of utterance, such that x is a boy, and x bears the temporal counterpart relation to Ted. Since there is such a stage, the claim is true. Despite being a stage, Ted *was* a boy; he has the historical property of *once being a boy*.

To illustrate further, let us return to the case of my front door. Let us say that it is not scratched at 08:00, when I leave the house, but scratched at 18:00 when I return. Making use of counterpart-theoretic talk, we could then say that my door is not scratched at 08:00 and a counterpart of the door is scratched at 18:00. While it is not true that the door that exists at 08:00 is numerically identical with the door that exists at 18:00, there is a weaker relation between the two doors, the counterpart relation, that although weaker than strict and literal identity, still serves to make true our claim that the door survives the change.

This view is one that is sometimes called 'exdurantism' or 'stage theory'. The idea, in a nutshell, is that we may talk truthfully about objects persisting through time provided the object that exists at this time has counterparts at other times. Objects-at-times can be thought of as very much like 'time slices'. An object can be said to have survived a change iff its counterparts at other times have different properties to the ones that it instantiates. So we may say that I persist through time because the time-slice that I picked out with the term 'I' has counterpart temporal slices at times other than the present. Thus, by avoiding making use of strict and literal numerical identity in our account of persistence, we are able to deny A1 and so preserve persistence.

# §8.2 Perdurance

There is a second view available to us that denies A1, but does so in a different way. This view is called 'perdurance'. To get a sense of what the perdurantist will say about persistence, let us consider a spatial case.

Imagine a coffee table. The table is made from oak, and has four legs. It's around a metre long and 50 centimetres wide. The table has been used for many years and has a number of dents in its upper surface. However, the table is well loved, and so is frequently polished, leaving much of the surface very smooth. It seems correct, intuitively, to say that the parts of the surface that have received damage are not smooth; they are bumpy, and it also seems true that the remainder of the surface of the table is smooth. This leaves us in the odd position of having to say that the table is both smooth and not smooth.

A moment's reflection, of course, reveals that this is not odd at all. Rather, what we should say is quite simply that some parts of the table's surface are smooth; other parts are not. There is no contradiction here once we understand the properties of smoothness and flatness to be properties of distinct parts of the table.

In the same way, claims the perdurantist, we should say that the properties of objects are properly understood as properties of *temporal parts* of objects. Thus we may say that one temporal part of my door has no scratch; a later part of my door has a scratch. In the spatial case we were happy that this led to no contradiction and so in the temporal case we should think likewise. There is no contradiction in saying that the door survives becoming scratched because the property of 'being scratched' is one that is born only by select temporal parts of the door.

With the distinction between exdurance and perdurance in mind, it's worth pausing just a moment to bring out a few points. First, notice that, according to the perdurantist, the door does not exist (at least, not fully) at any one time. Rather, we say that a part of the door exists at one time; another part exists at a later time. This, of course, is simply the mirror of our view about spatial objects; the table is spread out across space by virtue of having different parts at different regions. It is certainly not the case that the whole of the table is located at each spatial region! But in the temporal case that sounds a little odd, for it sounds a little odd to say of my door (and me, and all other persisting entities) that they do not exist at this time; rather, only a part of them does. Explaining away the pull of that intuition is a task that the perdurantist will have to consider carrying out.

Likewise, although the exdurantist can say that, at each moment, there is a wholly present object, there is a sense in which *that* object is not the same as the one in the future. So although the exdurantist will try to persuade us that any intuitive cost of denying A1 can either be soothed or outweighed by other considerations, it still seems as if there is some intuitive cost for them to bear by denying A1.

For the time being, though, let us see if we can find some way to make sense of objects persisting through change that does not require us to give up on the claim that a single entity survives the changes in its properties.

# §8.3 Endurance

All of which brings us neatly onto endurance as a theory of persistence. Endurantists will ask us to deny A2 (that a change in an object is understood as the object bearing incompatible properties at different times). The endurantist claims that objects persist through time by being at every time through which they persist. To give more colour, the idea is that the one and the same object exists at more than one moment. My front door, then, is located at many different times and it is strictly and literally the very same door at each of these times. One way in which the view is sometimes stated is as the view that an object endures iff it is 'wholly present' at each time through which it persists.[2]

So the endurantist will be able to preserve the intuition behind A1. This gives us a prima facie reason to prefer endurantism to its competitors. What matters, then, is the cost of denying A2. How, then, does the endurantist think we should make sense of this?

The basic idea that the endurantist deploys, to be refined and developed in a moment, is that the properties of objects are properties-at-times. Slightly more perspicuously, we can say that objects satisfy the predicates that they do by virtue of standing in particular relations to particular times.

Let's consider a new example – that of a metal rod being bent at one moment, and straight at another. One solution open to the endurantist is for them to say that the rod stands in the *relation* being-bent-at to the time *t*, and it stands in the relation *being-straight-at* to the time t*. In the case of my front door that we've been considering, we might say that the door stands in the relation 'being-matt-finished-at' to the time 08:00, but that it stands in the relation 'being-scratched-at' to the time 18:00.

We can caricature the endurantist position by saying that they have swapped the claim that objects bear properties, for the claim that objects stand in relations to times. Plainly, this avoids any contradiction for it is no longer true to say that the door is scratched and that the door is not scratched; rather, what we should say is that the door stands in two distinct relations: not-being-scratched-at to 08:00 and being-scratched-at to 18:00.

# §8.4 Objections to the endurantist solution

The first objection that we might make to swapping relations for properties is that it is grossly inappropriate. According to Lewis (1986a: 204) it's obvious to us that 'shape' is a property of objects. Indeed, shape is an intrinsic property. Of this we can be absolutely certain. Shape is a property, not a relation. Since the endurantist will have us believe that shape *is* a relation – it is a relation to a time – so endurantism is false.

This objection, at least as it stands, is too fast. This is made plain by Hawley (2001: 17). While it certainly seems clear that shape is not a relation to other concrete objects, it is altogether less clear that shape is not a relation to times. To see this, it's worth asking two questions. First, could the rod be bent without any other material object existing? It certainly seems so, yes. I can imagine the rod being bent quite independently of the existence of other objects. This seems to establish beyond doubt that shape cannot be a relation to other material objects. Now consider the second question. Could the rod be bent without the existence of a time? If the answer is 'yes', then shape cannot be a relation to a time. If shape is a relation to a time, then an object has a shape iff it stands in the requisite relation to a time. If there are no times, then it cannot stand in the requisite relation to a time. Thus, if a rod could be bent without existing at a time, then shape cannot be a relation to a time.

So what is the answer to the second question? It is, I think, rather hard to tell. It seems as if we are in a situation where all that we have to go on, if we have anything at all to go on, is a modal intuition to the effect that it is possible for there to exist a rod with a particular shape without the existence of a time (whatever 'a time' is). I will leave to the reader to assess just how great a cost denying this intuition is to bear for the endurantist. But it's hard to see, at least given what has been said so far, that this would be too substantial a cost. Certainly, we might be inclined to see this as a price worth paying in order to preserve A1.

A second objection to endurantism concerns whether or not the endurantist *should* deny A2. In our intuitive reflections on what it is for an object to undergo a change, we naturally suppose that a change requires an object to have incompatible properties at different times. As we have seen, above, the endurantist no longer claims this. Being F-at-t and ¬F-at-t* are not incompatible properties.

Although that seems right, it's not quite clear how much of a cost this is. If an object falls under one predicate, 'is F', at one time, and then falls under another, different predicate, at another time, 'is G', such that it would entail a contradiction to assert that the object 'is F & G', then we have provided an account of change to at least some extent. What the opponent of endurantism needs to do, in order to pursue this line, is show what is wrong with this account of change.

A further argument against endurantism, though one that is a little more exotic, is an argument from time travel. Suppose that, upon finishing reading this passage, you get up and climb into your time-machine and head back in time to a point at which you were sitting reading this book. At that moment in time, it is now true to say of you that you are sitting and that you are standing. The trouble, of course, is that if endurance is true, then you, the one and the same object, are standing in the relations 'is sitting at', and 'is not sitting at' to the very same time. These two incompatible relations are not such that a single entity can stand in both of them to the very same time. No object can be both

F-at-t and ¬F-at-t. Since this is precisely what the time-travel case forces upon them, the endurantist looks to be in trouble.

(At least *prima facie* neither perdurantism or exdurantism face this problem: the perdurantist will simply say that two distinct temporal parts have different properties; the exdurantist will say that two different objects that stand in a counterpart relation to one another have different properties. The problem is generated by the endurantist's insistence that there is *one* object and that it bears incompatible properties.)

At this point we must consider how serious an objection this really is. Can we, for instance, not simply deny that time travel is possible? Perhaps, but consider the dialectic here. We began, I assume, by thinking that time travel is perfectly possible (if a little odd). Now we find ourselves forced by our theory of persistence to conclude that it is not possible. Would it not be preferable were our theory of persistence compatible with those states of affairs that we think possible? And, if we think time travel possible, then our theory of persistence had better accommodate that. Further adjudication on this matter I leave to the reader.

# §8.5 Adverbialism

A solution taken by some endurantists is to deny that what we naturally think of as properties are, in fact, relations to times, and to instead assert that properties such as shape *are* intrinsic properties of objects, but to then further claim that particular instances of the property can stand in relations to times. This is adverbialism.

The way in which adverbialism is often expressed is to say that, rather than some object a 'being-F-at-t' as most endurantists will say, a should be said to be F-tly. One way to conceptualize this is to think of a's 'being F' standing in the 'instantiated at' relation to t. Thus, we can think of my door being scratched, and the door's being scratched being instantiated-at-18:00. To borrow from Hawley (2001: 22)

> *Being green* is a property, not a relation, but its particular instances can themselves stand in relations to times: the relation in question is that of *obtaining at*.

A putative advantage of adverbialism over treating properties as relations to times is that we preserve the intuition that objects do in fact have properties that are not mere relations to times. The advantage that adverbialism will then accrue is that if we think that the answer to the question 'can material objects bear properties in the absence of times?' is 'yes'. It is easy to accommodate this result for the adverbialist. Although most if not all of our property talk will require that objects are such that they bear their properties *and* that these then stand in the 'instantiated at' relation to some time or other, there is nothing conceptually prohibitive about their simply instantiating their properties and this not then being instantiated at any particular time. Thus, typically we will say that a's being F stands in the 'instantiated at' relation to some t. But there is no reason to think that this must be the case. It is perfectly conceivable that a's being F *not* stand in the 'instantiated at' relation to t. Rather, a could simply be F.

Of course, with advantages come costs. Here is one cost noted by Hawley (2001: 23). The endurantist who thinks that properties are relations to times has an explanation of why it is that abstract objects cannot have shape properties or other putative intrinsic properties of concrete objects. Abstract objects cannot bear such properties because, as we have already discussed, abstract objects do not exist in time, and such putative properties *are* relations to time. Since abstract objects do not exist in time, so they cannot stand in such relations. The adverbialist, in contrast, has no such distinction at hand. Why is it that, as a matter of fact, shape properties and the like are not instantiated by abstract objects (assuming they exist)? We have no ready explanation to hand.

Of course, there are options available to the adverbialist. They may say that they do not believe that there *are* abstracta, and so the argument here can get no purchase. There may be other ways to pursue this argument, but I shall leave this matter here.

# §8.6 The philosophy of time to the rescue?

On a slight tangent it's worth considering whether or not the endurantist has a ready response to hand to the principal objection we've been considering: the problem of treating properties as relations to times. It would also be good if we could make sense of the notion of being 'wholly present', that was mentioned in §8.3.

The natural response is presentism. In Chapter 7 we defined presentism as the view that only present objects exist. Suppose that we endorsed that view. If only present objects exist, then objects endure by simply existing – objects do not have non-existent parts. And since times other than the present do not exist, so there is no worry about generating a contradiction. Remember, the original problem was that objects appeared to be capable of bearing incompatible properties. Objects like my door seemed to be both scratched and not-scratched. But, if we endorse presentism, then this is readily resolved. My door, as it is in the present – scratched – exists. My door, as it was in the past – unscratched – does not. Thus, my door is not both 'scratched and not-scratched' because the door only exists as it is in the present: scratched.

So it seems that if endurantism is combined with presentism, then this does much to advantage endurantism. However, as we saw in the previous chapter, presentism also faces serious problems. In the end, whether or not we look to endorse the conjunction of presentism and endurantism is a question that will require us to balance up the pros and cons of both positions and weigh them against the competition; all of which suggests that we ought to now return our attention to the competition.

# §8.7 Returning to A1

Since we now have a sense of some of the problems associated with endurance, and have seen that there is the need for a careful weighing of our options, it looks as if it will be important for us to return our attention to exdurantism and perdurantism. Although these ideas were introduced above, we did not give much thought as to why we might be inclined to think that they are true.

A suite of arguments can be brought against endurantism and in favour of both perdurantism and exdurantism – though as we shall see, it may be the case that exdurantism is the ultimate winner here. We need to begin our study of these arguments with the consideration of two examples.

Here's a pretty famous case. Consider a statue made out of clay. It seems possible to us to destroy the statue without destroying the lump of clay. For instance, we could flatten the lump of clay. If we do so, then we destroy the statue, but not the lump of clay. This, some philosophers think, gives us reason to posit the existence of *two* objects in the original situation that I described. That is, we don't just have a statue that is made from clay; we have a statue *and* a lump of clay. Both of these things are co-located.

You might think this a bit quick: surely we don't think that there can be objects that are co-located, do we? It seems preposterous to think so. Well, matters are made more complex by consideration of some very plausible thoughts about identity. It seems correct to think that if two things are identical with one another, then they have the same properties. Thus, Barack Obama and America's first African-American president have the same properties, precisely because they are the same person. Everything that I can truthfully say about Barack Obama, I can truthfully say about America's first African-American president. So, if we had a single entity in the statue-lump case, then it should be the case that both statue and lump have the very same properties. But, as we have seen, they don't have the same properties. For one thing, we can squash the lump, but not the statue. Thus, it is not the case that everything that we can truthfully say about the statue we can truthfully say about the lump. This suggests that the statue and the lump are not the one and the same thing. Of course, we're still left with the thought that this is very odd, and that the co-location of two physical objects is in need of some explanation. Hold that thought while we consider the next example.

Suppose that brain transplants were viable, and that the following occurred. Half of Verity's brain is taken out of her body and put into a donor body. Let us suppose that, from this, Verity's memories, personality traits and the like, were then taken on by the donor. It seems that we have some reason to think that this new entity is Verity. Suppose, also, that the other half of her brain were taken out, and placed in an additional donor. Suppose that this person, too, came to have all of Verity's personality traits, memories and the like. (Let us also imagine that Verity's body does not survive the transplant; simply to complete the picture.) Intuitively, what we have here is a case where Verity fissions. We have a situation where we go from having one Verity in the world, to having two Veritys in the world.

This, in itself, is something that requires explanation. However, things become even more odd. There are various truths to which we assent, for instance:

(8) Only I can properly be punished for my crimes.
(9) Only I can properly be said to regret my past actions.
(10) Only I can properly be said to fear my future pains.

What all of these truths point to is seemingly a fact about our persistence; that where someone persists through time, there is a sense in which past and future events *matter* to them. And, given consideration of the three sentences above, it seems that what happens to a person only matters to us if they are identical to us.

We can, borrowing from Sider (2001: 144) summarize this as:

(=WM) Person x matters to person y iff x is identical to y.

Now, this seems to then generate the conclusion that, in fact, there were two Veritys all along! To see how, consider the following. After the fission, we agree that there are two Veritys. To check that, consider whether or not the future pain for one Verity will matter to the other; it seems not. Intuitively, at any rate, each Verity will care about different future states. Fission 1 Verity will not care about what happens to Fission 2 Verity in quite the same way as they care about what happens to Fission 1 Verity. Now it seems clear that there exist people in each Verity's past that matter to her: that is, each Verity-Fission will think that there are things in her past for which she should be punished, for instance. The natural thought, of course, is that there is only *one* person in the past, from which each of them fissioned. But a moment's reflection reveals that this cannot be right. Identity is a transitive relation, which means that if a is identical to b and b is identical to c, then a is identical to c. Were it the case that our first Verity fission were identical to some past Verity, and the very same past Verity were identical to the second Verity fission, then the first Verity fission would be identical to the second. And, as we've just seen via consideration of what matters to the two Verity fissions, the two Verity fissions are not identical to one another.

The result of this seems to be that there must have been two Veritys all along, one identical to each of the Verity fissions. This is something of a surprise. It appears that we have two Veritys occupying the very same regions of space at the very same time, thinking the very same thoughts.

It's hard, initially, to see what to say in response. However, what the perdurantist and exdurantist will say is that they can explain this perfectly well. This, they claim, gives them an advantage over the endurantist. We'll begin with the perdurance approach. To best appreciate the view, it's perhaps worth noting that the view is sometimes called the 'worm view' of persistence; so-called because 'objects' are identified with space–time worms – particular volumes of space–time.

The first case we considered was that of the statue and the lump. It is easy to see, given the worm view, how we can make sense of co-incidence. Another analogy: consider two roads that intersect one another. The two roads begin separately; come together for a while, and then separate once more. We clearly have two roads, even though the two roads share some common parts for a while. There is, we might think, nothing terribly surprising or complicated about this. Two roads can share the same spatial location for a while, and may do so without complication.

This, the worm theorist will claim, is very similar to the case of the statue and the lump. Suppose that we begin with a lump of clay. Out of the lump, we make a statue. Then, we destroy the statue. What we will have is two space–time worms. The space–time worm that is the statue occupies a particular volume of space–time. The space–time worm that is the clay occupies another volume of space–time: what is noticeable, of course, is that the two volumes are not identical with one another. The volume occupied by the statue is contained entirely within the volume occupied by the clay, but they are not the same volumes for the clay-worm is of greater duration than that of the statue.

But notice this: because we have two different volumes of space–time here, two different worms, so we have two different objects. The challenge, recall, was to explain how two different objects can co-locate. The answer, given per-durance, is that two different objects can co-locate *by sharing temporal parts*. In precisely the same way that two physically extended objects – like roads – can co-locate by virtue of sharing spatial parts, so two temporally extended objects can co-locate by virtue of sharing temporal parts.

It's easy to see, I take it, how this will extend to generate a solution to the problem of personal identity that we touched upon above. Both of the Verity fissions share a common part in their past: indeed, they share parts right up until the moment of fission. But, at that point, they cease to share parts and it is because of this that we can legitimately say that there are two temporally extended objects that merely overlap. They nonetheless co-locate without difficulty because to do so they must merely share temporal parts.

Notice that it *looks* as if there is no analogous solution for the endurantist. They must, or so it seems, simply bite the bullet and say that there really are co-located statues and lumps and that there really are two Veritys.

So much for the perdurantist solution. We will now consider the exduran-tist solution.

# §8.8 Exdurance

Given exdurance notice that at least while the statue and the lump are co-located the statue and the lump *are the same stages*. That is, once we have formed a statue from the lump, we may identify particular stages as both statue and lump. Now, if that's right (if, as it seems, the statue *is* the lump), then how can we make sense of their not being the same after the fission?

To get traction on their solution, consider two sentences:

(11) The statue will not exist tomorrow.
(12) The lump will exist tomorrow.

Then,

> 'Existing tomorrow' expresses different properties in different contexts since the relevant temporal counterpart relation can vary from context to context.
>
> A temporal counterpart relation specifies what sort of 'continuity' a thing must exhibit over time in order to continue to exist. But there are different kinds of continuity on which speakers focus. A certain kind of continuity is destroyed when a statue gets squashed, since the item has not retained a statue shape. Let us say that the *statue counterpart relation* does not hold between the statue stage before and the lump stage afterwards. But there is another kind of continuity that is not destroyed: the holding of a *lump-of-matter counterpart relation* underwrites our intuitive judgement that the same lump is present. (Sider 2001: 200)

So, return to our two sentences. The idea is that although there is no future 'statue counterpart' of the stage that presently exists, there are stages that are 'lump counterparts' of the stage that currently exists. Because of the existence of these counterparts we can solve the statue-lump case.

Similarly, it looks as if the case of fission in personal identity will admit of a satisfying solution. Our pre-fission Verity has two future counterparts: first fission Verity and second fission Verity. This seems the right result. Verity will, I assume, think that it 'matters' (in the relevant sense) what happens to both of the post-fission Veritys. Notice, though, that this does not require there to be two Veritys co-located pre-fission. It is not true that the counterpart relation is transitive. Thus, although first fission Verity is a counterpart of Verity's and second fission Verity is a counterpart of Verity's, it is not the case that first fission Verity is a counterpart of second fission Verity. This gives us at least some reason to prefer the stage view to the worm view. On the worm view, there really were two people there all along; there are, after all, two different space–time worms that are sharing the same parts. And although it is unremarkable that two objects can share the same region if they have the same parts, it nonetheless still seems a little odd to think that there were two people there. Certainly, if I had begun this chapter and said that if I *will* fission, then there are in fact two of me, you would have been rather surprised! On the stage view, there is only one person prior to fission; but, at the point of fission, there are two different counterpart relations going forward.

# §.8.9 In favour of exdurance?

There may be another reason to prefer stage theory to worm theory. We saw that worm theory gives us a handy solution to the problem of coincident entities, where the lump outlasts the statue. But matters are not so straightforward when it comes to another version of the same problem.

Suppose that, as a matter of fact, the lump and the statue persist for precisely the same length of time – that the time at which the lump comes into being is the same time at which the statue comes into being. Consider this scenario from the perspective of perdurance/worm theory. Plainly, it is *possible* for us to destroy the statue without destroying the lump even if we were not to in fact carry out this act of vandalism. This suggests that the statue and the lump are different objects. It is possible to squash the statue and destroy it, but not thereby destroy the lump. If they were identical with one another, that wouldn't look to be possible. We cannot, for instance, destroy Superman but leave Clark Kent unharmed.

Now what we have here, in the perdurantist case, is a situation in which the statue and lump share all of the same parts. Where two objects share all of the same parts, we might well think them identical. Indeed, although we might be happy to posit two roads, in the spatial case, where they only overlap for a short distance, were we to identify a single track as being 'two roads' despite there being no divergence, then we would likely object. Really, if 'two roads' share all of the same parts, then intuitively, there is only one road. The same sort of thoughts apply in the case of the statue and the lump. Intuitively it seems that, where the statue and lump persist through the same space–time, and share all of the same parts, we want to say that they are the one and the same – despite this new argument to the contrary. Thus, there is only one object because there is only one space–time worm. We seem to have conflicting intuitions. On the one hand, because they occupy precisely the same volume of space–time and share all of the same parts, we want to say that the statue and lump are identical. However, because it is possible to destroy the statue without also destroying the lump, we also want to say that they are different objects. Perdurantism looks to have no way to resolve this tension.

But it looks like stage theory can help us here. We must call upon counterpart theory once more. Each statue stage is also a lump stage; but there are a variety of different counterparts had by each stage. Suppose that we consider one stage from the perspective of its being a statue. What it is possible for that statue to do, and what it is possible for that statue to survive, will depend upon what counterparts exist. Since we are considering the stage *as a statue* we must ask what *statue counterparts* the stage has. Specifically, we must ask whether or not there are any (possible) statue counterpart stages that survive a squashing. If there are not, then it is not possible for the statue to survive a squashing.

Likewise, if we want to know what it's possible for the lump of clay to do, we must consider the stage *as a lump*: what (possible) lump counterparts does the stage have? Specifically, does the stage have (possible) lump counterparts that survive the squashing? The answer, of course, is 'yes'.

The result that we find, claim proponents of exdurance, is that there are (possible) lump counterparts that survive the squashing, but no (possible) statue counterparts that survive the squashing. Therefore, it is right to say that we *could* squash the lump and have it survive, but that we could not squash the statue and have it survive. Our analysis seems to leave us with at least some reason to prefer exdurance to perdurance. The thought is that it is the elegance of the *total solution* to all of these types of problem that make the stage theory, with its deployment of counterpart theory, so appealing.

# §8.10 Counterparts reconsidered

Of course, we might think that there is a problem with counterpart theory itself. What is clear from our discussion of stage theory is that the one and the same thing has different counterparts, depending upon how we think and talk about it. If we think of or talk about a stage as a lump, then 'the stage's' counterparts are one collection of entities; if we talk about a stage as a statue, then 'the stage' has different counterparts. But, look, there is only *one* stage. And, if there is only one stage, how can it have different counterparts *simply because we think and talk about it in two different ways*?

Sider (2001: 207) himself considers (and rejects) something very much like this objection. Here's how he puts it:

> Perhaps one of our deeply held beliefs about modality and temporality is that there is always a *single, univocal, non-conventional* answer to the questions 'What will happen to this thing tomorrow?' 'What might have happened to this thing?' The counterpart theorist must admit that pretty much any answer to these questions could, in principle, be correct, given an appropriate choice of counterpart relation. Actual spoken languages may well have significant restrictions on what counterpart relations are chosen, and it need not be that an individual speaker has the freedom to choose whatever counterpart relation she likes. Nevertheless, it

> seems that a counterpart theorist cannot accept the existence of 'deep', 'nonconventional' facts about *de re* persistence and modality.

The reply Sider gives to such an objection is straightforward – though I put it in my own words. The context of a question determines the propriety of any putative answer. If I ask you 'how many people are eating popcorn?' in a cinema, then *plainly* the context of my asking you the question goes some way to determining the answer. I'm not asking you about how many people *in the world* are eating popcorn; I'm asking you about how many people *in the cinema* are eating popcorn. Likewise, if I ask you whether or not it's *possible* for *that* to survive a squashing (and I point at the statue/lump on the table), it's unclear what is being asked. Are we asking 'is it possible for that *qua lump* to survive?' Or are we asking 'is it possible for that *qua statue* to survive?' Once we pick upon a question to ask, then, just as context determines that only certain people were appropriate to be counted in the popcorn case, context determines that only certain counterparts are salient in this case.

But perhaps there remains a feeling that it is precisely the elasticity of the counterpart relation that has generated these excellent results for exdurance, and modality, that is its Achilles' heel. For it might seem as if the counterpart relation is playing an analogous role to the 'God of the gaps'. The reference, here, is to a particular species of theology that, when faced with something seemingly inexplicable, simply claims that 'God explains it', or that 'it is God's will', and does not try to offer a further explanation or analysis. The feeling, here, in discussion of the counterpart relation is, you may think, very similar. We have, perhaps, some loose idea of what the counterpart relation is, but it now seems that, rather than trying to explain how it is that objects persist, we're *merely making do* with the idea that they persist *because they resemble other things in the right sort of way*. Notably, we are also staying pretty quiet on what is meant by 'the right sort of way'. Thus, when Sider (in the quote immediately above) says that 'A certain kind of continuity is destroyed when a statue gets squashed, since the item has not retained a statue shape', we might well object that it is opaque what is meant by 'a certain kind of continuity'. We might, we think, have some grasp of what continuity is; but as to what *kinds of continuity* are? Well, that looks a rather odd question. Were one feeling particularly petulant, one might even be inclined to say that the counterpart relation is *so* elastic, that it's hard to see it as a single relation at all.

If that's the intuition that you have, then caution is to be advised. Metaphysicians, in general, claim to be able to make sense of the counterpart relation. And it is a relation that performs a great service in many schemes. Were one to then wish to push the line that there is nothing substantial, or nothing comprehensible, about the counterpart relation, then it would require a good deal of further research. Articulating quite what is wrong with the concept would also need to be stated with great care and precision.

# §8.11 Conclusion

As we have seen, the conjunction of the three intuitive axioms, A1–A3 generates a serious problem. We have canvassed three solutions to the problem, but, as we have seen, each view carries with it attendant problems that must be faced.

It's perhaps worth alerting the reader to the close connection *sometimes* drawn between the philosophy of time one adopts and the account of persistence one chooses. If one thought endurance *obviously* the correct account of persistence, then it might be tempting to adopt presentism in order to do away with the various problems with properties being disguised relations to times. Likewise, if one thought that exdurance were the correct view then it might seem as if B-theory is an obvious and appropriate view. Because of such considerations it's sometimes hard to get a sense of which view is the correct view of either time or persistence without considering the relation between the two debates.

# Recommended reading

### General

Hawley, K. 2001. *How Things Persist*. Oxford: OUP, chapter 1.

Kurtz, R. 2006. 'Introduction to *Persistence*: What's the Problem?', in Haslanger, S. and Kurtz, R. eds. *Persistence*. Bradford: MIT, 1–26.

### Exdurance

Balashov, Y. 2002. 'On Stages, Worms and Relativity', in Callender, C. ed. *Time, Reality and Experience*. Cambridge: CUP, 233–52.

Hawley, K. 2002. *How Things Persist*. Oxford: OUP, esp. chapter 2.

Sider, T. 1996. 'All the World's a Stage', *Australasian Journal of Philosophy*, 74, 433–53.

Sider, T. 2001. *Four-Dimensionalism*. Oxford: OUP.

## Perdurance

Brogaard, B. 2000. 'Presentist Four-Dimensionalism', *The Monist*, 83, 341–56.

Hawley, K. 1999. 'Persistence and non-Supervenient Relations', *Mind*, 108, 53–67.

Lewis, D. 1986a. *On the Plurality of Worlds*. Oxford: Blackwell, 202–4.

Merricks, T. 2000. 'Perdurance and Psychological Continuity', *Philosophy and Phenomenological Research*, 61,195–9.

Rea, Michael C. 1998. 'Temporal Parts Unmotivated', *Philosophical Review*, 107, 225–60.

Sider, T. 1997. 'Four Dimensionalism', *Philosophical Review*, 106, 197–231.

## Endurance

Hinchliff, M. 1996. 'The Puzzle of Change', *Philosophical Perspectives*, 10, 119–36.

Lowe, E. J. 1998. *The Possibility of Metaphysics*. Oxford: OUP, chapter 5.

Mellor, D. H. 2006. 'Selections from *Real Time*', in Haslanger, S. and Kurtz, R. eds. *Persistence*. Bradford: MIT Press, 233–40.

Merricks, T. 1999b. 'Endurance, Psychological Continuity, and the Importance of Personal Identity', *Philosophy and Phenomenological Research*, 59, 983–97.

## 'Wholly present' and the distinction between endurance and other theories

Balashov, Y. 2007. 'Defining Exdurance', *Philosophical Studies* 133, 143–49.

Crisp, T. and Smith, D. 2005. '"Wholly Present" defined', *Philosophy and Phenomenological Research*, 71, 318–44.

Hofweber, T. and Velleman, D. forthcoming. 'How to Endure', *Philosophical Quarterly*.

McKinnon, N. 2002. 'The Endurance/Perdurance Distinction', *Australasian Journal of Philosophy*, 80, 288–306.

Merricks, T. 1999a. 'Persistence, Parts, and Presentism' *Noûs*, 33, 421–38.

## Time-travel cases and exotica

Eagle, A. 2010. 'Location and Perdurance', *Oxford Studies in Metaphysics*, 5, 53–94.

Effingham, N. and Melia, J. 2007. 'Endurantism and Timeless Worlds', *Analysis*, 67, 140–7.

Effingham, N. and Robson, J. 2007. 'A Mereological Challenge to Endurantism', *Australasian Journal of Philosophy*, 85, 633–40.

Gilmore, C. 2007, 'Time Travel, Coinciding Objects, and Persistence'. *Oxford Studies in Metaphysics*, 3,177–98.

Sider, T. 2001. *Four Dimensionalism*. Oxford: OUP, 96–8.

## Study questions

1) Write out each of the views covered in this chapter. Which view do you prefer? Why do you prefer that view?
2) The conjunction of A1–A3 seems to lead to a contradiction. Which axiom do you think it most reasonable to deny?
3) Do you think that it is advisable for the endurantist to endorse presentism?
4) Do you think that the idea of a counterpart relation is a useful one?

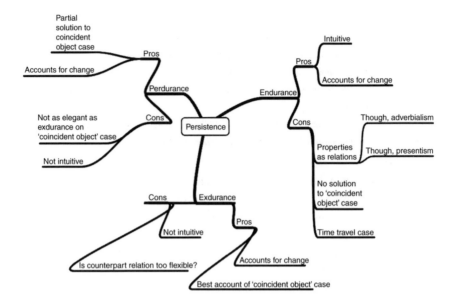

# 9

# Causation

To begin this chapter, let's consider an example. Suppose that we found ourselves in the trenches of the First World War. Our commanding officer, a captain, turns to us and shouts 'charge!'. As a result of this, we clamber out of our trench and proceed to charge across no-mans-land. Several hours later, back in our trench, we reflect: what *caused* us to charge? Although a variety of factors seem to have been involved, what seems true is that

    (1) The captain caused us to charge by shouting 'charge'.

Our topic in this chapter is, of course, causation, so what we must now concern ourselves with is what is distinctively *causal* about this picture. We do not mean to say, I suspect, merely that first the commanding officer shouted 'charge' and then we charged – for presumably we could have just ignored him. Rather, what we want to say is that there's some important connection between the shouting of 'charge' and the charging. It is not merely a coincidence that the charging occurred when it did. The case just described appears very different from one in which, say, I drop my pen and then the door blows shut. Plainly in this latter case there is no connection whatsoever between the two events. It is mere coincidence that one event occurred (the dropping of the pen) and then the other (the blowing shut of the door). In the war-like case just described the connection between the first event and the second seems causal; there is a particularly intimate connection between the two events. So, what should we consider to be the truth-makers for propositions expressed by sentences like (1)? What sort of connection do we have between the two events?

Intuitively, there seems to be some kind of necessary connection in play – or something like that, anyway. If the captain actually caused us to charge by shouting charge, then once he shouted charged *we had to charge*. If I cause you to fall over, then I *made you* fall over; if the flicking of the light switch caused the light to come on, then the light switch *made* the light come on. In all of these cases it seems that the result *had* to happen, if the first event caused it to. That, at least, is something that seems pretty intuitive. Perhaps, then, this connection in conjunction with the two events (the shouting 'charge' and the charging) is the truth-maker for the proposition expressed by (1).

So what we might think is that in describing (1) I've missed out on a few details. We don't just have the event of the commanding officer shouting 'charge', and the event of our unit charging: crucially, in addition to the events mentioned, there must be *a relation* ' . . . caused . . . ' that relates the event of captain's shouting to the event of the charging itself. Such a relation would be a two-place relation linking the event of the shouting and the event of the charging. Moreover, this relation will be something akin to necessitation; the first event in some way necessitates the occurrence of the second.

The first worry with such accounts of causation is epistemic. In the case that I described we would hear the captain shout his order; we would then see one another charging. But at no point would we *see* the causation; nor would we hear it, taste it, smell it or touch it. I do not hear myself being *caused* to charge. I simply hear the order, and then charge.

These sorts of consideration lead us to the first of Hume's remarks that we'll note, Hume famously claims:

> When we look about us towards external objects, and consider the operation of causes, we are never able, in a single instance, to discover any power or necessary connexion; any quality, which binds the effect to the cause, and renders the one an infallible consequence of the other. We only find, that the one does actually, in fact, follow the other. (Hume 1999: 136)

It would be deeply mysterious were we to have to posit the existence of such a relation as causation if we have no empirical *evidence* that such a relation exists. We might well think that, if we do not *perceive* a relation of causation, then we ought not to think that such a relation exists. And all that we seem to observe is that one event occurred and that another followed.

Of course, we might instead think that we could reason our way to the existence of a relation of causation. After all, we have seen in previous chapters (e.g. Chapter 3) that arguments can be put forward for the existence of entities that we do not perceive. If we can point to some explanatory role that needs to be played and that could only be played by an unobservable relation of causation, then that might give us a reason to posit a relation of causation.

So, let us reflect on an instance of causation – is there such a role that is in need of being played? Let us consider another case and see if we can reason our way to the existence of a relation of causation.

(2) I caused my cup to break by dropping it.

Slowly, and carefully, we should now think and reflect on this case. In the first instance, I release my cup. That doesn't suggest any particular idea of causation to me. I certainly don't need to posit a relation of causation between the dropping of the cup and the breaking of the cup to explain what's happened so far. Let us also then suppose that the cup falls away from my hand. Once more, that doesn't seem to be anything other than the cup falling. No need to posit a relation of causation. Then let us suppose that the cup strikes the floor and breaks. Again, we don't need to posit a relation of causation between the dropping of the cup and the breaking of the cup in order to explain what goes on. These sorts of consideration lead to another of Hume's (1999: 136) observations.

> There is not, in any single, particular instance of cause and effect, any thing which can suggest the idea of power or necessary connexion.

So it would seem that our quest to reason our way to the need for a causal relation has also failed us.

# §9.1 Reductive analysis

That being the case, it's then tempting to try to analyse causal talk in terms of other goings on. We seemingly don't need to posit a *distinct* relation that is the relation of causation. So maybe what we should try to do is to understand causation in terms of goings on that we do think occur.

As a first attempt we might then be inclined to say that the proposition expressed by (1) is true precisely *because* the event of the charging followed the event of the captain's shouting. We would be reductively analysing causation as the 'following on from' relation. But as tempting as such an account is, it is false. The claim is that causal sentences are true just in case they describe one event following another, and, as we saw in the case of the dropping pencil/door blowing shut mentioned a moment ago, merely that one event follows another does not give us any good reason to think that causation has occurred.

So let us re-focus our attention on the military case. It would be tempting, I think, to take the view that (1) is true because *whenever* the event of the captain's shouting occurs, it is *always* followed by the event of the soldiers responding. What we have is a constant conjunction of these two sorts of event. That doesn't require causation to be a distinct relation, or entity; it merely requires that we can say of two events that one caused the other, iff the one is always followed by the other.

Although something about this analysis is tempting, it's easy to see that it, too, fails. To see this, suppose that the first event is enacted, not in the trenches, but while the captain is at home, all alone. Thus, while seated in his living room, the captain shouts 'charge'. This event of the captain's shouting 'charge' is not followed by the event of troops charging. That means, of course, that the event of the captain's shouting is *not* always be followed by the event of the men's charging. According to the analysis suggested, that means that in the trenches, the captain's shouting 'charge' did not cause the troops to charge, and that makes this a poor analysis of such causal talk; it simply gives us the wrong result.

# §9.2 The counterfactual theory of causation illustrated

So the event of the captain's shouting is *not* constantly conjoined to the event of the troop's shouting. But what does seem right is that had the captain not shouted, then the soldiers would not have charged.[1]

Using this, we can formulate an analysis that we shall call the counterfactual theory of causation, CTC. For any two events, c and e, c causes e if and only if:

CTC: two events, c, and e, both occur, and, had c not occurred, then e would not have occurred.

To see how to make sense of the analysis, let us use the event of the captain's shouting the order to charge as event c, and the event of the soldiers charging as event e. Then we may say that the event of the captain's shouting causes the event of the soldiers charging iff (a) both events occur (which they do), and (b) had the event of the captain's shouting not occurred, then the event of the soldier's charging would not have occurred.

Happily, this appears to generate the right result, for in the case described it would very much appear that, had the captain not shouted his order, we would simply have remained in the trench. So it would appear that the CTC gives us a good analysis of causation, but does not require us to posit a primitive causal relation in order to preserve the truth of talk about causation.

This is another instance of a reductive theory. We are looking to analyse one thing (the relation of causation) in terms of another (a counterfactual relation). Notice, too, that because the second clause of the analysis talks about what *would* have happened, had the captain not given the order, so we are making a modal claim – a claim about what is possible. We find ourselves once more connecting back to the material on modality that we covered in Chapter 4.

But more detail will be required of us, for there are a number of counterexamples that threaten the CTC. The general shape that these counterexamples take is to give a case where it is pretty clear to us that we have an instance where causation has occurred, but where the last clause in the above is not satisfied; a case in which *had c not occurred, then e would not have occurred* is false. In other words, these counterexamples look to show that the conditions specified may be sufficient, but they are not necessary. The first few of these cases are merely ones that lead to the development of the CTC and were suggested by David Lewis in his attempts to formulate the CTC and, as such, are not *genuine* counterexamples. These are simply examples that help us get clear on the sorts of minor amendments that we must make to the CTC. As the objections develop we shall see that the criticisms become increasingly problematic and take on the form of genuine objections to the CTC. It is far from clear that the CTC can be saved from all of these objections.

To begin we might simply note that it's just not at all clear that 'had c not occurred, then e would not have occurred' is true. This part of the analysis involves a modal claim – a claim, not about what *is* the case, but about what *would be* the case. And, although it seems pretty clear to us that had the event of the captain's shouting the order not occurred, then the charging would not have occurred, this may simply be because we are not considering the full range of possibilities. For instance, it may be *possible* that the soldiers decide, all of their own accord, to simply exit the trench and charge towards the enemy. More realistically, it is *possible* for the attack to have been pre-arranged, such that the soldiers all knew to charge at the right time. If such a case is possible, and it certainly seems to be, then it's not at all clear that *had the captain not shouted his orders that the soldiers would not have charged.* If the plan *is* pre-arranged then the soldiers would charge regardless of any shouting of orders.

The strategy adopted by Lewis in response to this sort of concern is to try and ensure that the only possible worlds that are salient to the analysis of causation are those very worlds that gave us the right result. The way in which he does this trades upon the analysis of possibility as claims about sets of possible worlds (recall Chapter 4). The idea, then, is that the range of possible worlds that we are permitted to consider when trying to determine whether or not the counterfactual *is* true are the relevantly close possible worlds. The question, of course, is quite what 'relevant closeness' consists in.

There are four criteria that we might use for determining whether or not a world is 'relevantly similar' to our own.

(i) It is of the first importance to avoid big, widespread, diverse violations of law.
(ii) It is of the second importance to maximize the spatio-temporal region throughout which perfect match of particular fact prevails.
(iii) It is of the third importance to avoid even small, localized simple violations of law.
(iv) It is of little or no importance to secure approximate similarity of particular fact, even in matters that concern us greatly. (Lewis 1986b: 47–8)

We might then look to deploy these conditions to deal with both of the cases, above.

Consider the case where the soldiers have all been pre-issued their orders. Such a case clearly requires a divergence from the actual world, for in the actual world no such written orders were issued. Condition (ii) would seem to rule out such a world as salient to our analysis. What we are looking for in a relevantly similar possible world at which the captain does not shout his order is a world that varies as little as possible from the actual world. We must hold all (or as much as we can) fixed, aside from the captain's not shouting his order.

Although this is all very well, on the surface it does not appear to deal with the case in which the soldiers decide, entirely of their own accord, to all leave the trench at the same time, despite no orders to the contrary. This case appears to do very well on the four above conditions: it requires no obvious violations of law, it maximizes spatio-temporal region through which perfect match occurs, and we are giving little concern to approximate similarity of particular fact. This appearance turns out to be misleading, however. For what we must ask is how these soldiers all came to leave the trench at the same time. The explanation for their action will lie in their previous psychological make-up. This, in turn, will be brought about by conditions in the past, in conjunction with their unique genetic make-up. These past histories and varying psychological factors vary significantly from the ones the soldiers have in the actual world. So, to get to a situation in which all of the soldiers leave the trench *at the very same time* would require a massive divergence from this world in terms of the histories of each of the soldiers. Each solider will have to have had experiences very different from the ones that they have in the actual world. That means, of course, that this world cannot be reasonably said to be 'relevantly similar' to our own, and so provides no threat to the CTC.

As promised, now that we've developed the CTC, it's time to consider some more problematic counterexamples.

# §9.3 Counterexamples

As noted above, counterexamples to the CTC typically try to demonstrate that there are instances of causation that don't satisfy the analysis – thus showing the analysis false. To see one of these at work, let us revamp our military example slightly. In addition to the captain and other troops, suppose that we add a sergeant major. As before, the captain shouts the order to charge and, as before, the soldiers charge. However, what's new to this scenario is that the sergeant major *would* have shouted the order had the captain not done so. To give colour to the example, let us suppose that the attack is supposed to take place at 10:00 and the sergeant major has been briefed to give the order at 10.01 in case the captain is either unable or unwilling to do so.

As before, of course, the captain *does* give the order and so once again we have a case where both event e and event c occur. But, in this case, it seems that in the nearest possible world at which the captain does not give the order, nonetheless, the sergeant major, noticing that his commanding officer has not given the order when they were due to do so, goes on to give the order themselves. Being well trained, the soldiers respond to the order and charge. In this case, despite the fact that *at the actual world* it still seems right to say that the captain caused the men to charge by giving the order, this case is one where our analysis gets the wrong result. For if the captain had not shouted the order, then the sergeant major would have, and so the men *would have* charged. We thus have a situation in which event c does not occur, but event e occurs anyway. This means that given the CTC, the captain's shouting is not the cause of the men's charging. So the CTC is wrong.

There are ways to respond to this objection. One route open to us is to argue that in the case described, where the sergeant major would have given the order, had the captain not done so, the effect would not have been the same. Certainly, in the scenario described what we seem to have is a situation in which the sergeant major *waits* to see whether or not the captain gives the order. If the captain does not give the order, then the sergeant major commits to giving it on their behalf. But, of course, that will take some time; the sergeant major will have to wait to see whether or not the captain gives the order and, if they do not, *then* give it. Once the sergeant major gives the order, then of course the troops will charge. But, or so goes the thought, perhaps this charging – which will occur a little later than if the captain had given the order – is not *identical* to the earlier charging.

The idea is that at the relevantly close possible world under consideration, where we do not have c, we in fact do not have e, either; instead, the later charging that we have been considering is e*. Thus we preserve the analysis of causation. This response does seem plausible. It is intuitive to think that the two chargings that we are considering are different from one another. One (caused by the captain) occurs at 10:00, the other (caused by the sergeant major) occurs (suppose) at 10:01. If we then thought that it was essential to event e being event e that it occurred at the very time that it does, then it would be impossible for it to occur at any time other than 10:00. This enables us to deploy a bit of terminology. We may say of an event that it is 'fragile' if by trying to change the event in some way (for instance, by moving it to another time) we destroy the event in question and create a new event. Thus, we may say that our event, e – the charging of the troops– is fragile with respect to the time at which it occurs. If e doesn't occur at 10:00, then e does not occur at all.

However, even given that refinement it looks like we might be able to make trouble for the counterfactual theorist of causation. Here is a case due to Schaffer.

Imagine that it is a law of magic that the first spell cast on a given day match the enchantment that midnight. Suppose that at noon Merlin casts a spell (the first that day) to turn the prince into a frog, that at 6:00pm Morgana casts a spell (the only other that day) to turn the prince into a frog, and that at midnight the prince becomes a frog. Clearly, Merlin's spell (the first that day) is a cause of the prince's becoming a frog and Morgana's is not, because the laws say that the first spells are the consequential ones. Nevertheless, there is no counterfactual dependence of the prince's becoming a frog on Merlin's spell, because Morgana's spell is a dependency-breaking backup. Further, there is neither a failure of intermediary events along the Morgana process (we may dramatize this by stipulating that spells work directly, without any intermediaries), nor any would be difference in time or manner of the effect absent Merlin's spell, and thus nothing remains by which extant CACs might distinguish Merlin's spell from Morgana's in causal status. (Schaffer 2000a: 165)

The counterfactual case just described is one in which Merlin does not cast the spell, but in which the prince is still turned into a frog – and so the counterfactual dependence of Merlin's spell, which in fact surely causes the prince to turn into a frog, is blocked. This circumvents the defence by way of fragility, of course, because the event of the prince's turning into a frog – our putative event e – will occur at precisely the same time no matter whose spell is enacted: Merlin's or Morganna's.

Now, you might not think that such wizarding cases are of any relevance to us. What matters to *us* are far more mundane cases; cases involving the shouting of orders and the dropping of pencils. I don't mean to endorse this line here; I merely note that the case under discussion seems pretty far-fetched. In any case, Schaffer's case is such that it can be modified to make problems for more mundane cases, too. Consider an example of a more mundane sort that Schaffer has in mind,

Imagine that in a world that could well be our own, the major and the sergeant stand before the corporal, both shout 'Charge!' at the same time, and the corporal decides to charge. Orders from higher-ranking soldiers trump those of lower rank. I hope you agree that the major's order, and not the sergeant's, causes the corporal's decision to charge (for the same reasons as in the wizards and fields cases: ranking orders are like the first spells . . . ) (Schaffer 2000a: 175)

This case is not mysterious, and involves no magic. Indeed, it is a homespun case directly related to that with which we began this chapter. Once more, though, it appears to be a case in which we want to say that it is the major's order that causes the charging. But, in a close possible world where the major does not give the order, the troops still charge and, crucially in this case, the troops charge at the *exact same moment* that they do in our world. Thus, the fragility of event e will not avail us here. This is a case where c is the cause of e but had c not occurred, e still would have. The CTC is in trouble.

# §9.4 More troubles for the CTC: The analysis is insufficient

What all of these arguments have in common is that they try to show situations in which the counterfactual analysis is not satisfied, but where we still have causation. What none of these cases have disputed is that where we satisfy the analysis, we have causation. One way to think about this is in terms of necessary and sufficient conditions. We can agree that, so far, all of the arguments against the counterfactual theory have allowed that the satisfaction of the analysis is *sufficient* for causation to occur; the arguments considered simply suggest that it is not *necessary* for something to satisfy the analysis in order to count as causation. What we will look at now is a scenario in which we might at least be tempted to say that events can occur that satisfy the analysis, but that do not count as causation.

The case that we will consider is due to Barker (2003). Imagine a vertical, empty cylindrical tube. Within the tube we have a lead cylindrical slab, S1. S1 is supported in two ways. The first way it is supported is via a copper wire that runs up the inside of the tube. The second way in which it is supported is via an iron slab, S2. Specifically, S1 is resting upon S2. However, the support provided by S2 is only very minimal. Most of the supporting work is done by the copper wire. Strong soldered bonds in turn support S2. Suppose, then, that the wire snaps and that both S1 and S2 descend. It seems intuitively correct that S1 causes S2 to fall, and not vice versa. We do not think that S2 causes S1 to fall. This is where we might then encounter a problem, for it seems as if the following counterfactual is true:

(3) If S2 had not descended, S1 would not have.

In conjunction with the fact that, in this world, where S2 does fall, so does S1, this seems to satisfy Lewis' analysis. To see why this is the case we need simply note that S2 is blocking S1's path. S1 can only fall if S2 does. Thus, although it might be the case that the copper wire snapping is, intuitively, what causes S1 to fall, it turns out that, if the CTC is correct, S2 causes S1 to fall. It thus appears, entirely contra what we would have thought, S2's falling causes S1 to fall. This suggests, albeit tentatively, that Lewis' analysis is neither necessary nor sufficient for causation.

We will move on from the counterfactual theory, now. There is certainly more that can be said; I advise the reader to take a look at the recommended readings.

# §9.5 Elimination

There is a particular line of thought that now suggests itself. We can capture this thought by means of two quotations from Russell (1992).

> The law of causation, . . . is a relic of a bygone age, surviving, like the monarchy, only because it is erroneously supposed to do no harm. (1992: 193)
>
> In the motions of mutually gravitating bodies, there is nothing that can be called a cause, and nothing that can be called an effect; there is merely a formula. (1992: 202)

As the title of this section suggests, this is an eliminative view of causation. Unlike a reductive view, it simply denies that causation occurs. There is an obvious connection to the mereological Nihilism we surveyed in Chapter 2. There we saw that some philosophers are prepared to deny commonsense judgments to the effect that composition occurs in the world, and endorse an eliminative view: there are no composite objects. Here we see that some philosophers are prepared to say something very similar about causation: simply, there is no such thing. If this is correct then we ought to think that sentences such as (1) are all false.

The chief argument that we may give in favour of eliminativism is that, as implied in the second quotation, causation never appears in our fundamental physical theories. When physicists describe the world, using mathematical formulae, they make no mention of causation. Indeed, their theories simply make no reference to causation at all. That being the case, it does not seem that we have a reason to think that there is causation in the world.

But, at least so presented, that argument looks too fast. We do not necessarily need to think that, simply because something does not appear in the fundamental physical description of the world, it does not exist. It may be the case that the fundamental description of reality makes no mention of tables, but that need not mean that there are no tables. All it would mean is that the fundamental level of reality does not contain tables. And in many ways, that would be pretty unsurprising. We naturally suppose that tables are made from particles, at least some of which will be fundamental: some collections of particles will compose tables, others will not. But no matter: we do not expect the tables themselves to be a fundamental part of reality. The same might then be said of causation. We may simply grant that causation is no part of the fundamental level of reality.

And it is not too hard to find philosophers seeming to speak as if causation is an essential concept, one which we cannot do without. 'With regard to our total conceptual apparatus, causation is at the center of the center' (Carroll 1994: 118). Why might one be tempted to agree? Well, suppose you wanted to turn on the light. How would you do it? To begin, it seems that you will require some understanding of how to turn the light on. That is, you understand that by pressing the light switch, you will *cause* the light to come on. If you did not understand that the pressing of the light switch would *cause* the light to come on, then why would you press the light switch? Further, consider the concepts of explanation, responsibility and agency: each of these concepts appear to be intimately bound up with our concept of causation. Thus, unless one is willing to forgo these concepts as well, then it might appear that eliminativism is too bitter a pill to swallow.

# §9.6 Primitivism

Of course, just as our frustration with finding an analysis of causation might suggest elimination, so too, in conjunction with the claim that causation is not to be eliminated, might the difficulties we have been having point towards causation being a primitive.

What sort of argument might we offer, here? Consider the following:

(4) Causation cannot be analysed.
(5) If causation cannot be analysed, then causation is primitive.

Therefore,

(6) Causation is primitive.

Let us walk through the premises. Premise (4) is seemingly motivated by our inability to offer a complete conceptual analysis of causation. Salient to this are the sorts of concern that have been vexing us since the outset of this chapter. If we are to avoid the conclusion, then we must reject premise (5). One way to do that would be to endorse eliminativism – but we might not think the prospects too promising there in light of the previous section. We appear to be being corralled in the direction of endorsing (6).

But there is another way to resist. Why think that our inability to provide a conceptual analysis of causation entails that causation is a primitive?

> . . . ontological reduction does not require conceptual analysis . . . Perhaps our concept is insufficiently explicit, or our intuitions are misleading, or the analysis would require an infinite definition. From a failure of conceptual analysis, nothing follows about the world . . .
>
> One could imagine a creature wired to think of everything through the concepts of *edible* and *inedible* – what would that prove about the world? (Schaffer 2008: 87)

The point here, of course, is that merely because one of our familiar notions (causation) cannot be analysed – a notion which itself is plausibly gerrymandered and imprecise, and which lacks a fully rigorous definition that serves to map it onto the world – it does not follow that there is nothing that can be used to reductively analyse an important or central part of that concept. Thus, the prospects for primitivism also look a little bleak.

# §9.7 Agent Causation

A relatively little studied theory of causation, Agent Causation is worth mentioning here. Consider a case where I wave my hand at someone. How did I do it? What did I do to cause it to happen? In some senses, the question seems to miss an important point. I do not *do something to cause myself to wave my hand*; rather, I wave my hand! It is something that I simply *do*. As Lowe (2002: 201) points out, this seems radically unlike cases where we deal with inanimate objects. For instance, the causing of the motion of a boulder seems to be very different. In the case of the boulder it seems more natural to think that, in order to cause the boulder to move there are various things that I must do: exerting a force on the boulder by bracing my feet on the floor, and pushing with my arms – for instance. But to repeat, that *seems* very different from a case where I simply wave my hand – in that case, I just *do it*.

This *seeming* can be added to. Suppose that we thought that events were causes, and that we wanted to give an analysis of the case of the hand waving.

In that case, the event of my waving my hand would be caused by some other event; that, in turn, would be caused by another event and so on and so on. This would appear to suggest that, properly considered, I do not genuinely *perform* any actions at all. Rather, each of the events in which I am involved is compelled by a previous event. This seems to imply that no human being is the author of their own action. As Lowe (2002: 202) then points out,

> A human agent must then be seen as no freer, in reality, that the boulder which rolls into the tree, its rolling being caused by the action of some other object upon it, which action is in turn caused by yet earlier events – and so on back to the dawn of time.

This lack of freedom, and lack of differentiation between the animate and the inanimate, seems to get matters wrong. People are freer (or so we might think) than boulders.

This insight, that will serve to motivate Agent Causation, also gives us a first hint of how we might understand Agent Causation. These actions of animate agents appear spontaneous; there are particular actions that can simply be performed and are so basic that we cannot analyse them in terms of other causal relationships. Let us call these, 'basic actions'. These 'basic actions' are not caused; rather, they are simply *performed* by agents. From here, we can then give the following analysis of causation:

> Event c caused event e if and only if there was some agent, A, and some manner of acting, X, such that c consisted in A's Xing and A, by Xing, caused e. (Lowe 2002: 209)

Consider a case where a person – Verity – smashes a glass. We might then say that Verity, by engaging in a particular way of behaving – dropping the glass, say – caused the glass to smash. Given Lowe's definition, then, we should say that there is an event, c – the dropping of the glass – and another event, e – the smashing of the glass. In that case, the dropping of the glass caused a smashing of the glass iff there was some agent, Verity, such that the dropping of the glass consisted in her *dropping the glass*, and her *dropping the glass* caused the glass to smash. In this case, Verity's dropping of the glass might be treated as a basic action.

Some further remarks of clarification are required. First, so far as Lowe is concerned, 'agents' here can be taken to include both animate and inanimate objects. This apparent lapse can be defended via the observation that it is extremely hard to distinguish clearly between those entities that are capable of engaging in rational action, and those that are not. It would, therefore, be inappropriate to declare that only rational entities count as agents, for we have no definitive account of which entities fall under this description. Second, an example. Consider the case (borrowed from Lowe (2002: 209)) of a bomb exploding and thereby causing the bridge to collapse. According to the analysis suggested above, our intuition that this is a case of causation is correct:

> there was a certain agent (in the broad sense), namely, the bomb, and a certain manner of acting, namely exploding, such that the event which was the explosion of the bomb consisted in the agent's acting in that manner (that is, it consisted in the bomb's exploding) and the agent, by so acting, caused the collapse of the bridge – that is to say, the bomb, by exploding, caused the collapse of the bridge.

This is quite a turn around. The counterfactual theory of causation that we considered above treats causation as a relation between events. According to the agent theory, not only are we giving up on that counterfactual relation, and replacing it in our analysis with the behaviour agents, but we are no longer treating events as all that significant; we are analysing the claim that one event caused another *in terms of something more fundamental* – the behaviour of particulars.

Can we then say anything more in favour of Agent Causation? Lowe (2002: 207–8) certainly thinks that we can argue for Agent Causation's conceptual priority. Consider a purely passive being (Lowe asks us to try and imagine an intelligent tree – the core idea is simply an intelligent being that isn't able to actively interfere with its own environment). This being is capable of observing sequences of events, but, seemingly, will not be able to differentiate between a series of regularities that obtain purely by coincidence and a causal sequence. Unlike a purely passive being, we are able to tell the difference.

> For instance, one can attempt to interrupt the fall of the next object of the next kind in question, to see whether or not a flash of light will still occur even in the absence of the fall. . . . Because we are causal agents ourselves and are aware of our ability to intervene in and manipulate the course of nature in such ways, we are able to test causal hypotheses experimentally and thereby hope to distinguish, albeit not infallibly, between causal and non-causal sequences of events. (2002: 208)

The passive creature could not intervene and so would have no understanding of the nature of these interventions. Thus, the *only* concept that the passive creature will have is one of sequences of events; it simply will not have the concept of being able to intervene in nature, and so will not have the concept of causation. It is therefore only by being active, and engaging in causal behaviour in the world, that one comes to have any idea that there is such a thing as causation. The suggestion is that it is the concept of action, that is derived from our experience of it, that is essential to the concept of causation.

Of course, despite having said all of these positive things about Agent Causation it remains a little unclear why we ought to believe it. For everything that has been said, it simply *isn't* clear that human agents have free will. We may grant, of course, that human behaviour is extremely complex, but it is far from clear that this need motivate us to believe in something like Agent Causation. Equally, it is not *entirely* obvious why we should think that the inability of a passive creature to form a concept should tell us anything about the fundamental structure of reality. Even conceding to Lowe that this shows us that *our concept of causation* is one that is intimately linked to our concept of agency and interaction, as per the arguments considered with regards primitivism it is not obvious as to quite how this should be taken to tell us about the structure of the world. Our concepts do not *all* need to find correlates in the world.

# §9.8 Asking the right question

The forgoing might suggest that we have been asking the wrong question. We have, after all, been seeking a conceptual analysis. We have been looking for some reductive account of causation such that, for *any* sentence of the form 'x causes y', we can point to a truth-maker for that sentence. Perhaps that just isn't realistic. Perhaps we can only hope to find truth-makers for *particular* deployments of the term.

In place of conceptual analysis, Dowe (2000) engages in what he calls 'empirical analysis', the basic idea behind which is that we should draw on the results of the empirical sciences and use these to give an analysis of particular concepts. Dowe goes on to give an example of how we might do this with reference to the case of energy:

> science has shed light on the nature of energy. 'Energy' has today a technical scientific meaning. When asked the meaning of the term, we simply give the scientific definition. Adequate explication of that term took several centuries, but prior to that achievement, the term simply had a vague range of meaning in everyday language, somewhat as the word 'cause' does today. We can say that application of the scientific method of theorising and experimentation produced an 'empirical

analysis' of energy. In the same way, science may reasonably be expected to throw light on the language-independent entity called 'causation'. (Dowe 2000: 7)

Dowe goes on to make the Empirical Analysis of causation a more perspicuous task, for there appears to be an objection to the task of giving an Empirical Analysis of causation. As Dowe notes, there is a worry that in looking to provide an Empirical Analysis, the task upon which we are engaged is simply that of giving a conceptual analysis of scientists' use of the word 'causation'. Now although this is not quite the same as offering a 'straight-up' conceptual analysis of general usage, it is still the same sort of task. And, we might then wonder, is it really the case that Empirical Analysis is an interesting or worthwhile project? After all, scientists themselves may well lapse into the more common, general usage on occasion; there is no *obvious* way, then, of insulating ourselves from simply engaging in conceptual analysis when offering a theory of causation. Here is Dowe's response:

> 'The distinction between conceptual analysis and empirical analysis is not so cut-and-dried; any empirical analysis will still be a kind of conceptual analysis, for example, of the concept implicit in scientific theories. . . . I am happy to think of the task of empirical analysis as a conceptual analysis of a concept inherent in scientific theories. (2000: 11)

Thus, Dowe's analysis of causation will be one that analyses the concept of causation as it appears in the sciences.

One thing to keep in mind, therefore, is that it may well be the case that the sort of ontological ground that Dowe posits as sufficient for scientific causation is such that much of our everyday talk about causation turns out to be false. This may be a cost of the view. With that background in place, what sort of theory does Dowe propose?

# §9.9 Process theory

Dowe proposes what he calls a process theory of causation. This sort of idea first comes to the fore *substantially* in the work of David Fair (1979). To get to Dowe's preferred solution I want to follow the path that Dowe traces from Fair's work, through that of Salmon, and then show how Dowe's position seeks to make the best of both views.

Fair's idea, roughly, is that we should identify causation with the flow of energy. A causes B just in case 'energy flows *from A to B*, as defined in terms of its time derivative over spatial surfaces separating the A-objects from the B-objects' (1979: 240).

One of the concerns that we may level against this sort of theory is that it seems to rule out the possibility of backwards causation: causation where an earlier event is caused by a later event. It seems to be at least a physical *possibility* that there could be backwards causation (e.g. Feynman (1949)). That being the case we should look to avoid ruling it out *a priori*. And it seems as if Fair's analysis, which treats causation as a flow of energy *from* A, *to* B is such that it does rule out backwards causation. Simply, the analysis requires energy to flow *from* A, *to* B.

This leads us on to Salmon's Mark Transmission view of causation. Rather than thinking of causation as a relation that holds between events, Salmon treats causation as a product of the interaction of processes. A process is something that displays consistency of structure over time. Thus, I am a process; for I have displayed consistency of structure over time. The leaves that recently fell from the trees however do not. A pile of leaves does not display consistency of structure over time, for the leaves are forever being blown about.

We must then draw a distinction between causal processes and pseudo processes. Consider a shadow that is cast on a wall. That will display consistency in structure over time (given an intuitive understanding of what structure is). But we should not think of a shadow as being a causal process. The shadow that is cast on the wall is not capable of imparting any change in structure to any other process. For instance, the structure of the shadow cast on a wall will not have any particular impact on the structure of the wall itself.

Thus, let us say that a process is causal iff it is capable of making a difference to the structure of another process. Another way of saying this is to say that a process is causal iff it is capable of transmitting a 'mark'. We can get clearer on the notion of Mark Transmission, as follows:

> MT: Let *P* be a process that, in the absence of interactions with other processes would remain uniform with respect to a characteristic *Q*, which it would manifest consistently over an interval that includes both of the space-time points *A* and *B* (*A–B*). Then, a mark (consisting of a modification of *Q* into *Q\**), which has been introduced into process *P* by means of a single local interaction at a point *A*, is transmitted to point *B* if [and only if] *P* manifests the modification *Q\** at *B* and at all stages of the process between *A* and *B* without additional interactions. (Salmon 1984, p. 148)[2]

Dowe (1992: 200) then summarizes Salmon's position.

(I) A process is something which displays consistency of characteristics.

(II) A causal process is a process which can transmit a mark.

(III) A mark is transmitted over an interval when it appears at each spacetime point of that interval, in the absence of interactions.

(IV) A mark is an alteration to a characteristic, introduced by a single local interaction.

(V) An interaction is an intersection of two processes.

(VI) A causal interaction is an interaction where both processes are marked.

Let us consider an example in order to get a flavour of the view. Consider two massive bodies in a collision. Both bodies will have a particular consistency of characteristics and so will count as causal processes and both are capable of transmitting a mark – an alteration in characteristics – to another causal process. The collision of the two bodies is an intersection of two processes and, given the transmission of momentum (etc.) that will be generated by the interaction, so the interaction will be one where both processes are marked. Thus, what we have in the collision is an instance of a causal interaction. This sounds very plausible.

Dowe (1992: 201) thinks that there remain problems, however.

That is, are (IV) and (VI) circular? Logically, they are not unless by 'interaction' in (IV) we mean 'causal interaction', in which case the circularity is blatant. So, must a mark be introduced by a causal interaction or will any local intersection of processes suffice? Clearly, a genuine mark must be introduced by a causal interaction because a pseudo interaction could not produce a mark or else it could be a cause of something, a fact which would seriously undermine the pseudo/causal distinction on which Salmon's theory is built. Hence we must conclude that in (IV) 'interaction' means 'causal interaction', and thus Salmon's theory is circular.

If Dowe is right, and Salmon's theory is circular, then it will not do even to give an empirical analysis of causation.

Dowe's preferred account is one that then seeks to unite elements of both Fair's and Salmon's view. Dowe (1995: 323) calls the view the 'Conserved Quantity' of causation.

CQ1. A causal interaction is an intersection of world lines which involves exchange of a conserved quantity.

CQ2. A causal process is a world line of an object which possesses a conserved quantity.

Of obvious salience is the question of what exactly is a conserved quantity. Here, once more, is Dowe.

A 'conserved quantity' is any quantity which is universally conserved, and current scientific theory is our best guide as to what these are. Thus, we have good reason to believe that mass-energy, linear momentum, and charge are conserved quantities. (op cit)

Let us pause a moment to see how this theory preserves the insight of both Fair and Salmon's earlier attempts. The notion of a 'conserved quantity' appears to be a nod to Fair's claim that causation requires the transmission of energy. However, Dowe is a little more permissive in that he allows not just energy transference to count as causation, but the exchange of any conserved quantity. As per Salmon's approach, we are invited to think of this, not as an analysis of causation *simpliciter* but an account of when causation might be said to occur given a scientific understanding of the world. It is also worth noting that, like Salmon, Dowe treats processes as essential to causation. Dowe can also claim victory with regards to the two objections that we raised to competing theories of causation. It does not appear that his analysis is circular. The concepts of having and exchanging conserved quantities do not appear to require the concept of causation in order to be rendered intelligible. We can analyse what it is to 'have' and to 'exchange' quantities, without presupposing an analysis of causation. Nor does it appear that this account will rule out backwards causation. There is nothing built into the account that means that conserved quantities must flow *from one* process to another, across time. Rather, all that we require is a notion of an exchange of conserved quantities. Clearly, the concept of an exchange need not be read as presupposing that one event precede another.

# §9.10 Concerns for Dowe

Nonetheless, it remains the case that there are problems for Dowe's account. In particular, one species of problem appears especially pressing: causation by omission. Consider the following scenario. Verity goes away on holiday for a month and does not get anyone to water her houseplants. Unsurprisingly,

Verity's houseplants die. It seems that we want to say that the following sentence is true in the scenario:

(7) Verity caused her houseplants to die by not watering them.

If true, this sentence will create a problem for the process account for there is no causal process connecting Verity to the death of her houseplant. Verity is away on holiday and so is nowhere near them! Of course, that might seem a little unsurprising. It is more intuitive to think that Verity causes her houseplants to die in this scenario precisely because she withholds from engaging in a very specific causal process; that of watering the plants. And the withholding of that process is not itself a causal process. So much seems intuitively obvious. But it is that seemingly obvious point that then threatens the process accounts of causation. For Verity to cause their death, she must be connected (in the right sort of way) to the houseplants.

What might we do? One very blunt way in which we might respond is to deny that there is such a thing as causation by omission or absence. Thus, it is simply not the case that Verity caused her houseplant to die in the case that I described above, and (7) is false. That might strike some as extremely plausible even though we are forced to deny the truth of intuitively true sentences.

But, if you are inclined to think that's right, then there's another challenge in the vicinity. It would be natural to think that one is blameworthy for some event if one has caused it. Thus, if I cause someone to die by driving my car into them, then I am to blame; if I cause someone injury by striking them for not having done their seminar reading, then I am to blame. We thus have a well-established connection between causation and responsibility. But what if I do not cause an event? Suppose that it was not me that *caused* the car accident. Suppose that, although I was driving the car, what caused the accident was the malevolent behaviour of a mechanic. In that case, where I did *not cause the accident I am not to blame*.

This is interesting to us. For now consider a revised version of the houseplant case. Suppose that, in the revised case, it is not a houseplant that Verity leaves behind, but a small child. In the month of Verity's absence, the child dies due to an omission of adequate nutrition and care. This seems to be Verity's fault. We seem to want to blame Verity for the death of the child in this horrific incident. But, if omissions and absences do not count as causes, she did not cause the death. The death occurred because some level of care *was not* provided. Thus, Verity is not to blame. If we thought that this connection between causation and responsibility needed to be maintained, then this would give us the wrong result. This issue is one that the proponent of causal process theory will, therefore, have to pursue in more detail.

An option for a proponent of this style of analysis is to remind us that what we are after here is *not* a conceptual analysis of causation, but an analysis of the concept of causation as it appears to be deployed by scientists. It is not *entirely* clear that the case specified above is appropriately scientific and so it is not entirely clear that it constitutes a counterexample to this kind of project. Of course, such a riposte will only be successful if causation by omission is never mentioned in science. I leave it to the reader to adjudicate upon whether or not that is likely to be true.

The problem of what to say about causation by omission may turn out to plague more than just the process theory of causation. If we adopted the CTC then, given the example discussed, we would have to say that the event of Verity's not watering the houseplants caused them to die. But what *is* that event? It seems most natural to suppose that there is no such event, and that it's true to say that Verity did not water the houseplants despite there being no such event. The case of causation by omission may well turn out to be a problem that infects a whole variety of theories of causation.

# §9.11 Conclusions

The counterfactual theory of causation is powerful and popular, but as we have seen it also faces problems. It remains to be seen whether or not the CTC can do enough to overcome these problems. The other positions surveyed are rather more minority positions, I think. However, that is not to say that they face insuperable problems. As ever, we will require a careful weighing of our options. One view that I have not covered, probabilistic causation, is mentioned in the reading.

# Recommended reading

### General

Schaffer, J. 2008. 'Causation and Laws of Nature: Reductionism', in Sider, T., Hawthorne, J. and Zimmerman, D. eds. *Contemporary Debates in Metaphysics*. Oxford: Blackwell, 82–108.

## Counterfactual theory

Barker, S. 2003. 'Counterfactual Analyses of Causation: The Problem of Effects and Epiphenomena Revisited', *Noûs*, 37, 133–50.

Choi, S. 2007. 'Causation and Counterfactual Dependence', *Erkenntnis*, 67, 1–16.

Lewis, D. 1986c. 'Causation', in Lewis, D. *Philosophical Papers Volume II*. Oxford: OUP, 159–71.

Lewis, D. 1986d. 'Postscript', in Lewis, D. *Philosophical Papers Volume II*. Oxford: OUP, 172–213.

Lewis, D. 2000. 'Causation as Influence', *Journal of Philosophy*, 97, 182–97.

Schaffer, J. 2000a. 'Trumping Preemption', *Journal of Philosophy*, 97, 165–81.

## Process theory

Dowe, P. 1992. 'Wesley Salmon's Process Theory of Causality and the Conserved Quantity Theory', *Philosophy of Science*, 59, 195–216.

Dowe, P. 1995. 'Causality and Conserved Quantities: A Reply to Salmon', *Philosophy of Science*, 62, 321–33.

Dowe, P. 2000. *Physical Causation*. New York: CUP.

Fair, D. 1979. 'Causation and the Flow of Energy', *Erkenntnis*, 14, 219–50.

Salmon, W. 1984. *Scientific Explanation and the Causal Structure of the World*. Princeton: Princeton University Press.

Schaffer, J. 2001. 'Review of Physical Causation', *British Journal for the Philosophy of Science*, 52, 809–13.

## Agent theory

Lowe, E. J. 2002. *A Survey of Metaphysics*. Oxford: OUP, chapters 11 and 12.

Lowe, E. J. 2008. *Personal Agency: The Metaphysics of Mind and Action*. Oxford: OUP.

## Probabilistic causation

Lowe, E. J. 2002. *A Survey of Metaphysics*. Oxford: OUP, 162–3.

Mellor, D. H. 1995. *The Facts of Causation*. London: Routledge.

Schaffer, J. 2000b. 'Probability Raising without Causation', *Australasian Journal of Philosophy*, 78, 40–6.

Suppes, P. 1970. *A Probabilistic Theory of Causality*. Amsterdam: North Holland.

## Study questions

1) Write out a summary of each view covered in the chapter. Which view do you think is correct? Why do you think that view correct?

2) Do you think that Hume is right that we can never perceive causation?

3) The counterfactual theory of causation faces a number of problems. What do you think is the most serious? How do you think the proponent of the counterfactual theory should respond to the problem?

4) One of the arguments for the Agent theory required that we have free will. Do you think that this is a good or bad feature of the argument?

5) What do you think we should say about causation by absence?

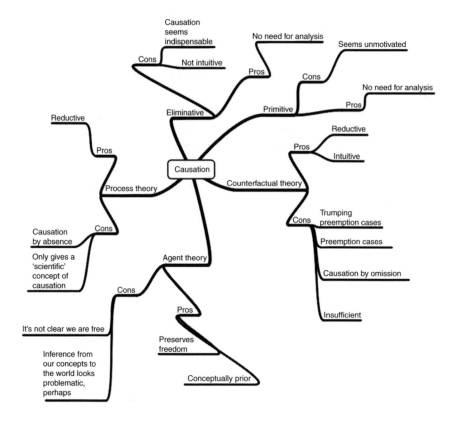

# Truth-making Reconsidered

Much of the preceding has laboured under the stricture, laid down in the first chapter, that truths have truth-makers and without existing entities to make true our propositions, our propositions would be false. The examples that we considered there, and the implications that we tried to draw, have taken us a *very* long way. At various points in this book we have considered the possibility of abstract objects; distinct possible worlds that are 'of a kind' with our own; properties as repeatable entities that exist in a realm of their own; the claim that there is only one substance. We have turned a critical gaze at a variety of theories that seek to account for the nature of composition, modality, time and so on; we have yet to turn that gaze onto the truth-maker theory itself. It is now time to turn our attention back to the material that we encountered in the first chapter.

I want to present you with a question: why not say that the modal truths, the truths about what is possible, do not require truth-makers? What would be so very bad about this? Let me be a little more clear. Suppose that we consider a sentence:

(1) It is possible for me to fall over.

I take it that in order for this to be true, it would be pretty intuitive that I would have to exist. So let's grant that. But, once we've done that, why think that anything makes it true that, given the particular properties that I have, I *could* fall over? Why not simply say that (1) is true iff I exist, and have a given set of properties *but that the proposition expressed by (1) does not have a truth-maker?* Why not just say that (1) is true just in case *I could fall over?*

Consider, also, the temporal case and sentence (2):

(2) There were dinosaurs.

Do we think that, in order to be true, the proposition expressed by (2) requires that something *exists?* Or do we merely require that some entity *existed* and that, because (suppose) presentism is true and only present objects exist, this is a truth without a truth-maker?

These are complex issues. The first thing for us to look at is whether or not there are good grounds for denying that all truths need truth-makers. If there are such grounds, then it may be that these arguments can be developed and extended to show that temporal and modal propositions (expressed by the likes of (1) and (2)) – and perhaps also many other propositions that we discussed in this book – do not require truth-makers.

# §10.1 Negative existentials

Consider the following two sentences:

(3) There are no arctic penguins.
(4) Everything is a physical object.

Sentence (3) is taken to be a humdrum claim to the effect that no penguins reside at the arctic. Sentence (4) is supposed to be a fast-and-loose way of stating physicalism, a position according to which there is nothing that is not a physical object. What both of these sentences have in common, though, is a commitment to there *not being* a particular sort of entity in the world. Thus, (3) claims that there are not any penguins at the arctic; (4) claims that there are no non-physical objects.

The natural question, then: what makes true the propositions expressed by these sentences? Let's consider (3). The first thing that we might consider as the correct truth-maker for the proposition expressed by (3) is the arctic itself. Thus, we might think, the arctic makes it true that there are no penguins at the arctic. But that won't do. The trouble is that the arctic is compatible with the existence of arctic penguins. Why would it be a problem if the arctic made true the proposition expressed by (3)? Well, suppose that due to various changes in the ecosystem at the Antarctic, penguins all migrated to the arctic. The *arctic* would still exist, thus would still – given what we've granted – make it true that <there are no arctic penguins>. But now there *would be* arctic penguins; this would obviously be ridiculous.

Now maybe you think that's a slightly odd case because it involves the migration of penguins, an alteration to the ecosystem at the Antarctic and so on. To try and persuade you that the problem can be forced closer to home, consider (5):

(5) There is no-one in the office next to mine.

At this moment in time, (5) is true. As with (3) and (4), (5) is a sentence about what is not; it is a claim that there does not exist a person in the office next to mine. So, we ask again: what makes this true? Suppose that we respond with the claim that it is *the office* that makes it true. What then happens when my colleague returns from their lunch? If their office is what makes it true that there is no-one in the office, and the office itself remains unchanged, then when they return (5) will still be true – this is a nonsense.

This might then give us pause for thought: do claims about what does not exist – so-called 'negative existentials' – require truth-makers? It is certain that there is no *obvious* truth-maker in the vicinity.

But as we have seen in the previous chapters, the absence of an obvious truth-maker does not always hinder a determined metaphysician. A determined metaphysician will simply hunt down an *unobvious* truth-maker. In fact, in this case, perhaps there *is* an obvious truth-maker for all of the above: an absence. Thus, what makes true (3) is an *absence of arctic penguins*; what makes true (4) is *absence of abstract objects*; what makes true (5) is an *absence of people in the room next to mine.* And, on the proposed model, these absences are reified; they are *things* in some sense of the word.

To flesh the account out a little, we might consider a 'states of affairs' ontology of the sort that we dealt with in Chapter 6. With regards (5) we might suggest that the truth-maker is the state of affairs composed from the thin particular 'the room' and the property 'not including any people'. This state of affairs is what makes it true that there are no people in the office next to mine.

But doesn't that sound a little odd? A property of *not including any people.* That doesn't sound like a property; rather, it sounds like the *absence* of a property of 'including people' (cf. §5.3). Indeed, this talk of 'negative properties', properties of states of affairs *not* being some particular way, all sounds rather suspicious. At least, so say the objectors:

> there is a strong intuition that everything that exists is 'positive'. (Mumford (2005: 265))

> There is implanted in the human breast an almost unquenchable desire to find some way of avoiding the admission that negative facts are as ultimate as those that are positive. (Russell 1956: 287)

> It is simply wrongheaded to think that there should be a truthmaker which corresponds to negative existential sentences. Intuitively, what makes a sentence such as 'There are no Fs' is a *lack* of Fs. (Melia 2005: 69)

We thus find ourselves in something of a quandary.

Molnar (2000: 84–5) puts the problem nicely when he says:

> (i) The world is everything that exists.
> (ii) Everything that exists is positive.
> (iii) Some negative claims about the world are true.
> (iv) Every true claim about the world is made true by something that exists.

At least intuitively, each of (i)–(iii) seems right. And so we must then consider (iv). It seems that we have a choice. We either find a truth-maker for negative claims about the world that is itself 'positive', or else we deny that *all* truths need truth-makers.

It's time to remind ourselves of some terminology: someone who claims that all truths require truth-makers is a 'truth-maker maximalist'; someone who thinks that only a restricted class of truths require truth-makers is a 'non-maximalist'.

# §10.2 Totality

Arguably the most prominent maximalist response to the problem of negative existentials is due to David Armstrong.

> If the world is a world of states of affairs alone, as I contend, then we have another Tot [totalling] relation holding between the very same whole and the 'property' *being any existent at all*. (2004: 74)

It's worth spelling out, here, rather more of the detail of Armstrong's proposal. Let us begin by considering a case. Consider an aggregate of electrons.

> The aggregate stands in a highly specific relation to the instantiated property . . . of *being an electron*. That property maybe said to *total* or to *all* that particular aggregate. (2004: 73)

Armstrong's thought is that we are perfectly familiar with the idea of a 'totalling' property or relation. In the case just described, the property 'being an electron' can be said to 'total' the aggregate.

This can then be developed into a useful tool for the truth-maker maximalist.

> If the world is a world of states of affairs alone, as I contend, then we have another Tot [totalling] relation holding between the very same whole and the 'property' *being any existent at all*. (2004: 74)

The 'totality' relation is a relation that takes all of the first order states of affairs and is then sufficient for the proposition <there is nothing else> to be true.

Here is the idea in action. Suppose that we consider sentence (5) once again. What makes it true that there is no-one in the office next to mine is the collection of all the positive states of affairs; the state of affairs of there being a table; being an office; being a chair and so on. But to all of these facts, we then add one further relation: the relation that *this is everything that there is*. This totalling relation will, in conjunction with all of the other facts, make true our propositions about what there is not. Thus Armstrong thinks that we can deal with the problem of negative existentials.

But it is not clear that we ought to agree with Armstrong. Consider this 'totality relation' that Armstrong posits. Should we think of this as positive or as negative? This totality relation appears to say that 'there is nothing more than these positive facts'; or, to put it another way, 'it is not the case that there is anything that is not positive'. This looks to be negative in the same way that the property of there being *not including any people*, looks negative. If we thought that the first sort of negative property was bad, it's not clear that Armstrong has offered us an advance.

So let us press this point. So far I've said nothing against negatives other than that they seem intuitively suspicious. Perhaps we can, and should, have something rather more powerful to say if we are to reject negative properties. Here, once again, is Melia (2005: 69)

> Armstrong tries to account for such truths by postulating states of affairs of total-ity. Besides the bizarre necessary connections that such states of affairs entail (how can something's mere existence necessarily prevent an object d from being *F*), and besides the implausible nature of the totality relation itself, it is just con-fused to think that we must account for a *lack* by postulating the *existence* of something else.

Melia seems to have three arguments, here. First, that there are bizarre neces-sary connections involved in positing a totality; second, that the nature of the relation is implausible; third, that it is 'just confused' to think that we must account for a lack by positing an existent. Let us consider these in turn.

## §10.2.1 Bizzare necessary connection

Suppose that I tell you that there is a cup on my table. It would be very odd to think that this entailed anything about, for instance, my bin. We do not think that, simply because there *is* a cup on my table, that there *could not be* a piece of paper in my bin. That sounds like a very odd thing to say! But the worry here is that this is precisely the sort of thing that Armstrong *is* saying. Armstrong is committed to the claim that if we have some positive states of affairs, and then some further entity – the totality relation – then there *cannot be any other positive states of affairs*. But since the positive states of affairs and totality relation are distinct from one another – much like my cup and my bin – it's really hard to see why we should think the totality relation capable of ruling out these distinct states of affairs.

## §10.2.2 Implausible nature

We are by now used to talk of relations. We think that there are lots of them: there is the relation of 'being to the north of'; there is the relation 'being the father of'; there is the relation 'being taller than'. All of these are perfectly ordinary. But notice: all of these relations are *positive*. They are positive additions to the fabric of being. It is simply unclear that this 'totality relation', which is negative, has any place on our inventory of existents. This argument, I assume, trades upon the idea that although we are familiar enough with positive relations, we simply don't have a conceptual grip upon what it would be like for a relation to *not* be like all those on our list; that is, to *not* be positive. It is, we might think, hard enough to grasp the idea of a negative property – the idea of a negative *relation* seems even harder to get our heads around.[1]

### §10.2.3 Wrongheaded

And, of course, the final objection – that it is wrongheaded to posit a truth-maker for a negative proposition – is just the claim that it is obviously foolish to look for truth-maker for claims that specify that things *not* exist.

> How about negative existential truths? It seems, offhand, that they are true not because things of some kind *do* exist, but rather because counterexamples *don't* exist. They are true for lack of falsemakers. Why defy this first impression?
>
> (Don't say: 'Aha! It's a *lack* that makes it true.' The noun is a happenstance of idiom, and to say that a negative existential is true for a lack of falsemakers is the same as to say that it's true because there aren't any falsemakers. The demand for truth-makers might lead one into ontological seriousness about lacks, but not *vice versa*.) (Lewis 1992: 216)

So, all in all, it would appear that we have some substantial problems to deal with *if* we are to endorse truth-maker maximalism. The problem of negative existentials is, as we have seen, something of a tricky problem for the maximalist. It seems as if we would do well to look for a better solution to the problem of negative existentials than the one that Armstrong proposes – either that, or we should give up on maximalism.

## §10.3 The world to the rescue

One solution to this problem comes from a view that we have already considered in another chapter: Schaffer's Priority Monism. Schaffer (2010b) defends the thesis that,

> M. For all worlds w: the one and only truthmaker at w is w. (2010b: 307)

Recall from §6.11 that, for Schaffer, the only *fundamental* existent is the one true substance. Thus, properly conceived, the substance will be the truth-maker for all of the positive existential claims about the world. But it will also generate the negative truths, as well. To see this, consider the true proposition <there are no dragons>. This is a true proposition. The fundament (the one existing substance), at our world, is not such as to make it true that <there are dragons>. Now, consider a possible world that is an expansion of our world: a world that duplicates our own and then adds dragons. That world does make it true that <there are dragons>. Our world can be conceived of as being a *part* of that world, by having a counterpart at that world.

Thus,

> Here is a reason to think the truth of <there are no dragons> has indeed found ground. While our world is contained in the expanded world (by counterpart), the expanded dragon world also has a dragon part. Thus our world cannot be the one fundament of the expanded world, because the one fundament there must also make a dragon. In general, any expansion (any more to the world) requires a different unique fundament – if the worlds in question did not differ, then they would be indiscernible, rather than contracted and expanded. So <there are no dragons> is true at actuality, in virtue of actuality's being the unique actual fundament. Once actuality is listed as the one fundamental entity, ground for the absence of dragons is assured. (2010b: 331)

Schaffer's proposal is hard to understand at first. The solution can be made more obvious, I think, by considering Schaffer's diagnosis of the source of the problem of negative existentials. Suppose that it were possible that wide range of fundamental substances could exist. Thus, let us suppose that the arctic exists, and that it is then possible for there to be penguins, but also possible for there to not be penguins. This means that it is possible for it to be true that <there are arctic penguins>, despite the fact that the actual world does not contain any arctic penguins.

But on Schaffer's model, this possibility simply is not available. Once we specify the nature of the one true fundament, we have fixed all of the facts. Our world, the actual world, cannot include dinosaurs, because none of its counterparts does.

> [A]ny difference in the truth of <there are no dragons> must stem from some difference in what is fundamental. If there can only be one fundament, and it is the world, then any difference in the truth of <there are no dragons> can only possibly

stem from a difference in the world. Fixing the one fundament as actuality fixes the world, and in so doing fixes the truth of <there are no dragons>. (Schaffer 2010b: 321–2)

I suspect that much of whether or not one is prepared to endorse Schaffer's solution to the problem of negative existentials will depend upon two things. First, whether or not one finds the proposed Monism independently plausible (though one would have to concede that this proposal, if successful, would add weight to the claim that we ought to endorse Monism); second, whether or not one thinks that there is a genuine problem here in the first place. As has been made clear earlier in the chapter (§10.2.3), there are those who remain resolutely sceptical about the problem and think, instead, that it is perfectly clear that not all truths require truth-makers.

We have said quite a bit about maximalism that is seeming to cast it in a negative light. Still, there are those who defend maximalism so we ought to consider why they do so. After all, we have seen in many of the cases that we've considered, first appearances can be deceptive, and that it is only once we engage in a careful weighing of our options that the optimal view became visible. Absent the positive reasons to endorse maximalism we simply cannot engage in such a weighing.

# §10.4 Motivations for maximalism

There are a number of reasons that have been advanced for endorsing maximalism. The first of these that we shall consider is due to Armstrong.

I do not have any direct argument. My hope is that philosophers of realist inclinations will be immediately attracted to the idea that a truth, any truth, should depend for its truth on something 'outside' it, in virtue of which it is true. (Armstrong (2004: 7))

Here Armstrong seems to be committed to saying that it is intuitive that all truths depend upon something *outside* them, in virtue of which they are true. As we saw when we were looking at the examples in the very first chapter, there is something pretty appealing about this. 'The cat is on the mat' seems the sort of truth that must depend upon there being a cat on the mat.

But we might question whether or not we really have this intuition *generally*. Do we really think that 'there are no arctic penguins' depends upon the *existence* of some entity? Some of the quotations in the previous sections might well lead us to think that such a presumption is not justified.

Cameron's (2008: 107–8) take on why to believe maximalism is slightly different:

> What possible reason could one have for thinking of some propositions that they need to be grounded in what there is that doesn't apply to all propositions? Why should it be okay for negative truths to go ungrounded and not okay for positive truths to go ungrounded? And if negative truths don't have truthmakers then make no mistake: they *are* ungrounded. It is no good to say that they are grounded in the *lack* of a truthmaker for the positive truth that is their negation. Unless we reify this absence of a truthmaker this is nothing but metaphysical smoke and mirrors. It's totally disingenuous to say that ¬p is true in virtue of the absence of a truthmaker for p unless there is *some thing* that is this absence. And if there *is* such a thing as the absence then it is a truthmaker for ¬p, so maximalism is vindicated.

Thus, Cameron seems to be of the mind (in this passage, at least) that whatever reason we have for thinking that some truths have truth-makers will extend to all truths.

But this might seem a rather surprising claim. Armstrong (2004: 7) introduces maximalism as a hypothesis to be tested. We might well think, then, that we find our hypothesis confirmed in a number of cases. In cases where we truthfully say that 'there is an F', then we require an existing F. But in cases where we say that, 'there is no F' our hypothesis fails. We find that these are truths that do not need truth-makers. So, why believe non-maximalism? Because we find situations in which truths do not obviously require truth-makers.

Perhaps a more powerful reason for believing in truth-makers is also suggested by Armstrong. Suppose that we thought that not all truths required truth-makers. Then we would have a theory that seemed to have two different kinds of truth: those truths that are related to the world via a truth-making relation, and those that are not. This, it might seem, is to make our theory of truth more complicated than it would be where we to simply endorse maximalism. If we endorse maximalism, after all, then we have only one type of truth: truths that are related to the world via the truth-maker relation. Speaking of truth-maker, Armstrong (2007: 99) then remarks:

> One advantage is that it permits an univocal theory of truth. (I take it that truthmaker theory, as opposed to suggestion about what particular truthmakers we should postulate, is part of the theory of truth.) Perhaps it is rather uneconomical

in what D.C. Williams wittily called the 'gross tonnage' sense, but I'd argue, as Williams did, that theoretical economy is very much more important than gross tonnage.

And this, Armstrong thinks, will help us to see our way to dismissing the objection to postulating a totality fact.

> The totalizer fact will be a negative fact, but it will be the only one. (It will be like a Sabbath, where God can rest.) Negative truths can flourish but in a sense there will only be one negative truthmaker . . .
>
> If you think that the totalizer fact is too big a fact, I reply that it is very big in a gross tonnage sense, but it helps towards giving us great theoretical simplification in truthmaking theory: a truthmaker for every truth. (2007: 100)

This will be another situation in which we must weigh our options. Do we think that the concerns raised above are sufficient to motivate a rejection of Armstrong's view, or do we think that the theoretical economy that we can preserve by endorsing truth-maker theory outweighs them?

# §10.5 Undermining the motivation for maximalism

The claim that considerations of simplicity can serve to motivate truth-maker maximalism, has been challenged. Goff (2008) begins by noting that a good number of truth-maker theorists offer us a theological metaphor of God instructing the angels.

> For the orthodox truthmaker [what we have been calling a 'maximalist'] theorist, God only tells His angels what to put in the world (remember, the explanation of truth 'bottoms out at existence facts') . . .

Goff then goes on:

> Why does He go in such a roundabout way to make true His favoured set of propositions ('Ok, Gabriel, listen carefully, because I will say this only once. . . . I need it to be true that there are no hobbits, so I want you to create all the things there are, and then create the fact that those things are all the things that there are. . . . ')? God's eccentric behaviour here seems inexplicable. Why doesn't He

> just tell Gabriel not to make any hobbits? Cameron's God certainly has His work
> cut out for him; I would be surprised if He has time spare to take Sunday off.
> (2008: 46–7)

Goff's point is an interesting one. Goff's point is that maximalism is an *over-simplification*. We might have thought that God *could* have created the world, and fixed all of the truths about what there is not, by simply getting the angels to *not* create some things. But if truth-maker theory is true, then it turns out that this is false. God is forced to create the world such that there are truth-makers for negative existentials. Nor is God an essential part of this story. We could simply say that we thought it metaphysically possible for there to be truths without truth-makers. Now it appears that this is not the case. As we have seen in earlier chapters, restrictions on metaphysical possibility are taken to be a negative consequence of a view (consider, for instance, our claim in Chapter 8 that the possibility of time travel raises problems for endurance theories of persistence).

This leads Goff (2008: 49) to his closing remarks:

> The supposed 'elegant theory of truth' which [maximalism] offers us is actually a
> very radical and unmotivated starting point for enquiry. This strange starting point
> comes with a radical restriction of the space of metaphysical possibility, which also
> seems unmotivated. The supposed advantages of [maximalism] turn out, on
> reflection, to be costs. Coupled with the significant ontological costs which inev-
> itably come with the theory, it is clear that [maximalism] can never be justified on
> a costs/benefits analysis.

If Goff is right about this, then it is hard to see how we could motivate a truth-maker maximalism by appeal to simplicity.

# §10.6 Maximalism and asymmetry

Yet another supposed motivation for endorsing maximalism is that it explains our sense that truth depends upon the world. It is pretty clear (at least intuitively) that a sentence is true *because of the way the world is*; the world is not a particular way *because a sentence is true*. To flesh this out a little more: it is not the case that the world is such as to have a cat on the mat *because* the sentence 'there is a cat on the mat' is true. But it is the case that the sentence 'there is a cat on the mat' is true, because the world is such as to have a cat on the mat.

This issue is discussed in Dodd (2007). The way that we might express our intuition is that:

(GT) <p> is true because p.

Dodd also claims that:

it is equally undeniable that such grounding is asymmetrical. Whilst we accept

(GT), we do not accept that reality is grounded in truth, that

(GR) p because <p> is true. (2007: 393)

The explanation of this asymmetry and the intuition (GT) is best explained by truth-maker. Again, to quote Dodd,

The filling in between '<p>' and 'p' in GT – is true because – turns out to be 'is made true by' in disguise. (2007: 393)

The asymmetry is established by there being no sense in which the truth of propositions 'makes real' any corresponding entity and truth-maker explains the correctness of (GT) as well; and, 'the correctness of (GT) is best explained by the fact that a true proposition has an ontological ground' (2007: 393).

Now, let us assume that we think that some truths have truth-makers. Let us also assume that we think this because we think that this asymmetry is important and that we think it best explained by truth-maker theory. In that case, it is hard to see how we might restrict truth-maker. In any situation in which we deny that a truth has a truth-maker, we look to contravene the intuition that there is an asymmetry between truth and world. But since this intuition is what is getting us to believe in truth-maker in the first place, so this is tantamount to a rejection of the motivation for truth-maker theory.

As is obvious, this argument will only be successful against truth-maker theory if one thinks that it is motivated by its ability to explain the asymmetry that truths depend upon the world, but not vice versa. If, however, one thought that truth-maker theory were a hypothesis to be tested, in the manner suggested above (§10.4), then one might not take this threat quite so seriously.

# §10.7 Catch the cheaters

A further, and much discussed, reason to believe in truth-maker theory is that it helps us to 'catch cheats'. Here, once again, is Cameron (2008: 113–14), this time discussing the truth-maker objection to presentism.

> Presentism says that the only time that exists is the present (and hence that the only things that exist in time are things that exist at the present time) . . . The presentist says that there were dinosaurs, but she refuses to admit that there are any past times containing dinosaurs that make it the case that there were dinosaurs . . . the objection is against accepting truths without accepting the corresponding parts of ontology that would make that truth true; the objection is to having truths without truthmakers.

By itself, of course, the truth-maker principle does nothing to cause any concern to the presentist. They may simply posit the Bigelow-style 'tensed properties' that we discussed in §7.6.1.

Cameron (2008: 115) goes on:

> if we are to have an argument against presentism we must be able to say what entities it is acceptable to believe in, and properties such as having previously contained dinosaurs (or the state of affairs of the world instantiating this property) must not be acceptable.

What sort of principle could play this role? What sort of principle could we use against the presentist who posits tensed properties, that will tell us what sorts of entities it is acceptable to believe in? The sort of principle that Cameron has in mind is something like the following, due to Sider (2001: 41)

> What seems common to all the cheats is that irreducibly *hypothetical* properties are postulated, whereas a proper ontology should invoke only *categorical*, or occurent, properties and relations. Categorical properties involve what objects are actually like, whereas hypothetical properties 'point beyond' their instances. The presentist's primitive tensed properties (or operators, or whatever) would be hypothetical. (2001: 41)

The point, then, is this: if we endorse both truth-maker theory *and* something like Sider's principle, then it looks like we will have an argument against 'dubious' or 'suspicious' metaphysics. Thus, it is because we want to rule out such dubious metaphysics that we should posit the truth-maker principle for it, in conjunction with Sider's principle for when something is hypothetical, will help us catch the cheats.

I think it's worth making two points by way of reply. First, it is unclear that a proponent of a so-called dubious ontology need feel compelled to endorse *both* truth-maker theory *and* something like Sider's principle. They could, quite straightforwardly, deny that Sider's principle is to be endorsed. One route that they might take here is to claim that this talk of 'pointing beyond' is all rather metaphorical. Properties do not point; they do not have fingers. Although this may appear slightly glib, it gestures towards an important point nonetheless. If the proponent of maximalism is to force us to believe in both Sider's principle *and* maximalism, then we might well want a clear specification of what it is for a property to 'point beyond' its instances.

The second objection that the proponent of these so-called suspicious properties might make is simply this. What, exactly, is supposed to be wrong with these properties? We have been told that they 'point beyond'. Perhaps we have some intuitive grasp of what is meant: the property *having been occupied by dinosaurs* is a property that (in some sense) makes no difference to how things are *now*; rather, it makes a difference only to how the world *was*. And perhaps that's what is meant. But so what? When we bought into these tensed properties it was clear to us that these properties made no difference to how the world is *now*; they only make a difference to the truths about the past. All that has happened since our initial adoption of the view is that these have come to be called suspicious. But this is nothing more than rhetoric. Absent some new reason to think that there is a problem here, a proponent of an ontology that is 'suspicious' may simply shrug their shoulders. A charge of suspicion is not the same as a guilty verdict, after all (though see discussion in Chapter 7 as to how we might refine this).

# §10.8 Restricted truth-maker theory

We've heard quite a bit in the previous section about why one might believe in maximalism and we've also considered some replies from the non-maximalist. We also saw, in an earlier section, why one might be inclined to endorse non-maximalism. At the moment, we might be inclined to the view that non-maximalism has a convincing lead when it comes to our choice of theory.

But, as things are presented in the literature, matters are not quite so simple. The proponent of a non-maximalist theory has (at least) two important questions to answer. First, which sentences (or propositions) do need truth-makers? It's particularly pressing that we get an answer to this question; if we were to lack one then we would not have a theory, so much as a vague and imprecise claim of the form 'not all truths need truth-makers, but we don't know which ones do'. That doesn't seem like much of a theory. Second, what are the consequences of endorsing a restricted theory?

It might appear very straightforward to answer the first question: those truths that do not need truth-makers are those that are *negative*. Those that do need truth-makers are those that are *positive*. But there are two problems with this. First, it is not actually clear what is meant by 'positive' and 'negative' in this scenario. At a first pass, we might think that propositions of the form <there are no . . .> do not need truth-makers in order to be true, but that propositions of the form <there is an. . . .> do require truth-makers. But this will not work

Suppose that we consider two sentences:

(6) There are no unicorns.
(7) There is an absence of unicorns.

Clearly, (6) and (7) seem to say the same thing – they might even be taken to express the same proposition. Sentence (6), of course, is a claim of the form 'there are no . . .'. So given our attempt at a criteria, the proposition expressed by this sentence would not need a truth-maker. But sentence (7) is a sentence of the form 'there is an. . . . ' and so, given the above criteria, it *will* need a truth-maker in order to be true. But sentence (7) is, intuitively, just as much a claim about what there is not as sentence (6) and, as we have said, the two sentences seem to say just the same thing. If the putative truth-makers for (6) were objectionable, and sentence (6) says just the same as sentence (7), then it is hard to see that the truth-makers for sentence (7) will be any less objectionable.

If that sketch of criteria will not do, what can the defender of non-maximalism do? One thing that they might do is respond with a more modest proposal: there is an intuitive distinction between propositions that say that something does exist, and something that does not exist. So, consider sentences (6) and (7): they say the same thing. They say that there are no unicorns. They do not say that there exists some entity that *is* an absence of unicorns. That much is a simple and intuitive insight into the nature of our language. Furthermore, we should exploit that insight. Sentences that make this sort of claim simply do not require truth-makers in order to be true. Sentences that say that there *are* particular sorts of entity; those sorts of sentences do require truth-makers in order to be true.

How successful this claim will be is unclear. A determined opponent might simply deny that they have this intuition and claim, instead, that they do not see that there is any principled difference here.

# §10.9 Problems with restriction

In any case, we might then consider the second question: what sort of problems might we face if this theory were viable? A pressing worry might be the following argument against a restricted form of truth-maker theory from Merricks (2007).

Consider the following two propositions:

> D: If glass G were struck, then G would shatter.
>
> NE: No sorcerer who is intent on preventing G from shattering, exists.

All proponents of truth-maker theory (either maximalism or non-maximalism truth-maker), claims Merricks, think that counterfactual conditionals such as D require truth-makers. However, if D is true, then that appears to entail that NE is true. After all, if D is true then there can be no sorcerer who would prevent G from shattering were G struck. Thus, whatever makes D true must also serve to make NE true.

As Merricks then notes,

> [a] commitment to truthmakers for dispositional conditionals brings with it a commitment to the claim that, at least for each negative existential entailed by a true dispositional conditional, there exists something that necessitates that negative existential, something neither constituted neither by suspicious properties . . . So truthmaker theorists should say that all such negative existentials have truthmakers. I think it would be unprincipled and unmotivated to persist in saying that other true negative existentials lack truthmakers. (Merricks 2007: 42–3)

Merricks is, then, explicit: 'Truthmaker theorists should say that negative existential truths have truthmakers' (2007: 43). Let me formalize, in the interests of clarity.

(8)  D has a truth-maker.
(9)  NE does not have a truth-maker.
(10) The truth of D entails the truth of NE.

Therefore,

(11) NE has a truth-maker.

This looks like a serious problem for proponents of non-maximalism.[2]

# §10.10 A defence and an extreme form of restriction

When we were trying to determine which truths need truth-makers, I suggested that only the 'positive' truths require truth-makers. That proved a troubling notion to spell out. But the basic gist seemed to be that only sentences that say how the world *is* require truth-makers. And this raises a further question – though one that might appear a little opaque at first sight: how do we read that 'is'?

Let me explain: we used the 'is' here to try and capture the difference between the 'positive' and 'negative'. But there are other distinctions that we could draw. When we say that only sentences that say how the world *is* require truth-makers, do we intend that 'is' to be present tensed? If we did, then the truth-maker objection to presentism would fall by the wayside. Only those truths about how the world *is-now* would require truth-makers. Likewise, do we hear that 'is' as signalling *how the world actually is*, or do we also hear it as signalling *how the world could be*? If we thought that the 'is' were only about those entities that are actual, then we would not need truth-makers for talk about what is merely possible (possible, but non-actual).

This would be quite a radical departure from much of contemporary metaphysics. The claim that there could be modal and temporal truths that do not require truth-makers is, seemingly, somewhat controversial – presumably, because it leaves it unclear what (for instance) possibility *is*. When we say that 'it is possible that p', on the account we're considering here, this claim has nothing that makes it true; if it is true, it is simply a matter of p's *being possible*, with no further claim as to what this amounts to in reality. This, we might be inclined to think, is deeply unsatisfactory.

Be that as it may, this strategy would help us deal with Merricks' objection. As Merricks notes, dispositional truths (truths about what *would* happen, *were* the glass struck by a stone) are modal truths. If it turned out that *modal* truths had no truth-makers, then 'D', in the above, would not have a truth-maker. Now, recall, it was the truth-maker for 'D' that was acting as the truth-maker for NE, so if we remove the truth-maker for D then there is no truth-maker for NE and we do not have a case where a negative existential gets a truth-maker. So, although the idea *might seem* to be a little unpalatable, it does carry with it something of a pay-off for the non-maximalist. It thus seems that in answering the second question, concerning the potential consequences of a restricted theory of truth-making, we find a result that might incline us to revise our account of which truths need truth-makers.

# §10.11 Consequences of extreme restriction

There is another worry waiting for us. We have seen, throughout, that truth-maker theory can be used to ask a range of metaphysical questions. Indeed, much of metaphysics seems to presuppose a connection between the truth of our utterances and the world, and, as we have seen, many of the interesting questions in metaphysics seem to arise from contemplating how the world would have to be in order for those claims to be true. In this final chapter we have been considering giving up truth-maker maximalism. Indeed, we have just considered giving up the truth-maker principle for an enormous class of truths. This might seem to put metaphysics in peril. If we don't think that all truths need truth-makers, why not simply say that *no* truths need truth-makers?

There are a variety of theories of truth on the market. Why not simply endorse deflationism about truth, according to which a proposition, <p> is true iff p. That is, <snow is white> is true, iff snow is white; <there were dinosaurs> is true iff there were dinosaurs; <there could have existed unicorns> is true iff there could have existed unicorns, and so on.

I suspect that there are a number of ways in which we might reply to this objection. First, we might note that not all metaphysical questions *need* to be framed in this way. Consider, for instance, our discourse about colour that played a role in the discussion of properties. I take it that what explains our asserting the sentence that 'these two objects are the same colour' is that the two objects under discussion appear to us to be identical. So, it is because of our perceptions that we endorse the sentence. If we could then find a way of explaining our perceptions, that did not require that the two objects were *literally the same* in any particular way (via, for instance, the shared instantiation of a universal) then we would have an explanation of why we assert the sentence and why we perceive the world as we do. Likewise, if we could explain why particular collections of particles appear to us as wholes – integrated objects – whereas others do not, then perhaps we would have an answer to the question 'what makes it true that *this* is a composite object, but *that* is not'. If we have an adequate explanation of the appearances, and the appearances then explain why we speak as we do, then that might be enough. We would then, in metaphysics, be engaged in the project of explaining how and why the world appears to us as it does. Thus, the complete loss of a truth-maker principle need not deal a devastating objection to metaphysical inquiry.

Second, it is not at all clear that the giving up of truth-maker in some domains entails the giving up of truth-maker in *all* domains. As we have seen throughout, it does seem to us that, in at least some situations, truths depend upon the world. It is hard to deny that the truth of the sentence 'there is an electron' depends, in some way, upon there existing an electron. Indeed, as I have suggested above, it might seem entirely appropriate to treat truth-maker itself as a hypothesis to be tested over a range of cases. In some cases, it will be obvious that there are truths that require truth-makers, in others it will be obvious that they do not; in others still it may require our careful weighing of the options. But such deliberations are still well within the purview of metaphysical deliberation.

Third, though clearly related to both of the two preceding points, metaphysics can, I think, be characterized as a study of the fundamental structure of reality. Truth-maker theory might then make a mistake with confusing metaphysics with ontology; ontology is the study of 'being' – the study of what there is. Now, a part of that reality is our language. But it is not clear that all of our true claims need terminate in the world. It is far from obvious that the way in which all of our true sentences get to be true *needs* to be by pointing at some existent. Some truths seem far more naturally suited to being truths only of our language: for instance, 'all unmarried men are bachelors'. This truth seems to be in some way – though I concede this is very difficult to spell out – a conceptual truth. But such concepts might well not need, for their truth, existents.

The relationship between truth and world is complex, but what seems clear is that metaphysics will survive even without so grand a tool as truth-maker maximalism.

## §10.12 Supervenience

In between these two views surveyed – maximalism and a large-scale restriction – is a softer view, one that I have not covered here and one that I lack the space to cover in any great detail. It is the supervenience theory of truth.

ST: Necessarily, if <p> is true, it would be impossible for <p> to be false unless at least one entity which does not exist were to exist, or at least one entity which exists were not to exist. (Bigelow 1988: 126)

Thus, the proposition <there is an electron> is true because it would be impossible for that proposition to be false unless all of the electrons failed to exist – at no possible world at which there are electrons is the proposition <there is an electron>, false. Likewise <there are no unicorns> is true, because at no possible worlds including a unicorn is the proposition <there are no unicorns>, true.

The view may be considered preferable to maximalism because, as we have just seen, the proposition <there are no unicorns> is true in the absence of there being any unicorns or any other truth-maker, for that matter.[3] Notice, also, that the view is extremely elegant.

I'll only consider one reason to reject ST in the form that it's stated (which is only a very crude and clearly inadequate formulation of the principle) and the reader should pursue matters in their own research. Consider the proposition <there is a cup on my desk>. That's a true proposition. But notice: to make the proposition false I do not (obviously) need to bring any new entity into existence, nor do I need to destroy anything. I can render the proposition false simply by picking up my cup in order to drink from it. Thus, ST looks (in this guise) to give us the wrong result. The proponent of ST will need to then add a clause to the effect that a change in how matters are arranged will also effect what is true. Spelling out the details of that clause, and putative problems with it, is something that I leave for the reader to pursue in the further reading.

# §10.13 Conclusions

Proponents of maximalism have put forward many reasons for thinking we should believe it to be true, but, as we have seen, it is not entirely obvious that we should agree with their arguments. Of course, it remains open that other arguments can be found or that the objections can be blocked. And perhaps you just find it overwhelmingly obvious that all truths require truth-makers and so think the objections to truth-maker theory *must* be overcome. Or, perhaps you think maximalism obviously false! In any case, we cannot settle matters here. What is clear is that the claim that all of our true propositions require truth-makers in order to be true, can, and has been, questioned. Whether or not it is the correct principle will, I suspect, determine the course of much future work in metaphysics. *I* do not think truth-maker maximalism is correct, but I may well be wrong.

# Recommended reading

## Pro-Maximalism

Armstrong, D. 2004. *Truth and Truthmakers*. Cambridge: CUP.

Cameron, R. 2008. 'Truthmakers, Realism and Ontology', in *Being: Contemporary Developments in Metaphysics*, Robin LePoidevin, R. ed. Royal Institute of Philosophy Supplement, 83, 107–28.

Rodriguez-Preyera, G. 2005. 'Why Truthmakers?', in Beebee and Dodd eds. *Truthmakers*. Oxford: OUP, 17–32.

Tallant, J. 2010b. 'Not a Total Failure', *Philosophia*, 38, 795–810.

## Negative existentials

Cameron, R. 2008b. 'How to Be a Truthmaker Maximalist', *Nous*, 44, 178–98.

Dodd, J. 2007. 'Negative Truths and Truthmaker Principles', *Synthese*, 156, 383–401.

Mumford, S. 2007. 'Negative Truth and Falsehood', *Proceedings of the Aristotelian Society*, CVII, 45–71.

Schaffer, J. 2010b. 'The Least Discerning and Most Promiscuous Truthmaker', *Philosophical Quarterly*, 60, 307–24.

Simons, P. 2008. 'Why the Negations of False Atomic Sentences are True', in T. de Mey and M. Keinänen, eds. *Essays on Armstrong. Acta Philosophica Fennica*, 84, 15–36.

## On the denial of maximalism

Daly, C. 2005. 'So Where's the Explanation?', in Beebee, H. and Dodd, J. eds. *Truthmakers*. Oxford: OUP, 85–103.

Melia, J. 2005. 'Truthmaking without Truthmakers', in Beebee, H. and Dodd, J. eds. *Truthmakers*. Oxford: OUP, 67–84.

Merricks, T. 2007. *Truth and Ontology*. Oxford: OUP.

Tallant, J. 2009. 'Ontological Cheats Might Just Prosper', *Analysis*, 69, 422–30.

Tallant, J. 2010c. 'There's No Existent Like "No Existence" Like No Existent I Know', *Philosophical Studies*, 148, 387–400.

Tallant, J. 2010d. 'Still Cheating, Still Prospering', *Analysis*, 70, 502–6.

## Supervenience theory

Bigelow, J. 1988. *The Reality of Numbers: A Physicalist's Philosophy of Mathematics*. Oxford: OUP, 128–34.

Dodd, J. 2002. 'Is Truth Supervenient on Being?', *Proceedings of the Aristotelian Society*, 102, 69–86.

Lewis, D. 1992. 'Critical Notice', *Australasian Journal of Philosophy*, 70, 211–24.

## Truth

Horwich, P. 1990. *Truth*. Oxford: Blackwell.

Kuune, W. 2003. *Conceptions of Truth*. Oxford: Clarendon.

Lynch, M. 2009. *Truth as One and Many*. Oxford: Clarendon.

## Recommended questions

1) Write out a summary of the various different positions covered in this chapter. Which do you think best? Why do you think that view best?
2) How do you think we should deal with the problem of negative existentials?
3) What do you think of the argument that we should be maximalists in order to catch cheaters?
4) In a number of early passages I quoted the views of philosophers on the idea that there are negative properties. Do you think that the fact that these quotes are from 'experts' ought to carry any weight?
5) What do you think are the consequences for metaphysics if we give up on maximalism?

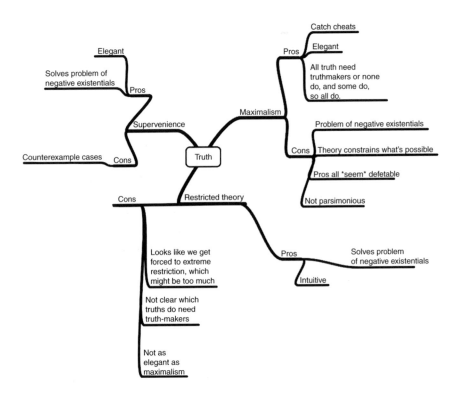

# Notes

## Chapter 1

1 Armstrong (2004: 4–5) offers some remarks as to the historical pedigree of TM, claiming to trace some early variant of it back as far as Aristotle.

2 Explicit defences of the view appear in Armstrong (2004) and Cameron (2008a).

3 The claim that the truth-maker relation is one of some kind of necessitation is controversial. Some have preferred to treat this as a relation of explanation – for example McFetridge (1989), Liggins (2005).

4 We return to these sorts of questions in Chapter 5.

5 Causation is discussed in Chapter 9.

6 There are certainly other arguments against the possibility of said dualism.

7 This line of reasoning will reappear for examination in Chapters 3 and 6.

## Chapter 2

1 A question that is formulated in a variety of ways in Van Inwagen (1990).

2 Van Inwagen (1990: 57–8) considers a case of two people shaking hands who are suddenly paralysed with their fingers locked together. They, he claims, do not compose an object, so *fastenation* doesn't seem right.

3 Where x overlaps y $=_{df}$ there is a z such that z is a part of x and z is a part of y.

4 It's less clear whether or not this can be used against the Universalist, since the Universalist seems to posit objects that don't do any causal work anyway – for example the Eiffel-tower-table.

5 And, for Van Inwagen, only things that are alive can think.

6 In fact, this is what Schaffer (2007) refers to as *Existence Monism*. As we shall see later, Schaffer prefers *Priority Monism*.

## Chapter 3

1 We can proceed with the assumption that if an object is not abstract, then it is concrete.

2 Notice that the sentences (10) through (13) are instances of this, while (8) and (9) are not. We'll return to this observation, below.

3 This section and the next borrow heavily from Melia (1995).

4 This section leans heavily on Liggins (2006).

5 For an overview of this, see Liggins (2006a).

# Chapter 4

1  See Chapter 6 for discussion of the distinction between universal and particular and Chapter 3 for a discussion of what sorts of thing an abstract object might be.

2  Lewis refines the rough and ready version of this principle (1986a: 88–90), but this will suffice for present purposes. The reader should explore for themselves the way in which Lewis carries out the refinement.

3  Even if you think that there are only finitely many, it is clear that the number of possibilities radically outstrips any written book.

# Chapter 5

1  It's worth noting that Lewis has another way of approaching the issue of intrinsicality and duplication. Cameron (2009b) offers a nice overview of this topic.

2  The definitions of the varieties of nominalism are drawn from Armstrong (1989b).

3  The Quine to which Armstrong refers is Quine (1953).

4  See Lewis (1986a: 56–7) for a more rounded discussion.

5  It's worth noting that Mumford himself is a dispositional Monist: that is, he believes that all properties are dispositional.

# Chapter 6

1  There might be another sense of 'support' intended by Locke. I'll return to this, below.

2  For a nice discussion of how this might be resolved, see Loux, M. (1998: 102–6).

3  Armstrong's preferred account of such properties and relations is that they are universals.

# Chapter 7

1  Because the A-properties include reference to the past, present and future, are, thus, frequently used to generate tensed sentences; the A-properties are also often referred to as 'tensed' properties. And, for similar reasons, the B-relations are often referred to as 'tenseless relations'. The locutions are clumsy, however. Tense, and tenselessness, are features of sentences in a language, not of properties. Properly speaking the locution 'the future' is not tensed; rather, it makes a semantic contribution to a sentence which, itself, may then properly be described as tensed. For this reason I will not be describing A-properties as 'tensed'.

2  Cf. Dyke (2002: 337) and see (2002: 331–6) for reasons to prefer this token reflexive analysis specified to the date analysis offered by Mellor (1998).

3　As a note of historical interest, B-theorists originally set themselves the task of translating tensed sentences using tenseless sentences, in order to demonstrate that tense plays no important role. Most B-theorists nowadays accept that tense is ineliminable from thought and language, but nonetheless deny the need for any A-theoretic ontological resources.

4　See Oaklander and Smith (1994: part III) for discussion.

5　Cf. Cameron (forthcoming, c).

6　Indeed, it makes a difference to its *intrinsic* nature.

7　Brogaard (2006) offers an interesting discussion of the problem.

8　The final analysis may have to be made more complex – for instance, we must also account for cases where x caused y and both x and y are in the past.

9　A similar problem will afflict growing block views, for the growing block view *also* endorses the claim that there is absolute simultaneity.

10　One exception to this line is Fine (2005: chapter 5).

11　The reader should beware, here, that I myself have defended presentism on occasion and so this concluding report may be a little more biased than is fully admirable.

# Chapter 8

1　The way in which I schematize this borrows heavily from Kurtz (2006).

2　I don't discuss what it is to be 'wholly present' in this chapter, though I do specify some readings.

# Chapter 9

1　Lewis (1986c) offers a superb discussion.

2　As per Sober (1987: 253) I include the 'and only if' clause that Salmon himself omits.

# Chapter 10

1　Compare this with the argument against the ersatz B-relation in §7.6.2.

2　Merricks' (2007: 163) own view is that we should deny that subjunctive conditionals of the sort specified in D require truth-makers, thus resolving the problem.

3　Such a tool may be useful (though notice that it's not clear that the principle will serve to help us argue against presentism, Kierland and Monton (2007)).

# Index